A FIELD GUIDE TO THE MAJOR NATIVE AND
INTRODUCED SPECIES NORTH OF MEXICO

TREES

OF NORTH AMERICA

by C. FRANK BROCKMAN

PROFESSOR OF FORESTRY, EMERITUS
COLLEGE OF FOREST RESOURCES
UNIVERSITY OF WASHINGTON

Illustrated by REBECCA MERRILEES

Under the Editorship of
HERBERT S. ZIM

 GOLDEN PRESS • NEW YORK
Western Publishing Company, Inc.
Racine, Wisconsin

FOREWORD

Reasons for the study of trees can be given by the score. All of them—scientific, cultural, economic, and aesthetic—are justifiable. Yet reasons are hardly necessary. Trees are too large, too majestic, too important, and too much a part of nature to be ignored. Man's dependence on trees, directly and indirectly, goes back to those distant times when the human species was first making its mark. The dependence continues into this age of synthetics. On a planet covered in good part by forests it is almost impossible to understand fully the many other groups of plants and animals without taking into account the natural biological role of trees. From the human point of view, trees are a multipurpose natural resource without equal.

TREES is the second volume of the Golden Field Guide series, developed to play a unique role in the natural sciences. Without the cooperation of dedicated individuals and organizations, the preparation of this guide would have been an impossible task. Special thanks are due E. S. Harrar, for his early review of the manuscript; Sally Kaicher, who did the illustrations of palms and yuccas; the Native Plant Workshop of South Florida, for checking the art of plants that grow in South Florida and in the Florida Keys. Daniel B. Ward checked range maps for the Southeast; Arturo Gomez Pompa, the maps for the Southwest and Mexico. Conrad Byrd, B. O. Mulligan, Carl English, Julia F. Morton, George B. Stevenson, Hugh B. Wycoff, Percy C. Everett, and Donald E. Stone were among those who supplied specimens. The U. S. Forest Service furnished many photographs to assist the artist.

C.F.B.

GOLDEN, GOLDEN FIELD GUIDE, and GOLDEN PRESS® are trademarks of Western Publishing Company, Inc.

HOW TO USE THIS BOOK

This is a field guide to the identification of 594 of some 865 species of trees native to North America north of Mexico. Included are the most common and most important species and also many that are less familiar but no less interesting. In addition, important foreign species that have become naturalized and some that are grown commercially or as ornamentals are also described and illustrated. In total, the guide includes more than 730 species in 76 families.

The criteria used to determine which species to describe and illustrate and which to only mention are based on the definition of a tree (p. 13). Native woody plants that regularly attain a height of 20 feet have been included, as have major introduced and naturalized species. A more difficult group were those woody plants that are treelike in only part of their range, in optimum habitats, or under special conditions. The more widespread, abundant, and important the plant, the better its chances for inclusion. Many of these smaller trees (to 15 feet) and some species that have limited ranges are mentioned, however.

Willows and hawthorns include many local species difficult to identify. Those that are of unquestionable tree size or that are the only representative in an area have been included.

To make this book most useful in the field, the text, range maps, and illustrations have been brought together so that all pertinent information can be seen at a glance. Because of limited space, the text is necessarily brief and therefore not complete in every detail, but the combination of text, range map, and illustrations will aid greatly in making identifications in the field.

Some trees have such distinctive forms that they can be identified at a glance, even at a considerable distance or from a moving car. A number of trees may be recognized quickly by their bark or by some unique character of the twigs, such as thorns or spines. Others may require a careful study of their flowers, fruits, buds, or detailed features of the foliage to confirm an identification. The range maps indicate the probability of finding a species in a particular area and, except for ornamentals planted outside their natural environment, are important, too, in tree identification. Range maps are especially helpful in identifying trees in such groups as the willows and hawthorns. These maps give only a general picture of where the species may be found, for within its range each species typically grows in a particular habitat, as in swamps, along rivers, or on alpine slopes. Some species are so tolerant of soil, moisture, and sunlight requirements that they are very widely distributed.

Each person develops his own method of tree identification. Often this is a combination of some characteristics that can be observed at a distance and others that need closer study. In most places, except in parks, a specimen of a leafy twig can be taken for study later at home or to show to a local authority on trees. A Bibliography (p. 271) is included to aid your further study.

Practice is the best way to learn to recognize trees. By observing the varied characteristics of different species and by reading further about them, distinctive features and descriptive botanical terms become commonplace. An awareness of the variations that might be expected of a species also develops with observation, for though leaves and other features of each species have a typical basic form, size, color, or other characteristic, often there is considerable variation in individuals of the same species. With field experience, the pleasure and satisfaction gained from this fascinating hobby is greatly increased. As a suggestion, underline in this book those field marks that are most helpful to you, especially those useful in differentiating a species from a similar species.

Technical terms have been held to a minimum in this field guide. In fact, an effort has been made to simplify terms wherever possible in the very brief descriptions and to emphasize only the most obvious field characteristics that may not be obvious in the illustration. Comparing a specimen with the illustrations and the description reduces considerably the need for these technical terms. Some of the most commonly used terms for parts of trees are given on pages 13-17, however. If a tree cannot be identified by quick reference to this guide, the use of such terminology will be of great help in conferring with tree experts or in using more technical references.

As a further aid to finding information quickly, this guide has a complete index to common and scientific names (pp. 272-280). And the illustrated guide to family characteristics on pages 5-12 will help in fitting a tree to its group and also in comparing features of the various families.

Common and scientific names in this book are based largely on the *Check List of Native and Naturalized Trees of the United States,* by Elbert L. Little, prepared under the direction of the Forest Service Tree and Range Plant Name Committee (see Bibliography, p. 271). Major departures from the *Check List* in this book are the division of Pinaceae into three families: Pinaceae, Taxodiaceae, and Cupressaceae; and the division of Cornaceae into two families: Cornaceae and Nyssaceae. Recognized botanical publications were consulted to determine the names for ornamental or naturalized species included in this guide but not in the *Check List.*

Many trees, as well as other plants, have several common names, varying with different localities. For this reason, botanists use scientific names that are written in Latin, a language that is no longer spoken and hence does not change with time. Each name consists of two parts—the genus and the species. Thus the scientific name of Sugar Maple is *Acer saccharum;* of Eastern Redcedar, *Juniperus virginiana;* of White Oak, *Quercus alba.* Regardless of nationality or native language, botanists anywhere in the world can recognize trees, as well as other plants and animals, by this naming system. Tree species also have varietal forms. A few examples of these are included in this book, as in Lodgepole Pine, *Pinus contorta* var. *latifolia.*

A GUIDE TO THE FAMILIES OF TREES

This is a guide to the families of trees in this book, presenting in abbreviated form their principal features. Major families are described in greater detail later; smaller families are described only here. In this condensed treatment, comparison of families is made easy. Often, of course, the precise botanical characteristics by which plants are classified are too small—flower details, for example—to be useful in field identification by the amateur. These are omitted.

GYMNOSPERMS

Gymnosperms do not have flowers in the commonly accepted sense; they produce naked seeds, usually on the scale of a cone. Many are evergreen, with needle-like, linear, or scalelike foliage.

Pages 20-65

YEW FAMILY (Taxaceae): leaves evergreen, linear (sides parallel), growing separately on twigs and not clustered; fruit one-seeded and drupaceous (plumlike) or with red, fleshy cup at base. *Yews, Torreyas.* **Page 20**

CYCAD FAMILY (Cycadaceae): tree-sized members palmlike; large, pinnate leaves; conelike male and female strobiles on separate trees; fruit a cone. *Sago Palm, Fern Palm.* **Page 20**

PINE FAMILY (Pinaceae): leaves evergreen (deciduous in larches), either needle-like or linear, single, in bundles (fascicles) or clusters; fruit a woody cone. *Pines, Larches, Spruces, Hemlocks, True Firs, Douglas-firs.* **Page 22**

REDWOOD FAMILY (Taxodiaceae): leaves linear or awl-like, single and in spirals on twig; most species evergreen; small woody cones. *Redwood, Sequoia, Baldcypress.* **Page 50**

CEDAR OR CYPRESS FAMILY (Cupressaceae): foliage evergreen, opposite or whorled, usually scalelike and overlapping, or awl-like and spreading, occasionally in 3's, sometimes both on same tree; fruit a woody, leathery, or semi-fleshy cone. *Cedars, Cypress, Junipers.* **Page 54**

GINKGO FAMILY (Ginkgoaceae): one species (not native to N.A.); fanlike leaves; male and female strobiles on separate trees—male in catkinlike cluster, paired female on spurlike shoots; fruit drupaceous (plumlike), with foul odor. **Page 64**

ARAUCARIA FAMILY (Araucariaceae): not native to N.A.; evergreen; cone disintegrates when mature. *Monkey Puzzle, Norfolk Island Pine.* **Page 64**

PODOCARP FAMILY (Podocarpaceae): evergreens; no native N.A. species. **Page 64**

ANGIOSPERMS

Angiosperms, true flowering plants, bear seeds within a closed vessel, often fleshy. Divided into Monocotyledons and Dicotyledons.
Pages 66-269

Monocotyledons: leaves evergreen, with parallel veins; flower parts in 3's; woody fibers irregularly distributed in stems, hence no annual rings.
Pages 66-75

PALM FAMILY (Palmae): tropical and subtropical trees; compound leaves, large and pinnate (feather-like) or palmate (fan-shaped) in a cluster at top of an unbranched trunk; fruits are berries (dates) or drupes (coconuts). *Palms, Palmettos.* **Page 66**

LILY FAMILY *(Liliaceae):* a large family with only a few tree-sized members; leaves tough, long, slim, and sharp-pointed; flowers in large, terminal panicles; fruit a papery, leathery, or woody capsule in some, berry-like in others. Yuccas. **Page 74**

Dicotyledons: leaves net-veined, mostly deciduous but some evergreen; stems increase in diameter by annual layers of wood of varying thickness, forming rings.
Pages 76-269

WILLOW FAMILY (Salicaceae): leaves simple, alternate, deciduous (leaves of *Willows* slender; leaves of most *Poplars* broad); staminate and pistillate catkins on different trees; fruits a capsule, with many small, tufted seeds. **Page 76**

WAXMYRTLE FAMILY (Myricaceae): shrubs or small trees; leaves evergreen, simple, alternate, aromatic, and with tiny resin dots; flowers in catkins; fruit a waxy drupe. *Bayberries.* **Page 90**

WALNUT FAMILY (Juglandaceae): large trees; leaves deciduous, alternate, pinnately compound; monoecious, staminate flowers in drooping catkins, pistillate, solitary or in small spikes; pith of twigs chambered in walnuts, solid in hickories; fruit a nut in husk. *Walnuts, Hickories.* **Page 92**

CORKWOOD FAMILY (Leitneriaceae): leaves deciduous, alternate, simple, hairy below; flowers dioecious, in catkins; fruit dry; wood light; one species, in Southeast. *Corkwood.* **Page 100**

BIRCH FAMILY (Betulaceae): leaves deciduous, simple, alternate, toothed; monoecious—staminate flowers in catkins, pistillate in catkins, clusters, or spikes; fruit a nutlet or nut, in a conelike strobile, leafy cluster, or husk. *Birches, Alders, Hornbeams, Hophornbeams, Hazelnut.* **Page 102**

BEECH FAMILY (Fagaceae): leaves mostly deciduous, simple, alternate; staminate and pistillate flowers on same tree—staminate in catkins or heads, pistillate in spikes—or in some genera both sexes in same catkin; fruit a nut or an acorn. *Beeches, Chestnuts, Chinkapins, Oaks, Tanoak.*

Page 114

ELM FAMILY (Ulmaceae): leaves deciduous (except in *Florida Trema*), simple, alternate, toothed; flowers inconspicuous, in greenish clusters; fruit dry, wafer-like *(Elms)*, nutlike *(Planertree)*, or a thin-fleshed drupe *(Hackberry, Trema)*.   **Page 138**

MULBERRY FAMILY (Moraceae): leaves simple and alternate, deciduous or evergreen; milky sap; flowers in spikes, heads, or hollow receptacles; multiple fruits in spikes, heads, or fleshy receptacles. *Mulberries, Osage-orange, Figs.*   **Page 144**

OLAX (TALLOWWOOD) FAMILY (Olacaceae): leaves evergreen, simple, alternate; axillary clusters of small, bell-shaped flowers; twigs thorny; fleshy fruit. *Tallowwood.*   **Page 148**

BUCKWHEAT FAMILY (Polygonaceae): low, sprawling shrubs or small trees, largely tropical; leaves leathery, evergreen, alternate, simple, oval to circular, margins smooth; edible, grapelike fruits. *Seagrapes.*   **Page 148**

FOUR-O'CLOCK FAMILY (Nyctaginaceae): largely tropical, with few trees; one tree species in Florida; leaves evergreen, simple, alternate or opposite, margins smooth; small flowers in clusters; fruit a nutlet in a fleshy, ribbed covering. *Longleaf Blolly.*   **Page 148**

MAGNOLIA FAMILY (Magnoliaceae): leaves alternate, simple, entire *(Magnolias)* or lobed *(Yellow-poplar)*, mostly deciduous; large, showy flowers; conelike, aggregate fruits; stipule scars encircle twigs.   **Page 150**

CUSTARD-APPLE (ANNONA) FAMILY (Annonaceae): small trees, largely in southeastern U.S.; leaves simple, alternate, entire; deciduous *(Pawpaw)* or evergreen *(Pond-apple)*; flowers large, solitary, yellow, white, or purple; large, fleshy fruits.   **Page 154**

LAUREL FAMILY (Lauraceae): mostly tropical and subtropical trees; leaves evergreen or deciduous, simple, alternate, lobed or unlobed with smooth margins, aromatic; flowers small, greenish yellow or white; fruit one-seeded berry or drupe. *Sassafras, California Laurel, Redbay.*   **Page 156**

WITCH-HAZEL FAMILY (Hamamelidaceae): leaves deciduous, alternate, simple, unlobed or palmately lobed; flowers in clusters or globose heads; fruit a woody capsule borne separately or in bur-like heads. *Witch-hazel, Sweetgum.*   **Page 158**

CAPER FAMILY (Capparidaceae): leaves evergreen, alternate, simple, scaly below, smooth margins; flowers, with elongated stamens, in terminal clusters; fruit an elongated berry-like pod; shrubs or small trees of tropics and subtropics. *Jamaica Caper.*   **Page 158**

SYCAMORE FAMILY (Platanaceae): leaves deciduous, alternate, simple, palmately lobed; flowers tiny, in heads; fruit a tight ball of achenes, each with a tuft of hair at its base; buds encircled by leaf scars, stipule scars encircling twigs. *Sycamores, Planetrees.*   **Page 160**

ROSE FAMILY (Rosaceae): a large family of trees, shrubs, herbs; leaves usually alternate, toothed, simple or pinnately compound, deciduous or evergreen; flower parts typically in 5's; fruit a drupe, pome, capsule, achene. *Apples, Plums, Cherries, Hawthorns, and others.*   **Page 162**

LEGUME FAMILY (Leguminosae): a large family; leaves alternate, simple, pinnate, or bipinnate; flowers regular or sweetpea-shaped; fruit a legume. *Acacias, Redbuds, Locusts, others.*   **Page 182**

RUE FAMILY (Rutaceae): leaves alternate (opposite in *Sea Amyris*), pinnately compound, evergreen or deciduous; twigs of some spiny; flowers small, clustered; fruit a capsule, samara, or thin-fleshed drupe. *Prickly-ashes and others.*   **Page 194**

BURSERA FAMILY (Burseraceae): tropical and subtropical trees and shrubs; leaves deciduous, alternate, pinnately compound; flowers in clusters; fruit small, with single seed. *Gumbo-limbo.*   **Page 196**

CALTROP FAMILY (Zygophyllaceae): leaves evergreen, opposite, pinnately compound; fruit a capsule; one U.S. species. *Lignumvitae.*   **Page 196**

AILANTHUS (QUASSIA) FAMILY (Simaroubaceae): tropical and subtropical trees; leaves evergreen (deciduous in *Ailanthus*), alternate, pinnately compound; fruit winged or thin-fleshed. *Paradise-tree and others.*   **Page 198**

MAHOGANY FAMILY (Meliaceae): shrubs and trees of tropics and subtropics; leaves alternate, pinnately compound, evergreen or deciduous. *West Indies Mahogany, Chinaberry.*   **Page 200**

SPURGE FAMILY (Euphorbiaceae): a large family of mainly tropical and subtropical herbs, shrubs, and trees with acrid sap. Few native to U.S.; leaves evergreen or tardily deciduous, simple, alternate; flowers in terminal spikes or axillary clusters; fruit a 3-lobed capsule or fleshy drupe. *Oysterwood, Guianaplum, Manchineel.*
Page 200

CASHEW (SUMAC) FAMILY (Anacardiaceae): deciduous or evergreen leaves, alternate, pinnately compound (simple in *American Smoketree*); flower clusters conspicuous. *Sumacs and others.*
Page 202

CYRILLA FAMILY (Cyrillaceae): a small family, with evergreen or tardily deciduous, simple, alternate, smooth-margined leaves; flowers in terminal racemes; fruit a capsule. *Swamp Cyrilla, Buckwheat-tree.*
Page 204

HOLLY FAMILY (Aquifoliaceae): leaves alternate, simple, usually evergreen with spiny-toothed (occasionally smooth) margins; mostly dioecious; flowers small, greenish white, in axillary clusters; fruit a red or purple drupe. *Hollies.*
Page 206

BITTERSWEET FAMILY (Celastraceae): leaves simple, opposite or alternate (leafless with spiny twigs in *Canotia*); flowers in stalked, axillary clusters; fruit a dry capsule or a thin-fleshed drupe. *Wahoo, Falsebox.*
Page 208

MAPLE FAMILY (Aceraceae): leaves deciduous, opposite, usually simple and palmately lobed (pinnately compound in *Boxelder*); flowers small, usually polygamous or dioecious, clustered; fruit double-seeded, each seed with propeller-like wing (samara). *Maples.*
Page 210

HORSECHESTNUT FAMILY (Hippocastanaceae): leaves deciduous, opposite, palmately compound; showy, tubular flowers in large clusters; fruit a leathery capsule with 1 or 2 large brown seeds. *Buckeyes, Horsechestnuts.*
Page 218

PAPAYA FAMILY (Caricaceae): leaves large, alternate, simple, palmately lobed; flowers unisexual, yellowish, clustered (staminate clusters elongated, many-flowered; pistillate short-stemmed, few-flowered); fruit large, fleshy, many-seeded; one N.A. species in Florida. *Papaya.*
Page 220

BUCKTHORN FAMILY (Rhamnaceae): leaves simple, alternate or opposite, deciduous or evergreen; small flowers in clusters; fruit drupaceous or capsular. *Buckthorns, Ceanothus, Leadwood, and others.*
Page 222

9

CANELLA (WILD CINNAMON) FAMILY (Canellaceae): leaves evergreen, simple, alternate, smooth margins; small flowers in clusters; fruit a red berry; tropical and subtropical trees, one N.A. species. *Canella.* **Page 226**

SOAPBERRY FAMILY (Sapindaceae): mainly tropical trees, shrubs, and herbs; leaves mostly evergreen, alternate, pinnately compound; flowers small, clustered; fruit fleshy, with one or many seeds or a 3-valved capsule. *Soapberry, Butterbough, and others.* **Page 226**

LINDEN FAMILY (Tiliaceae): leaves deciduous, alternate, simple, toothed, heart-shaped and unequal at base; pale-yellow, fragrant flowers in long-stemmed clusters, attached to a narrow leaflike bract; small, woody, nutlike fruit. *Basswoods* or *Lindens.* **Page 228**

TEA FAMILY (Theaceae): leaves mostly evergreen, alternate, simple, toothed; large, showy flowers; fruit a woody capsule. *Loblolly-bay, Mountain Stewartia, Franklinia.* **Page 230**

CACTUS FAMILY (Cactaceae): typically no leaves; spiny, fleshy trunks and stems; large, showy flowers; fruit a fleshy berry. *Saguaro and other cacti.* **Page 230**

MYRTLE FAMILY (Myrtaceae): leaves evergreen, usually opposite, simple, mostly smooth-margined and aromatic; flowers of most species showy; fruit a berry *(Cajeput-tree, Guava, Eugenias)* or capsule, *Eucalyptus.* **Page 232**

MANGROVE FAMILY (Rhizophoraceae): leaves evergreen, oval, leathery, opposite, smooth-margined; yellow flowers in clusters; fruit cone-shaped, leathery apex perforated by germinating embryo; roots stiltlike; in brackish coastal waters of tropics and subtropics. *Red Mangrove.* **Page 234**

COMBRETUM (WHITE-MANGROVE) FAMILY (Combretaceae): leaves evergreen, simple, alternate (opposite in *White-mangrove);* small flowers in spikes or heads; fruit leathery, one-seeded. *Button-mangrove, White-mangrove.* **Page 234**

DOGWOOD FAMILY (Cornaceae): leaves deciduous, simple, usually opposite; small, greenish-white flowers in terminal clusters, or in heads surrounded by showy bracts; the fruit is drupaceous. *Dogwoods.* **Page 236**

TUPELO FAMILY (Nyssaceae): leaves deciduous, simple, alternate; small, greenish flowers in clusters; fruit thin-fleshed, ovoid to oblong, the simple seed ridged or winged. *Tupelos.* **Page 238**

HEATH FAMILY (Ericaceae): leaves evergreen or deciduous, simple, alternate; flowers usually tubular to urn-shaped, solitary or in clusters; fruit fleshy and one-seeded (drupe), many-seeded (berry), or capsular. *Madrones, Rhododendrons, and others.* **Page 240**

GINSENG FAMILY (Araliaceae): leaves deciduous, alternate, bipinnately compound, toothed; small flowers in large clusters; fruit berry-like; twigs spiny. *Devils-walkingstick.* **Page 244**

MELASTOME (MEADOW BEAUTY) FAMILY (Melastomataceae): leaves evergreen, simple, opposite; flowers in clusters; fruit berry-like or capsular; mainly tropical species; rare in N.A. *Florida Tetrazygia.* **Page 244**

MYRSINE FAMILY (Myrsinaceae): leaves evergreen, simple, alternate, smooth-margined; flowers in clusters, fragrant in *Marbleberry*; fruit thin-fleshed, one-seeded; mainly tropical, rare in N.A. *Guiana Rapanea.* **Page 244**

SAPOTE (SAPODILLA) FAMILY (Sapotaceae): tropical and subtropical trees and shrubs; leaves simple, alternate, smooth-margined, evergreen (deciduous in *Bumelias*); milky sap; inconspicuous flowers in axillary clusters; fruit berry-like. *False-mastic, Willow Bustic, Satinleaf, Wild-dilly.* **Page 246**

THEOPHRASTA (JOEWOOD) FAMILY (Theophrastaceae): leaves evergreen, alternate, simple, smooth-margined, glandular-dotted; bell-shaped flowers in loose clusters; fruit an orange-red berry; small tropical family. *Joewood.* **Page 248**

SWEETLEAF FAMILY (Symplocaceae): leaves deciduous, simple, alternate, margins smooth or finely toothed; small flowers in small clusters; fruit thin-fleshed, one-seeded; one N.A. species is limited to South. *Common Sweetleaf.* **Page 248**

EBONY FAMILY (Ebenaceae): leaves deciduous, simple, alternate, smooth-margined; flowers dioecious (male in loose clusters, female solitary) or polygamous; fruit an orange-red or black edible berry; found mostly in warm climates. *Persimmons.* **Page 250**

SNOWBELL (STORAX) FAMILY (Styracaceae): southern trees; leaves deciduous, simple, alternate, margins smooth to finely toothed, hairy below; bell-shaped flowers in clusters; fruit single-seeded, ovoid (*Bigleaf Snowbell*), or elongated and winged (*Silverbells*). **Page 250**

OLIVE FAMILY (Oleaceae): leaves mostly deciduous, opposite, simple or, in ashes, pinnately compound; flowers perfect, dioecious or polygamous; fruit a dry, single-winged samara, or single-seeded, fleshy. *Ashes and others.* **Page 252**

BORAGE FAMILY (Boraginaceae): leaves evergreen or tardily deciduous, alternate, simple, margins smooth or toothed; showy flowers in clusters; fruit single-seeded and thin-fleshed; mostly herbs. *Bahama Strongbark, Geiger-tree, Anaqua.* **Page 260**

VERBENA FAMILY (Verbenaceae): leaves simple, opposite, entire, evergreen; flowers in clusters, fragrant in *Fiddlewood*; fruit a drupe or capsule; mainly herbs. *Black-mangrove.* **Page 262**

NIGHTSHADE FAMILY (Solanaceae): mostly herbs, a few trees; leaves of single native species (Florida) evergreen, simple, alternate, hairy, smooth-margined; flowers in clusters; fruit berry-like. *Mullein Nightshade.* **Page 262**

BIGNONIA (TRUMPET CREEPER) FAMILY (Bignoniaceae): leaves simple, mostly deciduous, opposite and whorled, or alternate; large flowers in showy clusters or solitary; fruit an elongated or ovoid capsule or berry; mostly tropical trees, shrubs, vines, herbs. *Catalpa, Black-Calabash, Desertwillow.* **Page 264**

HONEYSUCKLE FAMILY (Caprifoliaceae): leaves deciduous, opposite, simple or pinnately compound; flowers in showy clusters; fruits drupaceous; mainly shrubs and herbs of temperate regions, a few trees. *Elders, Viburnums.* **Page 266**

COMPOSITE (SUNFLOWER) FAMILY (Compositae): a very large family of mostly herbs and few shrub or small-tree-sized members; small flowers in compact heads. *Big Sagebrush.* **Page 266**

MADDER FAMILY (Rubiaceae): leaves simple, opposite or whorled, smooth-margined, deciduous or evergreen; flowers tubular, in clusters or globose heads; fruit a capsule or dry drupe. *Buttonbush and others.* **Page 268**

MISCELLANEOUS FAMILIES: Casuarinaceae, Stericuliaceae, Proteaceae, Malvaceae, Moringaceae, and Tamaricaceae. **Page 270**

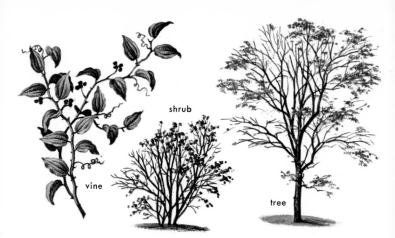

shrub

vine

tree

BASIC FEATURES OF TREES

Trees are woody plants at least 15 feet tall at maturity, with a well-developed crown and a single stem, or trunk, at least several inches in diameter. Shrubs, also woody plants, have several stems growing from a clump and are usually smaller than trees. Vines may have woody stems but do not have a distinct crown of upright branches.

Trees usually develop their typical shapes only when they grow in the open. Owing mainly to competition for light, those that grow in crowded forest conditions have a much greater "clear length" of trunk. Many trees that grow at timberline on high mountains are sprawling. Their irregular and twisted forms are a result of short growing seasons, deep snows, poor soils, and constant buffeting by strong winds. Many tree species have a characteristic shape, however, and with field experience it is possible to recognize them at a considerable distance. Some examples are shown below.

Leaves, flowers, fruits, bark, twigs, and buds are also important identification features. These parts are described and illustrated on the following pages. Although most technical terms are avoided in this book, an acquaintance with some of the most commonly used may be valuable in talking to tree specialists or in using other botanical references.

White Pine Blue Spruce Royal Palm Sugar Maple American Elm Live Oak

LEAVES may be deciduous (shed annually), or they may be ever-green or persistent (remaining on tree one to many years). Most cone-bearing trees and some broad-leaved trees are evergreen. Leaf arrangement may be obscure at growing tips, where leaves may not have reached full size. Leaves of some trees bear stipules (not shown), small leaflike appendages at base of petiole.

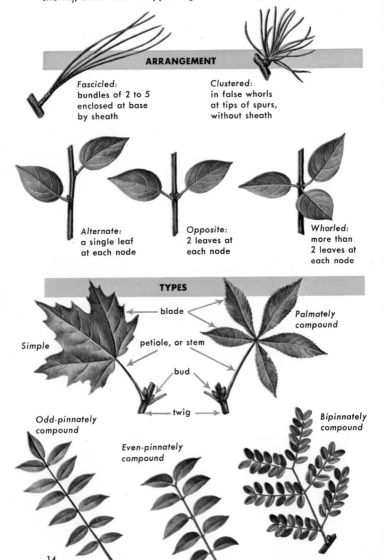

ARRANGEMENT

Fascicled:
bundles of 2 to 5
enclosed at base
by sheath

Clustered:
in false whorls
at tips of spurs,
without sheath

Alternate:
a single leaf
at each node

Opposite:
2 leaves at
each node

Whorled:
more than
2 leaves at
each node

TYPES

blade

*Palmately
compound*

Simple

petiole, or stem

bud

twig

*Odd-pinnately
compound*

*Even-pinnately
compound*

*Bipinnately
compound*

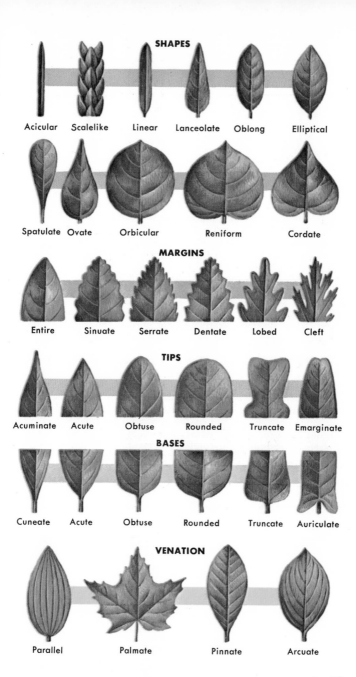

SHAPES

Acicular Scalelike Linear Lanceolate Oblong Elliptical

Spatulate Ovate Orbicular Reniform Cordate

MARGINS

Entire Sinuate Serrate Dentate Lobed Cleft

TIPS

Acuminate Acute Obtuse Rounded Truncate Emarginate

BASES

Cuneate Acute Obtuse Rounded Truncate Auriculate

VENATION

Parallel Palmate Pinnate Arcuate

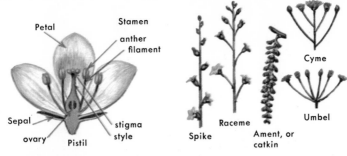

Petal
Stamen
anther
filament
Cyme
Sepal
ovary
Pistil
stigma
style
Raceme
Umbel
Spike
Ament, or
catkin

FLOWERS are a plant's reproductive organs. Those of some trees are small and inconspicuous; others are large and showy. *Complete* flowers have sepals, petals, and the two vital reproductive parts—the pollen-producing stamens (male) and pistils (female) with basal ovary enclosing ovules. *Incomplete* flowers lack one or more of these four parts. *Perfect* flowers have both stamens and pistils; sepals and petals may be present or not. *Imperfect,* or *unisexual,* flowers have either stamens or pistils. *Monoecious* species bear both sexes on the same tree—together in either complete or incomplete flowers, or separately in imperfect or unisexual flowers. *Dioecious* species have staminate and pistillate flowers on different trees. *Polygamous* species bear both perfect and unisexual flowers.

FRUITS bear the seeds. Seeds of gymnosperms are naked. In conifers they are borne in cones at the base of scales; in others a single seed is partly or wholly within a fleshy covering (aril). Angiosperm fruits bear seeds enclosed within the ripened ovary (sometimes including accessory parts). A *simple* fruit originates from a single pistil. Compound fruits are *aggregates* from two or more pistils of the same flower on a common receptacle, or *multiples* from pistils of separate flowers, often in a head.

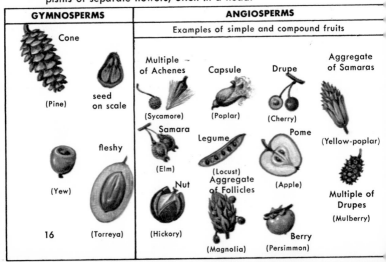

GYMNOSPERMS	ANGIOSPERMS
	Examples of simple and compound fruits

Cone

(Pine)

seed on scale

fleshy

(Yew)

(Torreya)

16

Multiple of Achenes

(Sycamore)

Samara

(Elm)

Nut

(Hickory)

Capsule

(Poplar)

Legume

(Locust)

Aggregate of Follicles

(Magnolia)

Drupe

(Cherry)

Pome

(Apple)

Berry

(Persimmon)

Aggregate of Samaras

(Yellow-poplar)

Multiple of Drupes

(Mulberry)

Smooth
Amer.
Beech

Furrowed
Black
Oak

Scaly
White
Pine

Plated
Ponderosa
Pine

Warty
Common
Hackberry

Shaggy
Shagbark
Hickory

Fibrous
Coast
Redwood

BARK often changes in appearance between small, young trees and larger, older specimens of the same species, between the trunk and twigs on the same tree, or even between individuals of the same species growing under different conditions. The bark of some trees is so distinctive that they can be easily identified, however.

Papery
Paper
Birch

TWIGS may be distinctive in color, odor, taste, lenticels (warty tissues for aeration), thorns, or spines, but the most helpful for identification are the position, size, and shape of the buds, leaf scars, vascular bundle scars, and pith. Buds of several types are scaly (or naked), gummy, fragrant, smooth, hairy, or, in some species, submerged beneath leaf scars. Buds are especially useful in identifying species in winter.

Red
Maple

Terminal buds: at apex of twig; usually larger than lateral buds

Pseudo-terminal bud: actually a lateral bud located at apex of the twig

American Sycamore

Imbricate scales: overlapping like shingles

Valvate scales: joined along edges; as in clam shell

Red Alder

Lateral buds: along twigs, in axils of previous season's leaves, at leaf scars

Leaf Scars indicate point of attachment of leaf stem. Shape may be distinctive

Pith forms core of twig. It varies in color, texture, and shape in cross section. May be solid,

chambered (open spaces with thin partitions), or diaphragmed (spongy with denser partitions)

pith solid

pith chambered

Black Walnut

FOREST REGIONS occurring in North America are based largely on climatic differences at different latitudes. Each of the major divisions may be divided into smaller areas, also with distinctive groups of trees. Species that have similar needs occur together, so learning these common associations of trees often helps in tree identification.

Variation in temperature, moisture, and soils are the principal factors that determine where trees grow. These climatic variations occur also with changes in altitude, which accounts for the extension in ranges of some northern trees into the southern Appalachians and, similarly, far southward in high western mountain ranges.

The map on the next page shows six basic forest regions. Also shown are the largely treeless regions (grasslands, desert, desert scrub and grass, and tundra).

NORTHERN Forest Region is typified by a short growing season and low temperatures. Far northern tree associations (boreal) consist largely of a few conifers, birches, and willows. To the southeast, especially where this region merges with adjacent areas, milder climates favor more complex mixtures of both cone-bearing and deciduous, broad-leaved trees.

Typical cone-bearing trees include White and Black spruces; Balsam Fir; Eastern Hemlock; Eastern White, Red, and Jack pines; Northern White Cedar; Tamarack. The principal broad-leaved trees are Paper, Sweet, and Yellow birches; Sugar Maple; Northern Red and other oaks; Quaking and Bigtooth aspens; American Beech; American Elm; Black Cherry.

SOUTHEASTERN Forest Region occurs mainly on the sandy coastal plain which is relatively dry despite the ample annual rainfall. The pines and broad-leaved trees here are adapted to drier soils than those of the coast and Mississippi Basin.

Shortleaf, Longleaf, Loblolly, and Slash pines, with Baldcypress in swamps and lowlands, are typical cone-bearers. Broad-leaved trees are magnolias; tupelos; Winged and Cedar elms; Sugarberry; Pecan and other hickories; oaks and hollies.

CENTRAL HARDWOOD Forest Region has a variable climate, rich soils, and fairly even precipitation. Much of the original forest cover of the area has been cleared for agriculture and other developments.

Typical trees of the many complex associations include Black Walnut; American Sycamore; Yellow-poplar; Sweetgum; Yellow Buckeye; and a variety of oaks, maples, ashes, hickories, basswoods, and some conifers.

ROCKY MOUNTAIN Forest Region, occurring chiefly on higher mountain slopes, is typified by cold winters and a short but warm growing season. A summer dry period is most pronounced in southern latitudes. Cone-bearing trees predominate.

Typical are Ponderosa, Lodgepole, Western White, Limber, and Pinyon pines; Engelmann and Blue spruces; Subalpine Fir; Douglas-fir; Western Larch; and a number of junipers. Quaking Aspen is the most conspicuous broad-leaved tree.

SUBTROPICAL Forest Region occurs along Florida's tip and the mouth of the Rio Grande in Texas. Tropical forests of broad-leaved, deciduous and evergreen trees occur southward.

Among the trees typical of the Florida subtropics are West Indies Mahogany; several mangroves; Sapodilla; Lignumvitae; and a number of species of palms.

Northern

Southeastern

Central Hardwood

Tundra

Grasslands

Subtropical

Rocky Mountain

Pacific Coast

Desert

Desert scrub and grass

PACIFIC COAST Forest Region from Alaska to northern California has a mild climate and abundant precipitation along the coasts. Here are dense forests, primarily of cone-bearing trees. Some typical coastal species range inland in the Pacific Northwest. Southward and inland the warmer, drier climate favors mixtures of cone-bearing trees on mountain slopes and broad-leaved trees at lower elevations.

Typical cone-bearing trees include Douglas-fir; true firs; Western and Mountain hemlocks; cedars (Western red, Port-Orford, and Alaska); Sugar, Ponderosa, Whitebark, and other pines; Western Larch; Redwood and Giant Sequoia; junipers and cypresses. Among the broadleaved trees are Black Cottonwood and Quaking Aspen; several oaks; Pacific Dogwood; Bigleaf Maple; Red Alder; and Oregon Ash.

GYMNOSPERMS

Gymnosperms bear naked seeds, often on a scale; angiosperm seeds, in contrast, are enclosed by the ovary (p. 66). Most familiar of the gymnosperms are pines, firs, and others of the pine family, but included in the nearly 700 species are the yews and cycads (below), plus the redwood family (p. 50), cedar family (p. 54), the Ginkgo and others (p. 64).

YEW FAMILY (Taxaceae)

Yews and torreyas are small trees and shrubs without cones but with flat, linear evergreen needles. Yews (Taxus) include about seven species. Three grow in North America; others in Europe, North Africa, and Asia. English Yew (T. baccata) and varieties are widely grown as ornamentals. Of five species of torreyas (Torreya), two grow in North America; others in Japan and China.

Pacific Yew

Florida Yew

California Torreya

Florida Torreya

PACIFIC (WESTERN) YEW (Taxus brevifolia) needles are 0.5 to 1 inch long, dark green above and light green below. Break from twig cleanly; similar Coast Redwood needles (p. 50) tear from twig and have two silvery bands below. Greenish seed, 0.3 of an inch, protrudes from scarlet, gelatinous cup (aril). Reddish-purple bark scales off in thin, irregular patches. Not abundant but widely distributed; grows 20 to 40 feet tall (rarely to 75), 1 to 2 feet in diameter, in moist forests. Florida Yew (T. floridana) is a rare, smaller, bushy tree, with short trunk and spreading branches.

CALIFORNIA TORREYA (Torreya californica) needles are 1 to 3.5 inches long, with a sharp tip. The plumlike fruit, streaked with purple, is 1 to 1.5 inches long and contains a large, brown seed. Sometimes called California Nutmeg. Bark is gray-brown, fissured to loosely scaly. Grows 30 to 90 feet tall, 1 to 3 feet in diameter, usually along streams. The rare Florida Torreya (T. taxifolia), also called Stinking-cedar because of the odor of its leaves, is smaller and has darker fruit.

CYCAD FAMILY (Cycadaceae)

CYCADS of about 100 species in 9 genera are primitive, palmlike plants of warm regions. A cluster of large, pinnate leaves is borne either on an erect trunk or on an underground stem. Staminate and pistillate flowers are in conelike structures on different plants. Four species of Zamia, or Coontie, grow in Florida. The Sago Palm (Cycas revoluta), from Java, and the slightly larger Fern Palm (C. circinalis), from southeastern Asia, East Africa, and the South Pacific islands, are cycads that are grown in southern U.S. as ornamentals.

GYMNOSPERMS

cone   naked seed
        on scale

branchlet
with fruit

seed protected
by ovary wall

ANGIOSPERMS

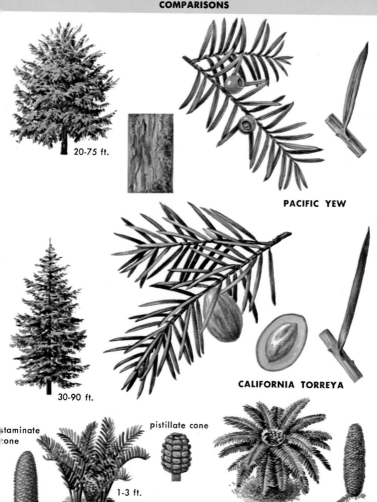

20-75 ft.

PACIFIC YEW

30-90 ft.

CALIFORNIA TORREYA

staminate
cone

pistillate cone

1-3 ft.

ZAMIA

to 10 ft.

SAGO PALM

staminate
cone

21

PINE FAMILY (Pinaceae)

Pines, larches, spruces, hemlocks, douglas-firs, and true firs represent the pine family in North America. Three other genera occur elsewhere. Needles of pines are in bundles (fascicles); those of larches (p. 36) in brushlike clusters on spur shoots; in other genera (pp. 38-48) needles are produced singly, either growing from persistent woody bases or directly from twigs. Based on wood and other features, about 35 species of North American pines *(Pinus)* are separated into two groups: soft (p. 22-25) and hard (p. 26-35).

SOFT PINES

EASTERN WHITE PINE *(Pinus strobus)* needles, in bundles of 5, are 3 to 5 inches long, soft, and flexible. They remain on the branches one to two years. Fine white lines of stomata are on two surfaces of each needle. The stalked, curved cones are 4 to 8 inches long (usually 5), and their scales lack spines. On young trees the bark is smooth and gray; on mature trunks it is broken into small rectangular blocks. This largest conifer in the Northeast grows 75 to 100 feet tall, 2 to 4 feet in diameter, with a pyramidal crown of whorled, horizontal branches. Prefers moist, sandy loam soils; often forms pure stands.

WESTERN WHITE PINE *(Pinus monticola)* needles resemble those of Eastern White Pine but may remain on the tree for as long as four years, making the crown denser. The stalked cones, which may be slightly curved, are 5 to 15 inches long (usually 8) with spineless scales. The bark resembles that of the Eastern White Pine. Grows 100 to 175 feet tall, 2 to 5 feet in diameter. Crown is open, with pyramidal whorls of horizontal branches.

SUGAR PINE *(Pinus lambertiana)* needles, usually twisted, resemble those of Eastern White Pine but have fine white lines on all surfaces. The stalked, columnar cones, with spineless scales, are 10 to 26 inches long (usually 16), the longest cones of any American conifer. The smooth, gray-green bark of young trees becomes grayish brown to purplish and is broken into scaly ridges. Sugar Pine grows 175 to 200 feet tall and 3 to 5 feet in diameter, the tallest American pine. Its pyramidal crown has whorls of horizontal branches, with several conspicuously longer than others. Its sap contains a sugary substance.

SOFT PINES

needles usually
in bundles of 5,
occasionally 1-4;
sheath is shed

seeds

cones usually
stalked and
scales without
prickles

HARD PINES

needles usually in
bundles of 2 or 3,
occasionally 5-8;
sheath persists

cones usually
with thick
woody scales
armed with prickles

COMPARISONS

EASTERN WHITE PINE

75-100 ft.

WESTERN WHITE PINE

100-175 ft.

SUGAR PINE

175-200 ft.

23

WHITEBARK PINE (*Pinus albicaulis*) has stout, stiff needles, 1 to 2.5 inches long, in bundles of 5. The ovoid cones, about 2.5 inches long, have scales with blunt, triangular tips. Unlike cones of other pines, they disintegrate when mature. The thin bark is scaly and gray to brown. An alpine tree, from altitudes of about 5,000 feet in the north to 10,000 feet or higher in California, Whitebark Pine may grow 50 to 60 feet tall and 1 to 2 feet in diameter. In rocky, exposed places, often a sprawling shrub. It grows slowly, requiring 200 years or longer to mature.

LIMBER PINE (*Pinus flexilis*) is a timberline tree of dry, rocky soil. Similar in appearance to Whitebark Pine. Cones are columnar, 3 to 8 inches long; they do not disintegrate and scales are thickened but not pointed at the ends. Bark scaly, dark brown to black. Limber Pine grows 25 to 50 feet tall and 1 to 2 feet in diameter. Like Whitebark Pine, it becomes twisted and dwarfed when growing in exposed locations.

FOXTAIL PINE (*Pinus balfouriana*) needles are 1 to 2 inches long and remain on the branches 10 to 12 years, giving them a bushy, foxtail appearance. Cones, 3 to 5 inches long, have scales tipped with a small, curved prickle. Bark of mature trees is gray to reddish brown, in scaly plates. Grows in poor, rocky soils at high elevations and is often contorted and windblown. On best sites, may grow 20 to 50 feet tall.

BRISTLECONE PINE (*Pinus aristata*) is a western alpine tree that may grow 20 to 60 feet tall and 1 to 2 feet in diameter. It resembles Foxtail Pine, but its needles remain on the branches even longer. Tiny, gray droplets of resin mark the needles and the 3-inch-long cones. Cone scales are tipped with long, stiff, incurved prickle. A gnarled specimen in California is believed to be 4,000 years old.

Singleleaf

Mexican

← Pinyon

Parry

PINYONS have large, edible seeds. All four species are small trees, 20 to 40 feet tall, with rounded crowns. Found in semi-arid regions of the West, they are typical of dry, rocky, or gravelly soils. The needles are 1 to 1.5 inches long, the cones round, resinous, and about 2 inches long. Singleleaf Pinyon (*Pinus monophylla*) bears needles singly; Parry Pinyon (*P. quadrifolia*) has needles in 4's. Pinyon (*P. edulis*) and Mexican Pinyon (*P. cembroides*) in 2's. Pinyon's needles have smooth margins; Mexican Pinyon's, finely toothed.

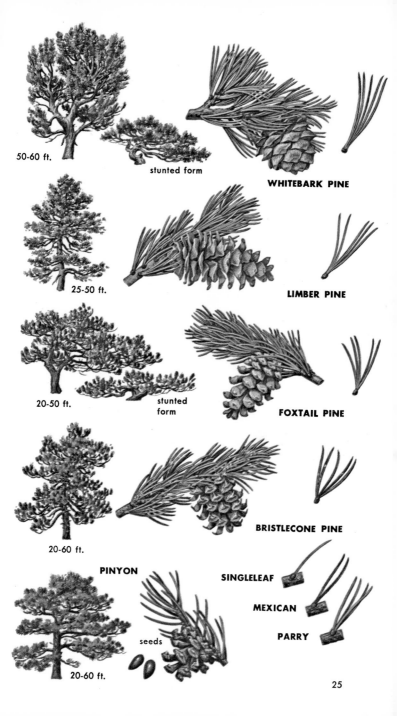

50-60 ft.

stunted form

WHITEBARK PINE

25-50 ft.

LIMBER PINE

20-50 ft.

stunted form

FOXTAIL PINE

20-60 ft.

BRISTLECONE PINE

PINYON

SINGLELEAF

seeds

MEXICAN

PARRY

20-60 ft.

25

HARD PINES

JACK PINE *(Pinus banksiana)* needles, in bundles of 2, are 1 to 1.5 inches long, stiff, and dark green. The cones, which may stay on the tree for many years, are 1 to 2 inches long and generally curve toward the tip of the branch. Each scale is tipped with a short, slender prickle. The scaly bark is dark gray to reddish brown. Jack Pine is a small to medium-sized tree, 70 to 80 feet tall and 1 to 1.5 feet in diameter. It is usually ragged in appearance, especially in the poor soils in which it commonly grows.

RED PINE *(Pinus resinosa)* needles, in bundles of 2, are 4 to 6 inches long, slender and flexible, but break readily when doubled. The 1- to 2.5-inch, conical-ovoid cones have unarmed scales. Twigs yellowish at first, changing to reddish brown. On mature trees, bark forms irregular, diamond-shaped, scaly plates. An important timber tree, 50 to 100 feet tall and 2 to 3 feet in diameter, Red Pine has a symmetrically oval crown. Another common name for this tree is Norway Pine, though it is a native of North America.

LODGEPOLE PINE *(Pinus contorta)* needles, in bundles of 2, are 1 to 3 inches long, stiff, and dark green. They stay on the branches for three years or longer. Each scale on the 1- to 2-inch cones is tipped with a stiff prickle. Cones remain closed and attached for years, but open when heated. Areas destroyed by ground fire are often reseeded quickly. The scaly bark is black to straw-colored. Lodgepole Pine grows in sandy soils, in bogs, and at high elevations in a wide range of conditions that also influence tree's form. Coastal form is 25 to 30 feet tall and 1 to 1.5 feet in diameter, with a ragged crown. A slender form of Lodgepole Pine *(P. contorta* var. *latifolia)* is 75 to 80 feet tall and 1 to 3 feet in diameter. In California, it is also called Tamarack Pine.

SHORTLEAF PINE *(Pinus echinata)* has needles 3 to 5 inches long, mostly in bundles of 2; they are dark yellow-green, slender, and flexible. The cones are 1.5 to 2.5 inches long, each scale tipped with a prickle. The bark is dark brown and in irregular, scaly plates. Grows 80 to 100 feet tall and 2 to 3 feet in diameter, with a narrow, pyramidal crown. An important timber tree, it grows in light, dry soils.

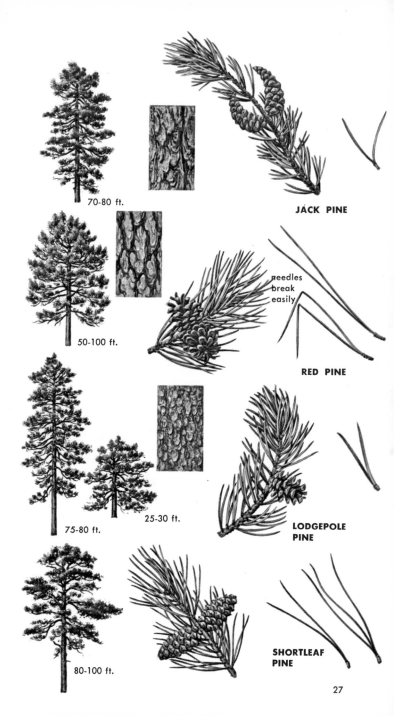

70-80 ft.

JACK PINE

50-100 ft.

needles
break
easily

RED PINE

75-80 ft.　　25-30 ft.

**LODGEPOLE
PINE**

80-100 ft.

**SHORTLEAF
PINE**

27

SLASH PINE *(Pinus elliottii)* needles are mostly in bundles of 2. They are stiff, 8 to 10 inches long, and dark blue-green. The scales on the 3- to 6-inch cones are tipped with prickles, and the gray to reddish-brown bark occurs in irregular, scaly plates. Slash Pine grows 80 to 100 feet tall, 2 to 3 feet in diameter, with a dense, rounded crown. It prefers relatively moist soils. Because of its vigor and rapid growth, Slash Pine is used in reforestation not only in southeastern United States but also in Australia, New Zealand, and South Africa.

BISHOP PINE *(Pinus muricata)* needles, in bundles of 2, are thick, rigid, and about 5 inches long. The 2- to 4-inch cones are usually in clusters of 3 to 5, the scales tipped with a stout, spurlike prickle. Bark is dark purple-brown and scaly or ridged. Bishop Pine grows 40 to 50 feet tall, 2 to 3 feet in diameter, with a spreading, pyramidal to flat-topped crown. Found in either dry or swampy soils, in pure stands.

SAND PINE *(Pinus clausa)* has slender, flexible needles, about 3 inches long, in bundles of 2. The ovoid-conical cones are 2 to 3.5 inches long. Bark is reddish brown, forming scaly plates and ridges. The Sand Pine is a scrubby tree, 15 to 20 feet tall, 1 foot in diameter, with a flat-topped crown; generally grows in poor soils.

VIRGINIA PINE *(Pinus virginiana)* is a small tree, 30 to 40 feet tall, 1 to 1.5 feet in diameter, with a ragged, flat-topped crown. Generally grows in poor soils. Needles, in bundles of 2, are 1 to 3 inches long and stiff. The 1.5- to 2.5-inch cones have a prickle on each scale; reddish-brown bark is scaly.

SPRUCE PINE *(Pinus glabra)* needles are 3 inches long, slender, flexible, and in bundles of 2. The globose cones, 2 to 3.5 inches long, have scales tipped with a minute prickle (often deciduous). Bark is dark gray and furrowed. Grows 80 to 100 feet tall and 2 to 2.5 feet in diameter. Generally found with hardwoods.

TABLE-MOUNTAIN PINE *(Pinus pungens)* grows to 60 feet tall, 2 to 3 feet in diameter, with a narrow, round-topped crown. Its needles, in bundles of 2, are 1.5 to 2.5 inches long, rigid, and twisted. Cones are 2.5 to 3.5 inches long, clustered, and persistent.

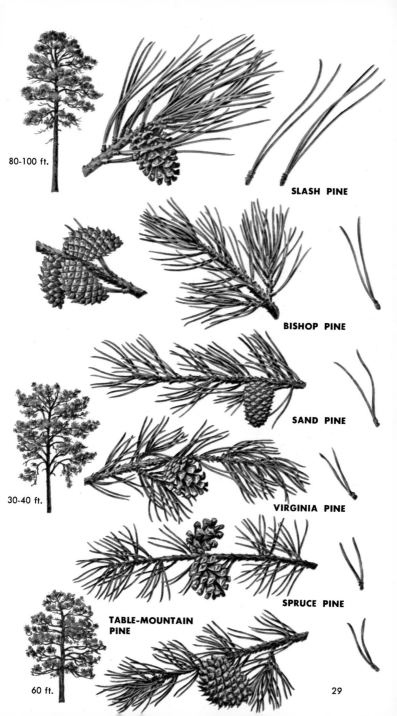

80-100 ft.

SLASH PINE

BISHOP PINE

SAND PINE

30-40 ft.

VIRGINIA PINE

SPRUCE PINE

TABLE-MOUNTAIN PINE

60 ft.

29

PONDEROSA PINE *(Pinus ponderosa)* needles may be in bundles of 3 or in 2's and 3's on same tree. They are 5 to 10 inches long, dark yellow-green, and form tufts near the end of the branches. Cones are oval, 3 to 6 inches long, the scales tipped with a stiff prickle. Bark on young, vigorous trees is dark brown or black. On mature trees, bright reddish-orange bark is in broad, irregular, scaly plates; scales fit together like jigsaw puzzle pieces. Grows 150 to 180 feet tall, 3 to 4 feet in diameter, with a broad, open crown. Ponderosa Pine is common throughout the West and is an important timber tree.

JEFFREY PINE *(Pinus jeffreyi)* resembles Ponderosa Pine but has darker needles that remain on the branches six to nine years, giving the tree a denser crown. Cones are 5 to 15 inches long, with incurved prickles on the scales. Bark of mature trees forms elongated plates. It has a distinctive odor of vanilla or pineapple. Jeffrey Pine is generally smaller than Ponderosa Pine and is found at a higher elevation. Washoe Pine *(P. washoensis)* is a closely related, rare species that grows only on the high eastern slopes of the Sierra Nevada.

KNOBCONE PINE *(Pinus attenuata)* has slender, stiff, yellow-green needles about 5 inches long, in bundles of 3. They cover the branches sparsely. The narrowly conical cones are 4 to 5 inches long, their scales tipped with a prickle and the basal scales knoblike. The cones remain closed and attached in clusters on the branches for long periods but open when heated, like Lodgepole Pine. Occasionally cones are found imbedded in wood as a branch has increased in diameter and grown around them. The gray-brown bark forms scaly ridges. Knobcone Pine grows 40 to 75 feet tall and 1 to 2 feet in diameter, with a sparse, irregular crown. It grows on dry foothill slopes.

COULTER PINE *(Pinus coulteri)* has stiff, blue-green needles, 10 inches long and in bundles of 3. The large, oval cones, heaviest of all pine cones, are 10 inches long, with thick, woody scales, each ending in a long, narrow, sharp, curved claw. Bark is black, scaly, and ridged. Generally found in dry, gravelly, or loamy soil at low elevations. Coulter Pine grows 40 to 80 feet tall and 1 to 3 feet in diameter, with a dense, broadly rounded crown.

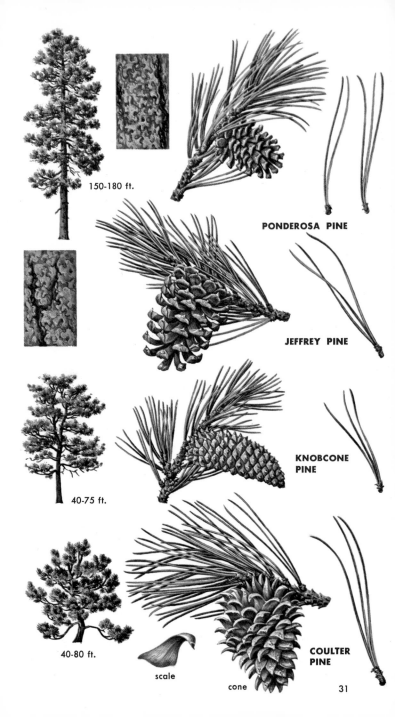

150-180 ft.

PONDEROSA PINE

JEFFREY PINE

40-75 ft.

KNOBCONE PINE

40-80 ft.

scale

cone

COULTER PINE

31

DIGGER PINE (*Pinus sabiniana*) needles, in bundles of 3, are stiff, gray-green, and 8 to 10 inches long. The oval cones are 5 to 8 inches long, with thick, woody scales that end in a broad, triangular claw. The scaly bark is black to reddish brown. Digger Pine grows 40 to 60 feet tall and 1 to 2 feet in diameter; trunk often forked. Common in Sierra foothills. The seeds were part of the diet of California Indians.

APACHE PINE (*Pinus engelmannii*) has 10- to 14-inch, dark-green needles, usually in 3's but sometimes in bundles of 2's or 5's. The oval cones, 4 to 6 inches long, are often asymmetrical at base; scales narrowly flattened at apex and tipped with a tiny prickle. The dark-brown bark is fissured. Grows 50 to 60 feet tall and 1 to 2 feet in diameter.

PITCH PINE (*Pinus rigida*) has stiff, yellow-green needles, 3 to 5 inches long, in 3's. Oval cones are 2 to 3.5 inches long, each scale tipped with a prickle. On mature trees the yellowish-brown bark is in scaly plates. Pitch Pine is a ragged, small to medium-sized tree, 50 to 60 feet tall and 1 to 2 feet in diameter. It generally grows in poor soils but may also have limited occurrence on better sites. Occasionally, and unusual for a conifer, it sprouts from base, especially after fire.

LOBLOLLY PINE (*Pinus taeda*) needles, usually in bundles of 3, are 6 to 9 inches long, slender but stiff, and yellow-green. The oval to conical cones are 2 to 6 inches long, each scale tipped with a prickle. Bark on mature trees is reddish brown and in scaly plates. Loblolly Pine is an important timber tree in southeastern United States. It grows 90 to 100 feet tall and 2 to 3 feet in diameter, with a relatively dense crown.

LONGLEAF PINE (*Pinus palustris*) has bright-green needles, 8 to 18 inches long, in 3's (or 5's in some parts of Gulf region), and tufted near ends of branches. Except early in the growing season, Longleaf Pine can be recognized by its white buds. Young trees grow slowly, forming deep roots and only a tuft of foliage near the ground; this is known as the "grass stage." Mature trees have cones 6 to 10 inches long, each scale tipped with a prickle. Bark is dark reddish brown in rough, scaly plates. Longleaf Pine grows 75 to 120 feet tall and 2 to 2.5 feet in diameter, with an open crown. It is important for lumber, pulp, and resin.

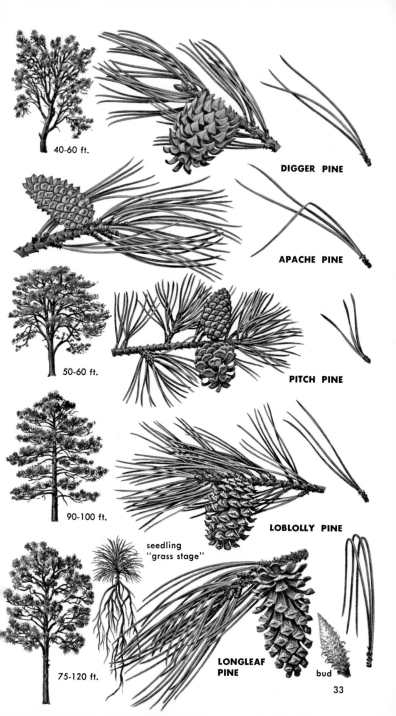

40-60 ft.

DIGGER PINE

APACHE PINE

50-60 ft.

PITCH PINE

90-100 ft.

LOBLOLLY PINE

seedling
"grass stage"

75-120 ft.

LONGLEAF PINE

bud

33

MONTEREY PINE *(Pinus radiata)* has slender, flexible, bright blue-green needles, 5 inches long, in bundles of 3 (rarely 2). Oval cones are 3 to 7 inches long, with light-brown, rounded scales tipped with a minute prickle. Bark is brown to black and fissured. Monterey Pine grows 40 to 100 feet tall and 1 to 3 feet in diameter, with a dense crown. Used for reforestation and as a timber tree in New Zealand, Australia, and South Africa, though in its native range the wood has little commercial value.

POND PINE *(Pinus serotina)* needles are 6 to 8 inches long, slender, flexible, and dark yellow-green; in 3's (occasionally 4's). Oval cones, 2 to 2.5 inches long, have flattened scales tipped with a prickle. Bark is dark reddish brown, scaly, and fissured. Usually grows in moist to swampy places. Pond Pine grows to an average height of 25 feet and occasionally 40 to 70 feet, with an open, round-topped crown.

CHIHUAHUA PINE *(Pinus leiophylla* var. *chihuahuana)* needles are in bundles of 3 and, unlike other hard pines, sheaths around bundles are shed. Needles 2 to 4 inches long, slender, and pale green. Cones 1.5 to 2.5 inches long, scales tipped with tiny, deciduous prickles; require three years to mature. Bark is dark reddish brown to black, scaly, and ridged. Grows 40 to 50 feet tall and 1 to 2 feet in diameter.

TORREY PINE *(Pinus torreyana)* needles, in bundles of 5, are 7 to 11 inches long, stiff, and dark green. The nearly round, chocolate-brown cones are 4 to 6 inches long and have scales ending in a thickened triangle with a rigid point. Bark is reddish brown, scaly, and fissured. Torrey Pine, a rare, protected tree, grows 20 to 60 feet tall and 1 to 1.5 feet in diameter, with a dense, bushy, round-topped crown.

SOME INTRODUCED PINES

SCOTCH PINE *(Pinus sylvestris)*, an important European timber tree, is widely planted in North America. Needles are stiff, yellow-green, 1.5 to 3 inches long, in bundles of 2. Cones, 2 to 5 inches long, have flat-topped scales tipped with a slender prickle. Bark scaly, bright orange-red; darker on older trees. Trunk often crooked. To 50 feet tall, 1.5 feet in diameter.

AUSTRIAN PINE *(Pinus nigra)*, a European species grown as an ornamental in North America, has dark-green needles, to 6 inches long, 2 per bundle; resemble those of Red Pine but are darker, heavier, and do not break cleanly. Cones, 2 to 4 inches long, have scales tipped with a tiny prickle. To 100 feet tall and 2.5 feet in diameter; stout branches, pyramidal crown.

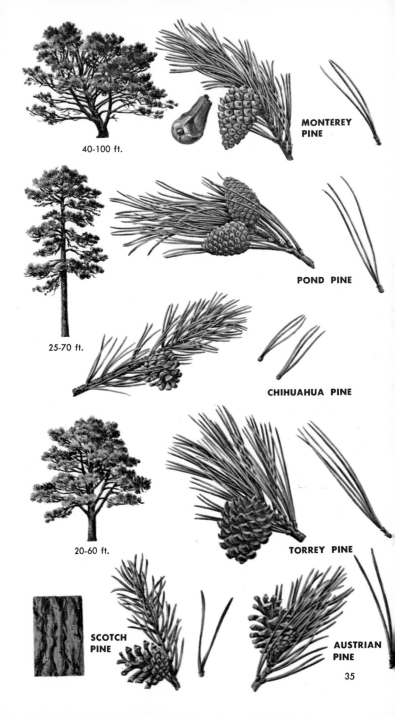

40-100 ft.

MONTEREY PINE

POND PINE

25-70 ft.

CHIHUAHUA PINE

20-60 ft.

TORREY PINE

SCOTCH PINE

AUSTRIAN PINE

35

LARCHES OR TAMARACKS *(Larix)*

Unlike most conifers, larches are deciduous. Their soft, flat needles grow in dense, brushlike clusters at tips of short, spurlike shoots (singly on new growth). Cones, 0.5 to 2 inches long, grow upright and may cling for several years. Needles resemble those of true cedars (see below), but true cedar needles are evergreen and plump in cross section. Ten species grow in cooler parts of Northern Hemisphere—three in Canada and northern United States. European Larch *(L. decidua)* is commonly planted as an ornamental.

TAMARACK *(Larix laricina)* has flat to slightly 3-angled, blue-green needles, 0.8 to 1.3 inches long; turn yellow in fall. Cones ovoid, 0.5 to 0.8 of an inch long, the 12 to 15 scales usually longer than broad and bracts shorter than scales. Bark thin, scaly, and gray to reddish brown. Grows 40 to 80 feet tall, 1 to 2 feet in diameter, usually in moist to boggy soils.

WESTERN LARCH *(Larix occidentalis)* needles are similar to Tamarack's but 1 to 1.8 inches long. Also, the 1- to 1.5-inch cones have more scales, usually broader than long; bracts are longer than scales. Bark thick, reddish brown, and in elongated, scaly plates. Grows to 150 feet tall, 3 to 4 feet in diameter. An important timber tree, it prefers moist mountain slopes but will grow in dry soils.

SUBALPINE LARCH *(Larix lyallii)* needles are somewhat 4-angled in cross section, otherwise resemble those of other larches. New-growth twigs are covered with white, cottony hairs. Cones, 2 inches long, appear bristly because bracts extend well beyond end of scales. Grows 15 to 60 feet tall and a foot in diameter. Branches often crooked and somewhat pendant, forming an irregularly shaped crown. Subalpine Larch is generally found in poor, rocky soils near timberline, often in pure stands.

TRUE CEDARS *(Cedrus spp.)* are not native to North America, but three species, and their varieties, are planted as ornamentals. Foliage resembles that of larches but is evergreen. Cones are upright, 3 to 5 inches long, barrel-shaped, and disintegrate after maturity (two years). Deodar Cedar *(C. deodara)*, from the Himalayas, has needles 1 to 2 inches long, downswept branches and a drooping tip. Both Atlas Cedar *(C. atlantica)*, from northern Africa, and Lebanon Cedar *(C. libani)*, from Asia Minor, have needles to 1.3 inches long, horizontal to uplifted branches, and a rather erect tip. All three grow to 100 feet tall. (See p. 54 for native species known as cedar.)

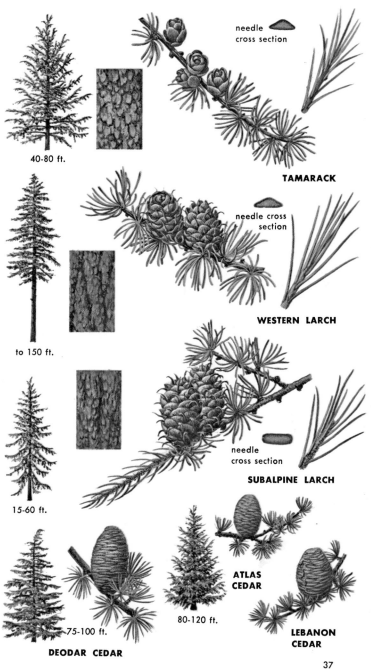

needle
cross section

40-80 ft.

TAMARACK

needle cross
section

to 150 ft.

WESTERN LARCH

needle
cross section

15-60 ft.

SUBALPINE LARCH

**ATLAS
CEDAR**

80-120 ft.

75-100 ft.

DEODAR CEDAR

**LEBANON
CEDAR**

·SPRUCES (Picea)

Spruces have sessile, rigid, often prickly, evergreen needles that grow singly from persistent, woody, peglike bases. Naked twigs are rough and warty. The pendant cones are composed of thin to light, woody scales. Seeds are ovoid or oblong. Bark typically thin and scaly. Spruces grow best in relatively moist soils, their crowns characteristically dense and spirelike.

About 40 species of spruces grow in the cooler and temperate parts of the Northern Hemisphere. Seven are native to the United States and Canada; others are found in Europe and Asia, most abundantly in China where there are about 18 species. Many spruces are commercially important, especially for paper pulp. Some spruces, including a number of introduced species, are planted as ornamentals.

BLACK SPRUCE (Picea mariana) needles are rigid but not prickly, dark green, plump to 4-sided in cross section and 0.3 to 0.5 of an inch long. Numerous short, brown hairs are typical on new growth of the twigs. The ovoid cones, 0.5 to 1 inch long, have brittle scales, rough along the outer margin. They often hang on branches for many years. The outer bark is reddish brown; the inner bark is olive green when freshly exposed. Black Spruce grows best in boggy situations, where it becomes 30 to 40 feet tall and a foot in diameter.

RED SPRUCE (Picea rubens) needles are similar to those of Black Spruce but are 0.5 to 0.7 of an inch long. New-growth twigs have only a few short, brown hairs. Cones, which fall soon after maturity, are 1.3 to 2 inches long and have thin, woody scales, generally smooth and rounded on the margin. Bark dark gray to brown; inner bark reddish brown. Red Spruce often grows along the edge of streams and bogs, where it attains a height of 60 to 70 feet and a diameter of 1 to 2 feet.

WHITE SPRUCE (Picea glauca) needles are similar to those of Black Spruce but are 1 inch long and generally crowded on the upperside of the branch. New twigs are not hairy. Cones are 1 to 2.5 inches long with thin, woody, but flexible scales, smooth on the rounded margin. Outer bark is ash brown; inner bark silvery when freshly exposed. White Spruce is found along the shores of streams and lakes, growing 75 feet tall and 2 feet in diameter.

sessile on woody "peg"

sessile; scar round, depressed

needles petiolate; on woody "cushions"

needles petiolate; scars round, raised

SPRUCES
Picea

TRUE FIRS
Abies

HEMLOCKS
Tsuga

DOUGLAS-FIRS
Pseudotsuga

pendant

upright

terminal

pendant, with bracts

COMPARISONS

30-40 ft.

needle cross section

scale with seeds

BLACK SPRUCE

60-70 ft.

needle cross section

scale with seeds

RED SPRUCE

75 ft.

needle cross section

WHITE SPRUCE

39

ENGELMANN SPRUCE *(Picea engelmannii)* foliage resembles White Spruce's, but the needles (plump to 4-sided in cross section) are often prickly; twigs minutely hairy. Cones, 1 to 2.5 inches long, are light chestnut-brown, the scales papery thin, stiff, ragged along outer edge. Bark scaly, purplish to reddish brown. Grows 100 to 125 feet tall, 1 to 3 feet in diameter, at high elevations in western mountains. Important timber tree.

BLUE SPRUCE *(Picea pungens)* needles are 1 to 1.5 inches long and stick out in all directions from branch. They are silvery blue, diamond-shaped in cross section, stiff, and very prickly. Twigs not hairy. Cones are similar to those of the Engelmann Spruce but 3.5 inches long. Bark dark gray. A medium-sized tree, 80 to 100 feet tall and 1 to 2 feet in diameter, Blue Spruce occurs on mountain slopes in Rocky Mountain regions, generally near streams. This tree is also widely used as an ornamental.

SITKA SPRUCE *(Picea sitchensis)* needles are flat in cross section, 0.5 to 1.5 inches long, extremely prickly and often silvery. Twigs not hairy. Cones resemble those of Engelmann Spruce, and the scaly bark is silvery to purplish gray. An important timber tree, grows 150 to 200 feet tall and 3 to 6 feet in diameter, occasionally larger. Crown of somewhat drooping branches. Grows at low elevations near sea level.

BREWER SPRUCE *(Picea breweriana)* needles are 0.8 to 1.3 inches long and flattened to 3-sided. The cones, 2 to 5 inches long, have thin, purplish-green scales, smooth and rounded on margin; later turn brown. Bark reddish brown. Brewer Spruce grows at elevation of 5,000 to 7,000 feet and reaches a height of 80 to 100 feet and a diameter of 2 to 3 feet. The long, pendant branches may touch the ground.

SOME INTRODUCED SPRUCES

NORWAY SPRUCE *(Picea abies)*, from Europe, is planted in the U.S. and Canada; many varieties. Needles are stiff, dark green, 0.5 to 0.8 of an inch long, flattened to triangular, usually point forward. Cones brown, 4 to 7 inches long. Bark reddish brown. Grows 125 feet tall, 2 feet in diameter.

TIGERTAIL SPRUCE *(Picea polita)*, from Orient, has spiny, dark-green, 1-inch needles, curved and often sticking out from stout branches that turn up—like "a tiger's tail." The 3- to 4-inch cones have broad scales with wavy or toothed margins; bark is dark. To 90 feet tall, 2 feet in diameter.

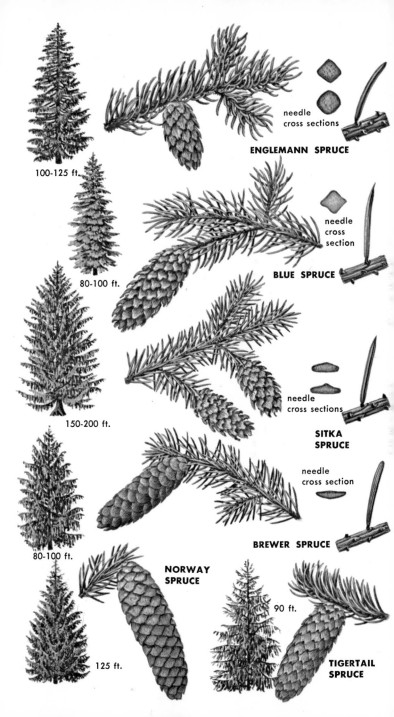

100-125 ft.

ENGLEMANN SPRUCE

needle cross sections

80-100 ft.

BLUE SPRUCE

needle cross section

150-200 ft.

SITKA SPRUCE

needle cross sections

BREWER SPRUCE

needle cross section

80-100 ft.

NORWAY SPRUCE

125 ft.

90 ft.

TIGERTAIL SPRUCE

HEMLOCKS *(Tsuga)*

Hemlocks are graceful trees, usually with soft, "lacy" foliage, and a drooping tip. The linear needles, generally flat and variable in length, are narrowed at the base into a short, slender stem. They grow from small, persistent, woody "cushions" on the twigs, as opposed to the more prominent woody "pegs" of spruces. Naked twigs are slightly roughened. The oval to oblong cones hang from the tips of the branchlets. Four of the 10 species are native to temperate North America; others grow in Japan, Taiwan, China, and the Himalayas. Some species are important for lumber and paper pulp, and because of their beauty, a number are planted as ornamentals.

EASTERN HEMLOCK *(Tsuga canadensis)* has flat needles, 0.3 to 0.7 of an inch long, tapering from base to apex, with two white bands of stomata below. Ovoid cones, 0.5 to 0.8 of an inch long, are attached by a short, slender stalk; outer margin of scales is smooth. Bark on mature trees is dark purplish brown, scaly, and deeply furrowed. Eastern Hemlock grows 60 to 75 feet tall and 1 to 3 feet in diameter, with a dense, pyramidal, "lacy" crown. It grows best in cool, moist locations.

CAROLINA HEMLOCK *(Tsuga caroliniana)* needles are flat but not tapered, about 0.8 of an inch long, grooved above, and with two white bands of stomata below. Oblong, stalked cones are 1 to 1.5 inches long. Bark is dark reddish brown, scaly, and furrowed. In rocky locations; to 50 feet tall, 2 feet in diameter.

WESTERN HEMLOCK *(Tsuga heterophylla)* needles resemble those of Eastern Hemlock but are not tapered. The cones, 0.8 to 1 inch long, are attached directly to branchlets, and their scales have wavy margins. Bark is dark reddish brown, scaly, and fissured; inner bark is reddish purple. Western Hemlock may grow 125 to 175 feet tall and 2 to 5 feet in diameter.

MOUNTAIN HEMLOCK *(Tsuga mertensiana)* needles are flat or plump in cross section, 0.8 of an inch long, curved, grooved and ribbed, and densely crowded on branches. Oblong cones, 0.8 to 3 inches long, at first green to purple, but turn brown to black with age. Dark purplish-brown bark. Where protected, Mountain Hemlock may be 75 to 100 feet tall, 2 to 3 feet in diameter; where exposed, may be a sprawling shrub.

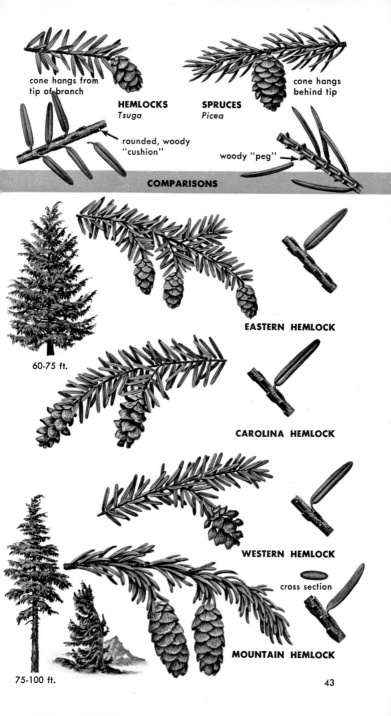

cone hangs from
tip of branch

HEMLOCKS
Tsuga

SPRUCES
Picea

cone hangs
behind tip

rounded, woody
"cushion"

woody "peg"

COMPARISONS

EASTERN HEMLOCK

60-75 ft.

CAROLINA HEMLOCK

WESTERN HEMLOCK

cross section

MOUNTAIN HEMLOCK

75-100 ft.

43

DOUGLAS-FIRS *(Pseudotsuga)*

Douglas-firs have flat, linear needles, with blunt to pointed tips. They grow directly from the branch and are narrowed at the base into a short, slender stem (petiole). When shed, a small, raised scar remains on the twig (see top of p. 39 and p. 45). Buds are ovoid, pointed, and shiny brown. The pendant, oblong-ovoid cones have distinctive 3-pointed bracts. Two douglas-fir species are native to western North America; three others grow in the Orient.

DOUGLAS-FIR *(Pseudotsuga menziesii)* needles, 1 to 1.5 inches long, stick out in all directions from the branches. Cones, 3 to 4 inches long, have 3-pointed bracts extending beyond ends of scales. Buds "cigar-shaped." Bark of young trees smooth and gray, with resin blisters; on mature trees, thick and furrowed, black to reddish brown outside and marbled cream-and-brown beneath. The compact, conical crown has drooping side branches. Forest trees have long, clear trunk. Grows rapidly, attaining greatest size—250 feet tall, 8 feet in diameter—in moist Pacific Coast region. In drier inland areas, grows slower and smaller —100 to 130 feet tall, 2 to 3 feet in diameter. Inland form sometimes considered a separate species; smaller cones, with bracts bent backward. Douglas-fir is an important timber tree; its strong, durable wood has many uses. One of the most distinctive trees in the Pacific Northwest, it is also prized as an ornamental, as a Christmas tree, and for reforestation.

BIGCONE DOUGLAS-FIR *(Pseudotsuga macrocarpa)* resembles Douglas-fir, but foliage is more nearly 2-ranked and the cones, 4 to 6 inches long, have bracts extending only to about the ends of the scales. Bigcone Douglas-fir grows 60 to 75 feet tall and 1 to 2 feet in diameter. Limited in distribution, Bigcone Douglas-fir is of no economic importance and is primarily of botanical interest.

SEEDS OF TREES IN PINE FAMILY

These seeds are borne in pairs at the base of cone scales. They vary in shape and weight; they also differ in how long they can remain dormant and still germinate. Seeds of some species in the pine family are wingless, but most are winged. Wings aid in dispersal by the wind.

Cone-hoarding squirrels also help to spread and to plant the seeds. Good seed crops are produced every few years. At such times foresters collect seeds for use in reforestation of burned and logged-off lands. (Also see pp. 52-53 for comparisons of seeds of other conifers.)

leaf scar large, round, and depressed; needle lacks petiole

TRUE FIRS
Abies

leaf scar small, raised; needle with petiole

DOUGLAS-FIRS
Pseudotsuga

COMPARISONS

DOUGLAS-FIR

100-250 ft.

60-75 ft.

bud

BIGCONE DOUGLAS-FIR

Red Pine	Balsam Fir	Western Larch
Pinyon	Noble Fir	Western Hemlock
Ponderosa Pine	Red Spruce	Douglas-fir

45

TRUE FIRS (Abies)

True firs have dense, compact, often spirelike crowns. Needles, flat to plump in cross section, grow directly from the branch. They have an expanded base, like a suction cup, and leave a distinctive, round, depressed scar on the twig. Location of silvery lines or bands of stomata on needles is an aid in identifying species. Erect cone disintegrates at maturity leaving a spikelike axis on branch. Buds plump, blunt at apex, often resinous. Though not highly regarded for lumber many true firs are sources of paper pulp. Others are prized as ornamentals or as Christmas trees. About 40 species of true firs grow in various parts of the world; nine are native to the area covered by this book (p. 3).

BALSAM FIR (Abies balsamea) needles are flat, 0.8 to 1.5 inches long, usually blunt or notched at the tip, with 2 silvery bands of stomata on the underside only. Needles 2-ranked except on topmost branches, where they are crowded on upperside of the twigs. Cylindrical, purplish cones are 2 to 4 inches long, the bracts shorter than the scales. On young trees, bark has many resin blisters; on mature trees, it is gray to reddish brown and in scaly plates. Balsam Fir may be 40 to 60 feet tall and 1 to 1.5 feet in diameter, attaining its best growth in moist soils near lakes and streams.

FRASER FIR (Abies fraseri) resembles Balsam Fir, but bracts of cones are longer than scales.

GRAND FIR (Abies grandis) needles, 0.5 to 2 inches long, are flat, blunt, or notched at tip, with stomata on the lower surface only. Distinctly 2-ranked and variable in length on lower branches. The cylindrical, greenish cones, 2 to 4 inches long, have bracts shorter than the scales. Bark on mature trees is gray to reddish brown, ridged, and furrowed. Grows 125 to 150 feet tall, 2 to 4 feet in diameter, the crown becoming rounded in older trees.

PACIFIC SILVER FIR (Abies amabilis) needles are flat and uniform in length (1 to 1.5 in.), with stomata on lower surface only; clothe top and sides of twigs. Purple, barrel-shaped cones, 3 to 6 inches long, have bracts shorter than scales. Bark, silvery to ash gray, is smooth, rarely furrowed. Pacific Silver Fir grows 100 to 150 feet tall, 1 to 3 feet in diameter; crown dense, spirelike.

cone upright, disintegrates at maturity

TRUE FIRS
Abies

cone pendant; does not disintegrate at maturity

DOUGLAS-FIRS
Pseudotsuga

COMPARISONS

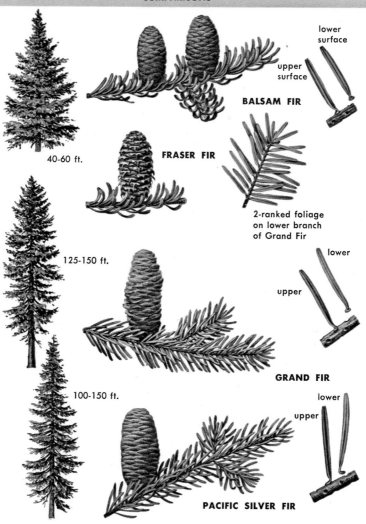

lower surface

upper surface

BALSAM FIR

40-60 ft.

FRASER FIR

2-ranked foliage on lower branch of Grand Fir

125-150 ft.

lower

upper

GRAND FIR

100-150 ft.

lower

upper

PACIFIC SILVER FIR

47

WHITE FIR *(Abies concolor)* has bluish-green needles that are 2 to 3 inches in length. They are flat, blunt to pointed, loosely 2-ranked, with stomata on both surfaces. The oblong, olive-green to purple cones are 3 to 5 inches long, their bracts shorter than their scales. The dark-gray bark is heavily ridged. White Fir grows 125 to 150 feet tall and 2 to 4 feet in diameter, with a dome-shaped crown. It occurs at low elevations, usually in drier soils than other firs.

BRISTLECONE FIR *(Abies bracteata)* has flat, often curved needles, 1.5 to 2.5 inches long, with stomata on lower surface only. Oval, purple-brown cones, 3 to 4 inches long, appear bristly due to long, slender bracts. Bark reddish brown. Bristlecone Fir is usually small but may grow 150 feet tall and 3 feet in diameter. The sharp spire of its crown is one of this tree's distinctive features.

NOBLE FIR *(Abies procera)* has 1- to 1.5-inch needles, flat on lower branches and plump to 4-angled on upper branches; on topmost branches erect and crowded on upper side. Needles silvery, stomata occurring on all surfaces. Cylindrical cones, 4 to 6 inches long, are "shingled" with long, reflexed greenish-brown bracts. Bark dark gray, in small, rectangular blocks. Grows 100 to 150 feet tall, 3 to 5 feet in diameter, with a dense, domelike crown. Noble Fir prefers deep, moist soils, at 2,000 to 5,000 feet.

CALIFORNIA RED FIR *(Abies magnifica)* needles resemble Noble Fir's, but the cones are 6 to 9 inches long, cylindrical to barrel-shaped, purple, with bracts shorter than the scales. Outer bark is reddish brown; inner bark reddish purple. Grows 100 to 150 feet tall, 2 to 4 feet in diameter, with a spirelike crown. California Red Fir grows between elevations of 5,000 and 10,000 feet, reaching its maximum size in moist, well-drained soils. A variety, Shasta Red Fir *(A. magnifica shastensis)*, has cones with reflexed bracts that are longer than the scales.

SUBALPINE FIR *(Abies lasiocarpa)* needles are flat, 1 to 1.8 inches long, with silvery lines of stomata on both surfaces. Cones, with bracts shorter than scales, are 2 to 4 inches long, purple, and cylindrical. Bark on mature trees is gray-brown, scaly, and furrowed. At timberline, often twisted and contorted; elsewhere grows 40 to 100 feet tall and 1 to 2 feet in diameter, with a compact, spirelike crown.

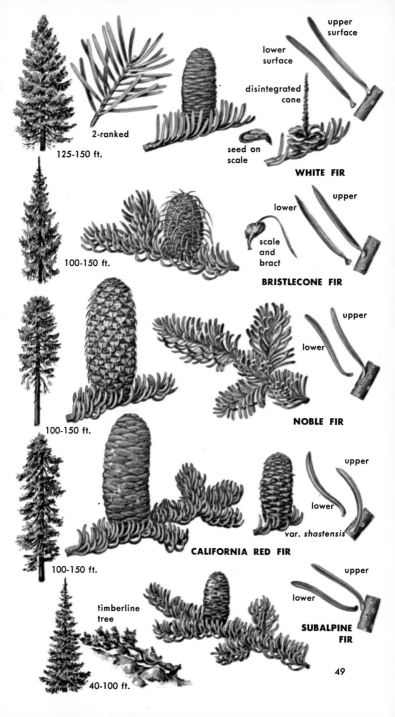

upper surface

lower surface

2-ranked

disintegrated cone

seed on scale

125-150 ft.

WHITE FIR

lower

upper

scale and bract

100-150 ft.

BRISTLECONE FIR

upper

lower

100-150 ft.

NOBLE FIR

upper

lower

var. *shastensis*

100-150 ft.

CALIFORNIA RED FIR

upper

lower

SUBALPINE FIR

timberline tree

40-100 ft.

49

REDWOOD FAMILY (Taxodiaceae)

About 40 species of sequoias *(Sequoia)* flourished in Northern Hemisphere forests some 60 million years ago. Only two species survive. Both are evergreen trees found principally in California; both have a high resistance to fire, insects, and disease, which accounts largely for their great age. Baldcypresses *(Taxodium)* are the only other native North American members of the redwood family. Other genera occur in Asia.

GIANT SEQUOIA *(Sequoia gigantea)* foliage is blue-green; leaves awl-like, 0.2 of an inch long (at ends of branches lance-shaped, 0.5 of an inch long). The egg-shaped cones, 2 to 3.5 inches long and with 24 to 40 woody, wedge-shaped, roughly flattened scales, reach full size in one season. Seeds do not mature until second season. Bark is fibrous, reddish brown, and furrowed; it may be 2 feet thick at base of columnar trunk of large trees. Young trees have a tapered trunk. Limited to groves on west side of Sierra Nevada, between 4,000 and 8,000 feet. The General Sherman Tree, in Sequoia National Park, is 272 feet tall, has an average basal diameter of 30.7 feet, and is estimated to be 3,800 years old. Placed in separate genus, *Sequoiadendron,* by some botanists.

REDWOOD *(Sequoia sempervirens)* needles are flat, 0.5 to 1 inch long, with a pointed tip; base extends down twig. Foliage resembles Pacific Yew's (p. 21), but Redwood needles tear rather than break from the branch and have two prominent, silvery bands on their underside. The cones are 0.8 to 1 inch long and have 15 to 20 scales; they mature in one season. Seeds do not germinate well, but the tree reproduces readily by sprouts from the stump, uncommon in conifers. The fibrous, reddish-brown bark is 3 to 10 inches thick. Commonly grows 200 to 275 feet tall, 8 to 10 feet in diameter, with a narrow, conical crown; exceptional specimens have exceeded 350 feet.

INTRODUCED RELATIVES OF SEQUOIA

JAPANESE CEDAR, SUGI, OR CRYPTOMERIA *(Cryptomeria japonica)* is a common and highly important evergreen tree native to Japan. Grown as an ornamental in parts of U.S. and southern Canada. The foliage resembles the Giant Sequoia's, and the oval, bristly cones are 0.8 to 1 inch long.

METASEQUOIA OR DAWN REDWOOD *(Metasequoia glyptostroboides)* was thought to be extinct until living specimens were found in an isolated valley in central China in 1948. The foliage resembles the Redwood's, but it is deciduous and the linear needles are somewhat longer.

REDWOOD
Sequoia sempervirens
p. 50

needles tear
from branch

silvery bands
on underside

PACIFIC YEW
Taxus brevifolia
p. 20

needles break
from branch

underside
greenish

COMPARISONS

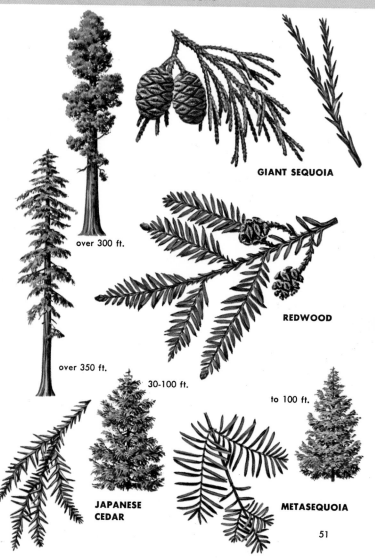

GIANT SEQUOIA

over 300 ft.

REDWOOD

over 350 ft.

30-100 ft.

to 100 ft.

JAPANESE CEDAR

METASEQUOIA

51

BALDCYPRESSES *(Taxodium)*

Like the redwoods (p. 51), baldcypresses are of ancient lineage, attain large size, and reach venerable age. There are only two species, found in southern United States and Mexico.

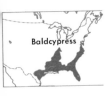

BALDCYPRESS *(Taxodium distichum)* has yellow-green 2-ranked, linear needles 0.5 to 0.8 of an inch long on lateral branchlets; they turn brown before falling with the branchlets in autumn. The tree also has shorter scalelike foliage, usually on fertile branchlets. Cones nearly round, 0.8 to 1 inch in diameter, the surface wrinkled; mature in one season, then usually disintegrate. Bark ash gray to reddish brown, fibrous or scaly. Baldcypress grows 100 to 125 feet tall and 3 to 5 feet in diameter. Trunk swollen, fluted, tapered; crown pyramidal to irregular. Typical of swamplands of southeastern U.S., but not confined to that environment. Branches often draped with Spanish Moss. Woody "knees," from a few inches to several feet tall, protrude above water from shallow, wide-spreading root system.

Pondcypress *(T. distichum* var. *nutans)* is a smaller variety of Baldcypress. Its branches are horizontal or ascending, and the shorter foliage is mostly awl-like and closely appressed to the slender twigs.

MONTEZUMA BALDCYPRESS *(Taxodium mucronatum)* resembles Baldcypress but has slightly larger cones and lacks "knees." Except in colder parts of range essentially an evergreen, as new needles develop before older needles drop. Not a swamp species, but needs ample moisture. Seeds germinate only in water or wet soil. Usually in small groups, or as single trees above 1,000 feet. Mexico's national tree, the largest and most famous is the Tule Cypress in Santa Maria del Tule, near Oaxaca. Although only 140 feet tall, this giant is between 35 and 40 feet in diameter, and its age has been estimated variously at from 2,000 to 5,000 years.

SEED COMPARISONS OF CONIFERS

Redwood and cypress trees bear from 1 to about 20 seeds on each cone scale. Each seed usually has two narrow, lateral wings. Juniper seeds are wingless; Baldcypress seeds have ridges rather than wings and are spread by water. Giant Sequoia seeds range from about 3,000 to more than 8,000 per ounce, yet each has the potential to become the largest of all living things.

Trees of the yew family do not bear cones. They produce single, relatively large seeds, either fully or partly enclosed by a fleshy covering, or aril. (See pp. 44-45.)

52 CEDAR OR CYPRESS FAMILY

COMPARISONS

leaves 2-ranked, deciduous; cones round, disintegrate

needle clusters on spur shoots; deciduous; cones oblong, persist

BALDCYPRESS
Taxodium

LARCHES
Larix

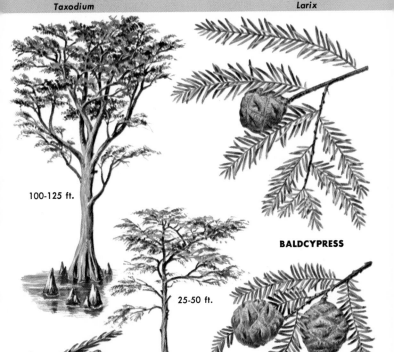

100-125 ft.

25-50 ft.

BALDCYPRESS

PONDCYPRESS

MONTEZUMA BALDCYPRESS

CYPRESS FAMILY

 Western Redcedar

Incense Cedar

 Common Juniper

 Port-Orford-Cedar

REDWOOD FAMILY

 Redwood

Giant Sequoia

 Baldcypress

YEW FAMILY

Pacific Yew

California Torreya

53

CEDAR OR CYPRESS FAMILY (Cupressaceae)

Cedar is the common name given trees of various genera in several families. Most familiar are native American species of the genera *Libocedrus, Thuja, Chamaecyparis* (p. 56) and several junipers (pp. 60-64). All these, together with cypresses, also in this family, have scalelike foliage on flattened or rounded branchlets. Species in the genus *Cedrus* (p. 36) of the pine family and *Cryptomeria* (p. 50) of the redwood family are also called cedar. The wood of most trees known as cedar is aromatic.

INCENSE-CEDAR *(Libocedrus decurrens)* has flattened branchlets covered with elongated (0.1 to 0.5 of an inch) closely overlapping, lustrous, dark-green scales in whorls of 4. The oblong cones, 0.8 to 1.5 inches long, are at first bright green, turning brown and opening wide when mature. They hang from the tips of the branchlets. On mature trees, the bark is dark brown, fibrous, deeply and irregularly furrowed. Young trees have a dense, conical crown; in older trees, which may grow 100 to 150 feet tall and 3 to 4 feet in diameter, crown becomes rounded.

NORTHERN WHITE-CEDAR *(Thuja occidentalis)* has flattened branchlets clothed by alternate pairs (at right angles to the pairs above and below) of closely overlapping, yellowish-green, aromatic scales, 0.1 to 0.3 of an inch long and glandular below. Oblong cones, 0.3 to 0.5 of an inch long, stand erect on branchlets; fibrous, gray to reddish-brown bark is ridged and furrowed. Typical of limestone soils but common also in moist or boggy situations. Usually has a compact, conical crown and may grow 40 to 50 feet tall, 2 to 3 feet in diameter.

WESTERN REDCEDAR *(Thuja plicata)* foliage is similar to Northern White-cedar's but a darker, more lustrous green. The cones, similar in size to those of Northern White-cedar, have a small spine just below tip of outer scales. Dark reddish-brown bark is fibrous, shreddy, and vertically ridged. In moist bottomland soils, this tree reaches its largest size—150 to 200 feet tall and 3 to 8 feet in diameter. The downswept branches that form the dense crown turn up at the ends; they look like giant fern fronds. Because of its durable, straight-grained wood, Western Redcedar is an important timber tree.

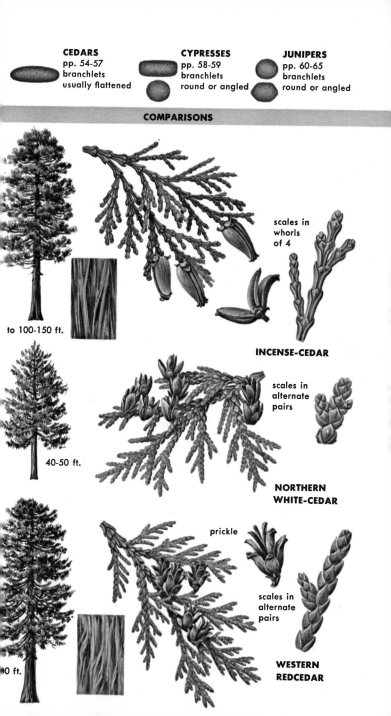

CEDARS
pp. 54-57
branchlets
usually flattened

CYPRESSES
pp. 58-59
branchlets
round or angled

JUNIPERS
pp. 60-65
branchlets
round or angled

COMPARISONS

scales in
whorls
of 4

to 100-150 ft.

INCENSE-CEDAR

scales in
alternate
pairs

40-50 ft.

**NORTHERN
WHITE-CEDAR**

prickle

scales in
alternate
pairs

0 ft.

**WESTERN
REDCEDAR**

PORT-ORFORD-CEDAR *(Chamaecyparis lawsoniana)* has flattened branchlets with closely overlapping, lustrous, dark-green scales, 0.1 of an inch long, in alternate pairs. Foliage similar to Western Redcedar's, but the smaller scales are marked on underside by stomata in conspicuous silvery X's. Round cones, 0.3 of an inch in diameter, have several wedge-shaped scales, each with a small, curved point in the center. At first bright green, cones turn brown at maturity. Bark on mature trunks is silver-brown, fibrous, and vertically ridged. Grows 140 to 180 feet tall and 4 to 6 feet in diameter, with a dense crown of short, somewhat pendant branches. An important timber tree and also planted as an ornamental, with several varieties developed especially for this purpose. Port-Orford-Cedar is often called Lawson Cypress.

ALASKA-CEDAR *(Chamaecyparis nootkatensis)* has scale-like, yellow-green foliage without silvery X's on underside and with a rougher texture (scales loose at ends) than Port-Orford-Cedar's. The cones resemble those of Port-Orford-Cedar but mature in two seasons and point in center of cone scales is usually erect. On mature trees, gray, shaggy bark is in thin, elongated, vertical scales loose at the ends. A medium-sized tree, 70 to 100 feet tall and 2 to 3 feet in diameter, the drooping branches give Alaska-cedar a "wilted" appearance. Lemon-yellow wood used for interior finish.

ATLANTIC WHITE-CEDAR *(Chamaecyparis thyoides)* has small, bluish-green scales, 0.06 to 0.1 of an inch long. The branchlets are not conspicuously flattened. The cones, 0.3 of an inch in diameter, are somewhat fleshy and wrinkled (raisin-like). On mature trees, the thin bark is ash gray to reddish brown. Usually grows in coastal fresh-water swamps or bogs. It may be 80 to 85 feet tall and 1 to 1.5 feet in diameter, with a crown of short, horizontal branches.

SOME INTRODUCED "CEDARS"

CHINESE, OR ORIENTAL, ARBORVITAE *(Thuja orientalis)* has foliage like American trees in the same genus (p. 55). Oblong cones, 0.5 to 1 inch long, have curved, hornlike projections near scale ends. Native to China and Taiwan; numerous varieties. May reach 60 feet.

HIBA ARBORVITAE *(Thujopsis dolobrata)* scales are nearly 0.3 of an inch long, lustrous dark green above and with silvery patches of stomata below. Cones are ovoid but flat-topped. Native to Japan, several varieties are grown in U.S. To 50 feet tall.

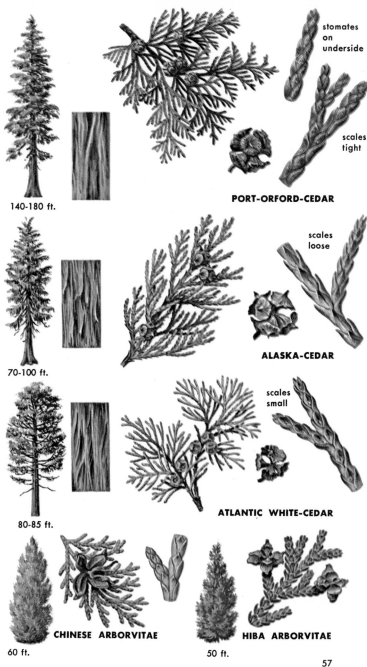

stomates on underside

scales tight

PORT-ORFORD-CEDAR

140-180 ft.

scales loose

ALASKA-CEDAR

70-100 ft.

scales small

ATLANTIC WHITE-CEDAR

80-85 ft.

CHINESE ARBORVITAE

60 ft.

HIBA ARBORVITAE

50 ft.

CYPRESSES (*Cupressus*)

Cypresses are evergreen trees or shrubs with round to 4-sided branchlets clothed with small, closely overlapping, alternate pairs of scalelike foliage; surface of scales often glandular. The cones, 0.5 to 1.5 inches in diameter, are composed of woody, wedge-shaped scales. All species of cypress native to the United States occur in the West. A number of these, as well as some foreign species, are cultivated as ornamentals.

MONTEREY CYPRESS (*Cupressus macrocarpa*) has dark blue-green foliage without glandular pits; woody cones 1 to 1.5 inches in diameter. It grows 20 to 70 feet tall and 3 to 4 feet in diameter, with dark-brown to light-gray, scaly, ridged bark. In the Monterey Bay region of California, this picturesque tree occurs on rocky headlands where it is often misshapen by the buffeting of high winds. Old trees have broad, flat-topped crowns with stout branches. Crowns of young trees growing in sheltered places are narrower, bushy, and pyramidal. This tree is extensively planted as an ornamental or for a windbreak.

GOWEN CYPRESS (*Cupressus goveniana*) has dark-green, nonglandular foliage, and cones 0.5 to 0.8 of an inch in diameter. It is a many-stemmed shrub or small tree, to 25 feet tall and 1.5 feet in diameter, with reddish-brown, scaly, ridged bark. Usually grows in dry, alkaline soils. (Sargent Cypress, *C. sargentii*, is a synonym of this species in *Check List*.)

MACNAB CYPRESS (*Cupressus macnabiana*) has light-green foliage with glandular pits. Cones, 0.5 to 0.8 of an inch in diameter, have long projections on scales. Bark reddish brown, fibrous, often with a purplish tinge. MacNab Cypress, often a shrub, may be a small tree to 40 feet tall and 3 feet in diameter. Modoc Cypress (*C. bakeri*) is similar, more northern.

TECATE CYPRESS (*Cupressus guadalupensis*) has blue-green, obscurely glandular foliage and cones 0.8 to 1.5 inches in diameter. The purplish to reddish-brown bark sheds in scales or strips. To 20 or 25 feet tall, 2 to 3 feet in diameter.

ARIZONA CYPRESS (*Cupressus arizonica*) has gray-green, generally glandless foliage; cones are 0.8 to 1 inch in diameter. Mature trees have brown, fibrous bark. In protected sites, grows 60 feet tall and 2 feet in diameter, with a dense, conical crown.

BALDCYPRESS
large woody cones;
needle-like foliage
deciduous with
lateral branchlets

CYPRESS
large woody cones;
scalelike, evergreen
foliage on plump
or angled branchlets

CHAMAECYPARIS
small woody cones;
scalelike evergreen
foliage on flattened
branchlets

JUNIPER
small fleshy cones;
scalelike evergreen
foliage on plump or
angled branchlets

20-70 ft.

MONTEREY CYPRESS

GOWEN CYPRESS

MACNAB CYPRESS

TECATE CYPRESS

ARIZONA CYPRESS

to 60 ft.

59

JUNIPERS *(Juniperus)*

About 70 species of evergreen trees and shrubs. They are widely distributed in the Northern Hemisphere, with 13 species native to the United States. Several are called "cedars." Junipers usually grow in dry, rocky soils. Their foliage is either scalelike and variously glandular, covering the rounded or 4-sided branchlets in closely overlapping, alternate pairs (occasionally 3's), or is awl-like and pointed outward. In some cases both kinds of foliage are found on the same tree. The semi-fleshy, bluish or reddish-brown cones are often called "juniper berries." They are 0.2 of an inch in diameter, covered with a gray, waxy substance, and reach maturity in from one to three seasons.

ROCKY MOUNTAIN JUNIPER *(Juniperus scopulorum)* has scalelike, obscurely glandular foliage about 0.1 inch long covering the rounded to 4-sided branchlets in closely overlapping, alternate pairs. On new growth, the foliage is pointed and awl-like. The fleshy cones, 0.2 inch in diameter, are blue with a gray, waxy covering; they mature in two seasons. Rocky Mountain Juniper grows 30 to 40 feet tall and 1 to 3 feet in diameter, with a short, stout, often divided trunk and a bushy crown of horizontal or ascending branches. Its gray-brown to reddish-brown bark is broken into narrow, flat, interlacing ridges with shreddy scales on the surface. Rocky Mountain Juniper is found widely throughout the Rocky Mountain region and, unusually, in a localized dry area of the Puget Sound region noted for its moist climate.

WESTERN JUNIPER *(Juniperus occidentalis)* resembles Rocky Mountain Juniper, but the foliage is conspicuously glandular, occurring both in pairs and in 3's. Also the bark is cinnamon brown and divided into large, irregular, scaly plates. A small tree, 20 to 60 feet tall and 1 to 3 feet in diameter, with a short, twisted trunk and a broad crown of stout, horizontal to ascending branches. Found on rocky slopes. Ashe Juniper *(J. ashei)* resembles Western Juniper but has less conspicuously glandular foliage and is more southern in distribution.

ONE-SEED JUNIPER *(Juniperus monosperma)* foliage is commonly glandular. The cones resemble those of Western Juniper but usually contain only one seed. Common on semi-arid, rocky soils. Usually grows as a much-branched shrub on very poor sites. In suitable locations, grows 20 to 30 feet tall and 1 to 3 feet in diameter, with a short, often twisted trunk and an open crown of stout branches.

JUNIPER

cones
fleshy
about 0.2 in.
in diameter

CYPRESS

cones woody,
0.5-1.5 in.
in diameter

COMPARISONS

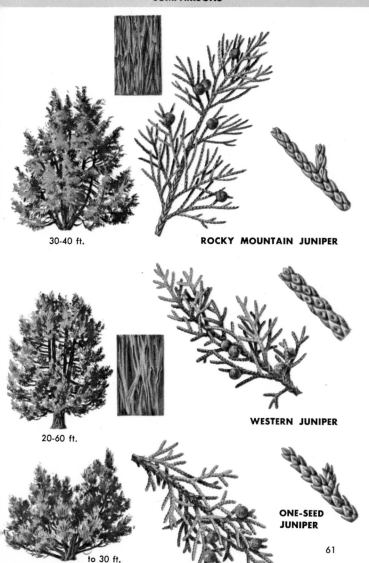

30-40 ft.

ROCKY MOUNTAIN JUNIPER

20-60 ft.

WESTERN JUNIPER

to 30 ft.

ONE-SEED JUNIPER

61

UTAH JUNIPER *(Juniperus osteosperma)* has scale-like, yellow-green, usually glandular foliage. Its oblong cones, 0.2 to 0.3 of an inch long, are reddish brown beneath their gray, waxy covering; mature in two seasons. The gray bark is broken into thin, fibrous, elongated scales. Grows to 20 feet tall and 1.5 feet in diameter, with a short, twisted trunk and slender, ascending branches that form a broad, open crown. California Juniper *(J. californica)* resembles Utah Juniper, but foliage is in 3's, not pairs.

ALLIGATOR JUNIPER *(Juniperus deppeana)* has blue-green, occasionally glandular, scalelike foliage. Its cones resemble Utah Juniper's. On mature trees, the reddish-brown bark may be 4 inches thick and divided by deep fissures into scaly squares, 1 to 2 inches long, like an alligator's hide. The trunk is short, and the tree's slender branches form a pyramidal or round-topped crown. Alligator Juniper may grow 50 to 60 feet tall and 3 to 5 feet in diameter.

COMMON JUNIPER *(Juniperus communis)* has lanceolate, sharp-pointed, concave needles, 0.3 to 0.5 of an inch long, marked with silvery bands of stomata above. They grow in whorls of 3. The cones, 0.2 inch in diameter, are blue beneath their gray, waxy covering; mature in three seasons. A sprawling shrub and very rarely a small tree, it usually grows on rocky soils. Common Juniper is widely distributed in the Northern Hemisphere. Some of the many varieties of this species are planted as ornamentals.

PINCHOT JUNIPER *(Juniperus pinchotii)* has dark yellow-green, conspicuously glandular, scalelike foliage. The scales, usually in 3's, are 0.1 inch long. Red cones, 0.2 of an inch in diameter, mature in one season. Light-brown bark has distinctive long, narrow, thin scales. To 20 feet tall and a foot in diameter, with stout, wide-spreading branches.

DROOPING JUNIPER *(Juniperus flaccida)* foliage may or may not have glands. The scales are 0.1 inch long, sometimes longer on young, rapidly growing branchlets and somewhat spreading at the apex. Dull, reddish-brown cones, 0.5 of an inch in diameter, are covered with a waxy bloom. Bark is cinnamon brown with thin, narrow scales. Drooping Juniper grows 30 feet tall and 1 foot in diameter. The wide-spreading crown of hanging branchlets give the tree a "weeping" appearance that is unique among the junipers.

UTAH JUNIPER

20 ft.

ALLIGATOR JUNIPER

50-60 ft.

COMMON JUNIPER

shrubby to 20 ft.

PINCHOT JUNIPER

to 20 ft.

DROOPING JUNIPER

30 ft.

Eastern Redcedar

Southern Redcedar

EASTERN REDCEDAR (*Juniperus virginiana*) has rounded to 4-sided branchlets covered by closely overlapping, dark-green, occasionally glandular scales about 0.06 of an inch long and in alternate pairs. New foliage near tips of branches is pointed and prickly. Round cones, 0.3 of an inch in diameter, are somewhat fleshy; green at first, turning blue at maturity, and covered with a gray, waxy substance. Ash-gray to reddish-brown bark is fibrous or in long, narrow, fringed scales. Small to medium-sized, 40 to 50 feet tall and 1 to 2 feet in diameter, with a dense, pyramidal crown. Common in poor soils, but grows best in limestone regions. Many varieties grown as ornamentals. Southern Redcedar (*J. silicicola*) resembles Eastern Redcedar, but has somewhat pendant branches and smaller cones. Prefers moist to swampy soils.

SOME INTRODUCED GYMNOSPERMS

GINKGO FAMILY
(Ginkgoaceae)

GINKGO (*Ginkgo biloba*) is the only remaining species of a group of trees widely distributed in prehistoric times. Fan-shaped leaves are deciduous, 2 to 3.5 inches wide, and bright yellow in fall. Dioecious; the plumlike fruit is about 1 inch long, orange-yellow when ripe. Its thin, pulpy flesh encloses a large white seed and gives off a foul odor as it disintegrates. Native to the Orient, where it is cultivated. Often planted as an ornamental in the United States. Grows to 100 feet tall, 3 feet in diameter.

PODOCARP FAMILY
(Podocarpaceae)

PODOCARPS (*Podocarpus* spp.), about 100 species of evergreen trees and shrubs, grow mainly in the Southern Hemisphere. Foliage linear to ovate, dark green above and lighter below; commonly alternate. Usually dioecious, staminate flowers yellow, in catkin-like spikes; pistillate greenish, solitary. Single-seeded fruit at apex of a swollen base. Ornamentals in warmer parts of U.S. include *P. nagi*, with opposite, elliptical leaves, and *P. macrophyllus*, with alternate, linear foliage. Both native to Japan.

ARAUCARIA FAMILY (Araucariaceae)

MONKEY PUZZLE (*Araucaria imbricata*) is a striking evergreen with stiff, leathery, dark-green, scalelike foliage. Sharp-tipped, overlapping scales are 1 inch long or less on branchlets, to 2 inches on large branches. Dioecious, producing ovoid to globose cones, 5 to 8 inches long, which disintegrate at maturity. Monkey Puzzle's pyramidal crown is formed of whorls of long, stiff branches. Grows to 100 feet tall. Native to South America but is grown as an ornamental in U.S.

NORFOLK ISLAND PINE (*Araucaria excelsa*) has evergreen foliage to 0.5 of an inch long—curved, sharp-pointed, spreading, and overlapping on the branches. Subglobose cones are 4 to 6 inches broad. Norfolk Island Pine grows to 70 feet tall, its slightly upturned branches in regular whorls of 4 to 7 and with pendant side branchlets. Native of Norfolk Island, northernmost of the New Zealand group; grown outdoors in warmer parts of the U.S. or indoors as a potted plant.

new foliage

old foliage

EASTERN REDCEDAR

40-50 ft.

GINKGO

PODOCARPS

P. nagi

P. macrophyllus

MONKEY PUZZLE

to 100 ft.

NORFOLK ISLAND PINE

to 70 ft.

ANGIOSPERMS

Angiosperms include most of the common flowering plants. This large group, composed of about 300 families and nearly 200,000 species, dominates the earth's vegetation. Angiosperms are divided into two classes: monocots (Monocotyledoneae) and dicots (Dicotyledoneae). Their differences are compared in the examples illustrated at the top of p. 67.

MONOCOTS include members of the grass, palm, lily, pineapple, banana, and orchid families. In northern North America, only the palm and lily families contain plants that attain tree size.

DICOTS include members of the oak, willow, ash, maple, hickory, birch, elm, and other families. Most of the tree-sized angiosperms that grow in northern North America are members of the dicot group.

PALM FAMILY (Palmae)

The palm family contains about 4,000 species of vines, shrubs, and trees in a wide range of sizes and forms. They are most abundant in the tropics of America and Asia; a few occur in tropical Africa, in the Mediterranean region, and in Chile, Japan, and Korea. Palms provide food, shelter, and clothing for people living in the tropics. Copra, coconuts, dates, oils, and waxes are familiar palm products. Native North American species and many exotics are grown as ornamentals in warm parts of the United States.

Palms are separated into two groups: fan palms, the leaf segments (pinnae) of the broad, fanlike leaves radiating from a common point; and feather palms, the numerous narrow, pinnate segments arising at right angles to the central leaf stalk.

JAMAICA THATCHPALM (*Thrinax parviflora*) has fan-shaped leaves, 2 to 3 feet wide, lustrous green above and pale below. The many narrow, tapering, pointed segments extend nearly to the center. Stiff, flat stems are about 4 feet long. New foliage densely covered with gray hairs. In early spring, white, fragrant, short-stalked flowers occur in narrow clusters about 3 feet long. Fruits, which mature in the fall, are smooth, ivory-white, nearly round, and about 0.5 inch in diameter; single chestnut-brown seed is enclosed in dry, thick flesh. Jamaica Thatchpalm grows 30 feet tall and 4 to 8 inches in diameter. The foliage is clustered at the top of the slender, gray trunk, which is commonly thatched with dead leaf bases.

BRITTLE THATCHPALM (*Thrinax microcarpa*) is similar to Jamaica Thatchpalm but foliage silvery below and fruits smaller, about 0.1 of an inch in diameter.

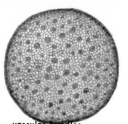

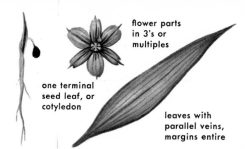

flower parts
in 3's or
multiples

one terminal
seed leaf, or
cotyledon

leaves with
parallel veins,
margins entire

vascular bundles
scattered, not appearing
as rings in cross section

MONOCOTS

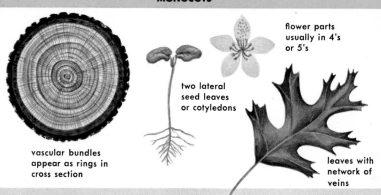

flower parts
usually in 4's
or 5's

two lateral
seed leaves
or cotyledons

leaves with
network of
veins

vascular bundles
appear as rings in
cross section

DICOTS

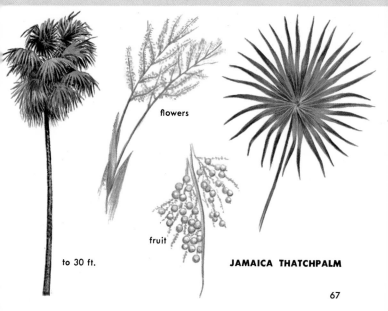

flowers

fruit

to 30 ft.

JAMAICA THATCHPALM

FLORIDA SILVERPALM (*Coccothrinax argentata*) has drooping foliage similar to that of thatchpalms, but somewhat smaller and with orange midribs. Flowers are produced in clusters about 2 feet long. Fruit, 0.5 to 0.8 of an inch in diameter, turns lustrous black when mature. Each contains a single brown seed. Florida Silverpalm grows 15 to 25 feet tall and 4 to 6 inches in diameter. Its smooth trunk is gray-blue to brownish.

Cabbage Palmetto

CABBAGE PALMETTO (*Sabal palmetto*) has fan-shaped leaves with stiff, half-rounded stems 6 to 7 feet long. The margins of the lustrous, dark-green blades, 5 to 8 feet long, are cut into numerous long, drooping segments bearing many threadlike fibers. The fragrant, white flowers, about 0.3 of an inch in diameter, are produced in spring, in drooping clusters about 2 to 2.5 feet long. Fruits, which ripen in the fall, are smooth, round to oval, almost black and about 0.3 of an inch in diameter; each encloses a single chestnut-brown seed. Cabbage Palmetto may grow to 80 feet tall and 1 to 2 feet in diameter, with a brownish to gray trunk. At first the leaf bases cling to the trunk, or it is ringed with leaf scars. Trunk eventually becomes smooth. Texas Palmetto (*S. texana*) resembles Cabbage Palmetto but is smaller, 30 to 50 feet tall and 2 feet in diameter, with flower clusters to 8 feet long and fruits often lobed. Louisiana Palmetto (*S. louisiana*) ordinarily grows from an underground stem but occasionally develops a short, upright trunk to 8 feet tall.

Texas Palmetto

Louisiana Palmetto

SAW-PALMETTO (*Serenoa repens*), most abundant native palm, often forms dense growths on sandy soils or in pine forests. Usually a shrub, but stems may grow to 25 feet tall. Leaves fan-shaped, about 2 feet in diameter, the leafstalks armed with sharp, rigid, curved spines.

PAUROTIS (*Paurotis wrightii*) has fan-shaped leaves 2 to 3 feet in diameter, light yellow-green above, bluish to silver-green below, and split almost to their base. Leaf stems, 18 to 24 inches long, are bordered with stout, flattened, orange-colored teeth. Small, greenish flowers are in drooping, branched clusters 4 to 6 feet long; the fruit, 0.3 of an inch in diameter, is orange-red, turning black when ripe. Paurotis, a native of the Florida Everglades, grows to 30 feet tall, often less, with clustered stems 4 inches in diameter.

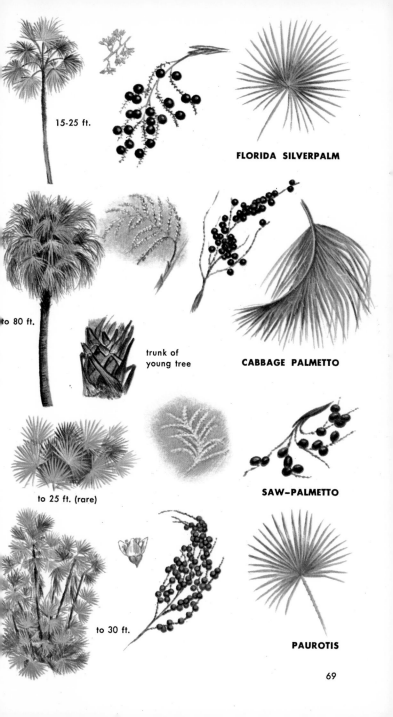

15-25 ft.

FLORIDA SILVERPALM

to 80 ft.

trunk of
young tree

CABBAGE PALMETTO

to 25 ft. (rare)

SAW–PALMETTO

to 30 ft.

PAUROTIS

69

CALIFORNIA WASHINGTONIA *(Washingtonia fili-fera)* has fan-shaped leaves, 5 to 6 feet long and 3 to 6 feet broad. The leaves are light green, with numerous folds and narrow, recurved segments that extend half to two-thirds of the way to the base and have many threadlike fibers along their margins. The stout, spiny leaf stems are 3 to 5 feet long and 1 to 3 inches wide. The somewhat fragrant flowers, which open from May to June, occur in branched clusters 8 to 10 feet long. The fruits are oval, 0.3 of an inch long and black at maturity. This is a large palm, 20 to 75 feet tall and 2 to 3 feet in diameter, with a thick, reddish-brown trunk. The dead leaves commonly hang on the tree, forming a brown skirt around the trunk. Both the California Washingtonia and a Mexican species (*W. robusta*) are grown as ornamentals.

FLORIDA CHERRYPALM *(Pseudophoenix sargentii)* has feather-like leaves, 5 to 6 feet long. They are dark yellow-green above, but paler and somewhat silvery below, with a short fibrous stem that is concave on its upper surface. Narrow, pointed leaflets are about 18 inches long and an inch wide, longest and widest at the center of the leaf. Yellowish flowers are widely spaced in loose clusters, and the orange to red fruits are 0.3 to 0.8 of an inch in diameter. Grows to 25 feet tall but usually shorter, with a ringed trunk.

FLORIDA ROYALPALM *(Roystonea elata)* has dark-green leaves, 10 to 12 feet long. The pointed leaflets are 2.5 to 3 feet long, becoming shorter toward end of the leaf. They extend in two ranks from the round leaf stalk that is flattened to concave at its base. In late winter to early spring, white, fragrant flowers, 0.3 of an inch in diameter, occur in densely branched, drooping clusters about 2 feet long. The smooth, purple fruits, about 0.5 of an inch long, are rounded at the tip and narrowed at the base. The thin, light-brown seed is embedded in fibrous flesh. This striking palm grows 80 to 100 feet tall. Its smooth, concrete-gray trunk, often conspicuously and abruptly swollen along its length, may be 2 feet in diameter. The Cuban Royal-palm (*R. regia*), Caribbean Royalpalm (*R. oleracea*), and Puerto Rican Palm (*R. borinquena*) are introduced species planted as ornamentals. All are stately trees much like the Florida Royalpalm in appearance.

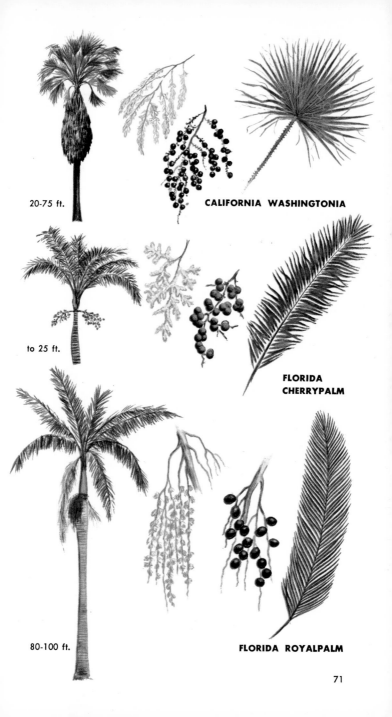

20-75 ft.

CALIFORNIA WASHINGTONIA

to 25 ft.

FLORIDA CHERRYPALM

80-100 ft.

FLORIDA ROYALPALM

SOME INTRODUCED PALMS

COCONUT PALM (*Cocos nucifera*) has feather-like leaves up to 18 feet long, with numerous long, linear, gracefully drooping leaflets. The creamy-white to yellowish flowers are in large, dense clusters (panicles). The familiar fruit is oval to somewhat 3-sided, 10 to 12 inches long and 6 to 8 inches in diameter. The large seed, or nut, is enclosed in a thick, fibrous husk. Inside the woody shell of the seed is a layer of creamy-white meat; inside that, the whitish "milk." The Coconut Palm may reach a height of 100 feet, its smooth trunk as much as 2 feet in diameter, often curved. The Coconut Palm's precise origin is not known; some say the Indo-Pacific, others the American tropics. It was naturalized before the discovery of America by Europeans.

MANILA PALM (*Veitchia merrillii*) has a stocky, usually straight trunk to 20 feet tall and 10 inches in diameter. It is crowned with strongly arched, feather-like leaves, each with numerous upswept leaflets that are widest at their middle. Clusters of white flowers form below the leaves. The striking, crimson fruit, more than 1 inch long, ripen in December or January. Manila Palm is one of 18 species of a genus native to South Pacific.

MADAGASCAR PALM (*Chrysalidocarpus lutescens*) forms an attractive loose clump consisting of several smooth, yellow-ringed stems, each up to 2 inches in diameter and 20 feet tall. These bear an elongated crown of long, graceful, arching, glossy-green, feather-like leaves, each with 30 or more pointed pinnae along central shaft. Small, yellowish flowers occur in clusters among the foliage; fruit is yellowish or red. Native to the island of Madagascar and quite sensitive to cold. Often cultivated in southern Florida, where it is known also as Areca Palm.

DATE PALM (*Phoenix dactylifera*) has feather-like, gray-green leaves, 15 to 20 feet long. The upper leaves stand more or less upright; the lower leaves arch outward and downward. Dioecious, the small, yellowish flowers produced in large clusters (panicles). Fruits, about 3 inches long, consist of a hard, grooved seed in a soft, pulpy, edible flesh. Grows 75 feet tall and 1 to 5 feet in diameter, the trunk usually roughened by bases of dead leaves. Native to northern Africa and western Asia, the Date Palm grows commonly as an ornamental in the warm parts of North America. The similar Canary Island Date Palm (*P. canariensis*) has inedible fruit but more graceful, arching foliage. Date Palm is the most common species of palm planted in Florida.

QUEEN PALM (*Arecastrum romanzoffianum*) has a slender trunk to 40 feet tall and 12 inches in diameter. It has a crown of erect, loosely spread, and somewhat recurved, feather-like leaves to 15 feet long. The soft, flexible leaf segments are about 18 inches long and 1 inch wide. Clusters of yellow flowers, 2 to 3 feet long, occur among the leaves. Orange fruits, about 1 inch long, are nearly round. Native to South America.

FISHTAIL PALM (*Caryota urens*) has a single stout, ringed trunk, to 50 feet tall and 1.5 feet in diameter. It bears an elongated terminal cluster of gracefully spreading, bipinnate leaves, to 20 feet long, with pinnae as much as 6 feet wide. Segments of pinnae are wedge-shaped with toothed tips, resembling a fish's tail. Clusters of flowers, to 12 feet long and 2 feet wide, form first in leaf axils near top of trunk, then develop progressively downward. Fruit is globular and red. A smaller species, *C. mitis*, has clustered trunks, black fruit.

to 100 ft.

ripe

green

COCONUT PALM

to 75 ft.

DATE PALM

to 40 ft.

to 20 ft.

MANILA PALM

QUEEN PALM

to 20 ft.

MADAGASCAR PALM

to 50 ft.

FISHTAIL PALM

73

LILY FAMILY (Liliaceae)

YUCCAS (Yucca)

Yuccas have light to dark-green, stiff, bayonet-like, often concave leaves. Bases may be thickened and clasping, margins toothed or fibrous; tips sharp-pointed. Clusters of cup-shaped flowers open during the night, the 6 white segments often streaked with green or purple. Fruit is an oval to oblong capsule containing numerous smooth, flat, black seeds. Yuccas occur only in Western Hemisphere, in dry soils. Of about 30 species, 11 reach tree size; the 4 most common are described here. The closely related Bigelow Nolina (Nolina bigelovii), which resembles a yucca, grows to tree size in southwestern Arizona and southeastern California.

JOSHUA-TREE (Yucca brevifolia) has dark-green leaves, 6 to 10 inches long, with pointed tips and finely toothed margins. They are clustered at ends of thick, irregularly formed branches. White flowers, about 2 inches long, produced in dense clusters about a foot long. Fruit somewhat 3-angled; bark divided into oblong plates. Grows 15 to 30 feet tall, 1 to 3 feet in diameter.

SOAPTREE YUCCA (Yucca elata) has pale yellow-green, grasslike leaves, 1 to 2.5 feet long and less than 0.5 inch wide; tipped with a sharp spine; smooth margins fringed with fine filaments. Flowers, 1.5 to 2 inches long, produced in branched clusters, 3 to 6 feet long. Fruit 3-celled, about 2 inches long and 1 to 1.5 inches in diameter; tipped with a stout point. Soaptree Yucca usually grows 3 to 6 feet tall; occasionally to 20 feet. Trunk gray.

SCHOTTS YUCCA (Yucca schottii) has flat, blue-green, bayonet-like leaves, 1.5 to 2.5 feet long and 1 to 2 inches wide, with a sharp-tipped spine and smooth, reddish-brown margins without threads. Flowers, 1 to 1.5 inches long, are in erect, branched clusters 1 to 2.5 feet long. Fleshy fruit, 4 to 5 inches long and 1.3 to 2 inches in diameter, has a pointed tip. Often branched, to 20 feet tall; trunk gray to brown.

ALOE YUCCA (Yucca aloifolia) has slightly concave, dark-green leaves, 18 to 32 inches long. Tips stiff and brown, margins toothed. Flowers, 1 to 1.5 inches long and 3 to 4 inches wide, in clusters 18 to 24 inches long. Oblong, light-green fruit about 3 to 4 inches long, black when ripe. Aloe Yucca grows 25 feet tall, 6 inches in diameter.

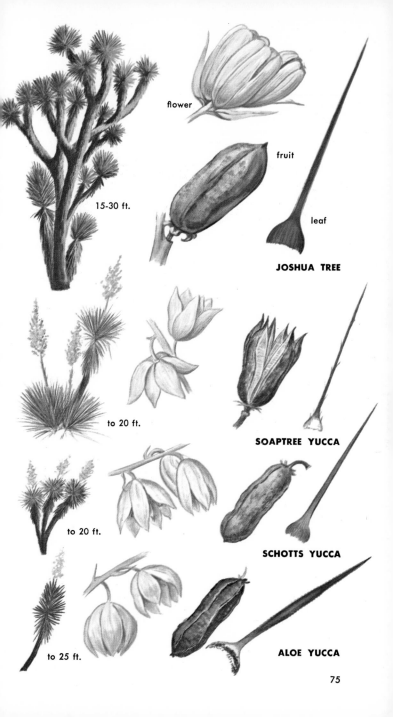

flower

fruit

leaf

JOSHUA TREE

15-30 ft.

to 20 ft.

SOAPTREE YUCCA

to 20 ft.

SCHOTTS YUCCA

to 25 ft.

ALOE YUCCA

75

WILLOW FAMILY (Salicaceae)

More than 325 species of willows (*Salix*), poplars or cottonwoods, and aspens (*Populus*) are widely distributed in the world but occur most abundantly in the cooler parts of the Northern Hemisphere. All are deciduous, rapid-growing but relatively short-lived, and dioecious—that is, staminate and pistillate flowers, both in aments, or catkins, are produced on separate plants.

WILLOWS (Salix)

Willow leaves are alternate, have short stems, and are usually much longer than broad. Each tiny flower of the staminate or pistillate aments is attached to a nectar-producing, hairy bract. The fruit is a small, 2-valved capsule that contains many minute, hairy seeds. Buds, excellent features for winter identification, usually hug the twigs and are covered by a single scale. More than 100 species are native to North America. Most are shrubs, but about 40 species attain tree size, 15 of them described and illustrated here. Willows root easily and occasionally form dense thickets. They are often planted to help hold stream banks in danger of erosion by floods. Bees obtain nectar from the blossoms in early spring, and the flexible twigs of some are used in basketry. A few kinds are planted as ornamentals; the catkins of those called "pussy willows" are used in decorations.

Willows generally grow along streams or in similar places where the soil is moist. As the many species of willows are so similar that exact identification is extremely difficult, check range maps carefully to determine where the species can be expected to occur.

BLACK WILLOW (*Salix nigra*) has lanceolate leaves, 3 to 6 inches long, 0.5 to 0.8 of an inch wide, with finely toothed margins. They are smooth and green, more lustrous above and slightly paler below. Twigs of the current year are a reddish to gray-brown. Capsule about 0.3 of an inch long. Bark of large trees is dark brown to black and heavily ridged. Usually grows 30 to 40 feet tall and 12 to 14 inches in diameter, with an irregular crown and often several trunks. This is the only willow important for lumber, used for boxes and similar purposes not requiring strength.

PACIFIC WILLOW (*Salix lasiandra*) resembles Black Willow, but the leaves are gray-green on the underside, with glands at the base of the blade. Twigs of the current year are yellow. Grows 15 to 50 feet tall and 12 to 14 inches in diameter, with an irregular crown of ascending, spreading branches.

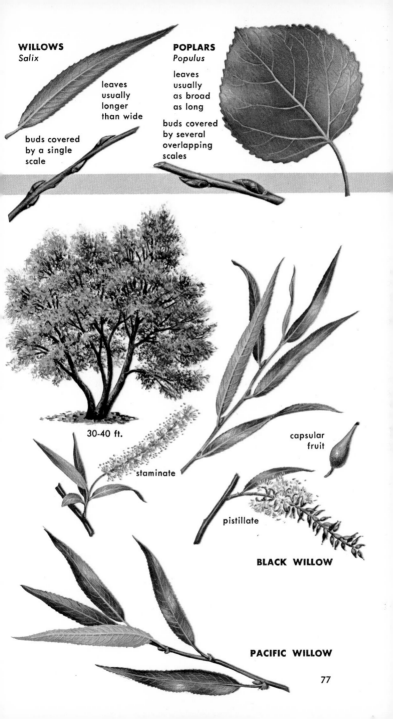

WILLOWS
Salix

leaves usually longer than wide

buds covered by a single scale

POPLARS
Populus

leaves usually as broad as long

buds covered by several overlapping scales

30-40 ft.

staminate

capsular fruit

pistillate

BLACK WILLOW

PACIFIC WILLOW

77

PEACHLEAF WILLOW *(Salix amygdaloides)* has broadly lanceolate leaves, 2 to 5 inches long and 0.8 to 1.3 inches wide, with finely toothed margins. They are light green above and grayish below, with a yellow or orange midrib. Bark of large trunks is black, ridged, and furrowed. Peachleaf Willow grows 10 to 60 feet tall, 12 to 15 inches in diameter, and has a crown of ascending branches. It is commonly found along prairie watercourses.

RED WILLOW *(Salix laevigata)* leaves are broadly lanceolate, 2 to 7 inches long and 0.8 to 1.5 inches wide, with obscurely toothed margins. Leaves are shiny green above, gray-green below, with yellow midrib. Red Willows grow 20 to 50 feet tall and 1 to 2 feet in diameter, with a spreading crown of slender, reddish-brown branches. The black, furrowed bark is somewhat scaly.

SANDBAR WILLOW *(Salix interior)* has narrowly lanceolate leaves, 2 to 6 inches long and 0.3 to 0.5 inch wide. Somewhat curved, the leaves are yellow-green but darker above than below, with a yellowish midrib and wide-spaced marginal teeth. The dark, reddish-brown bark is scaly. Sandbar Willow is commonly shrubby, often forming dense, riverside thickets. Occasionally it grows to 30 feet tall and 3 to 6 inches in diameter, with short, slender, orange to purplish-red, erect branches.

ARROYO WILLOW *(Salix lasiolepis)* leaves are lanceolate to oblanceolate, 3 to 6 inches long and 0.5 to 1 inch wide, dark green above and somewhat hairy and gray below. Their margins are slightly curled under and smooth or occasionally toothed. Bark is gray-brown on branches and on young trees; thick, ridged, and black on mature trees. Arroyo Willow is a large shrub or small tree, to 30 feet tall and 6 inches in diameter, with a loose open crown of slender, erect branches.

MACKENZIE WILLOW *(Salix mackenzieana)* has lanceolate to elliptical leaves, 1.5 to 4 inches long and 0.8 to 1.5 inches wide. They are light green above and pale green below, with small, rounded, marginal teeth. A shrub or small tree, 15 to 20 feet tall and 6 inches in diameter, the Mackenzie Willow has a narrow crown of slender, upright, yellowish to lustrous reddish-brown branches. Bark gray.

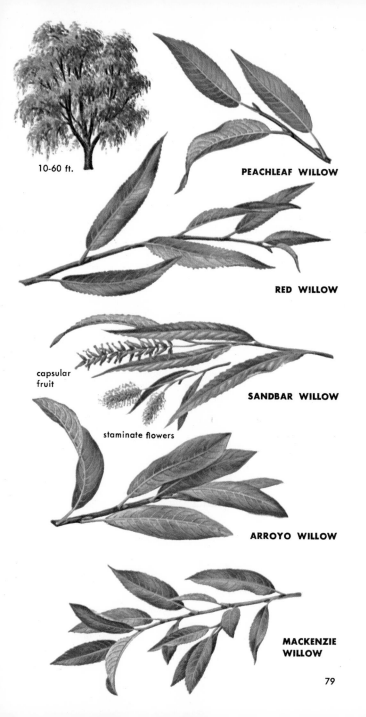

10-60 ft.

PEACHLEAF WILLOW

RED WILLOW

capsular
fruit

SANDBAR WILLOW

staminate flowers

ARROYO WILLOW

MACKENZIE
WILLOW

79

PUSSY WILLOW *(Salix discolor)* leaves are lanceolate to elliptical, 3 to 5 inches long and 0.8 to 1.5 inches wide, with wide-spaced marginal teeth and a yellow midrib. They are light green above, somewhat silvery below and often hairy. The flowers appear in late winter or early spring, the staminate flowers (aments, or catkins) soft and silky. Pussy Willow may be a shrub or a small tree, to 25 feet tall and 6 inches in diameter, with an open, rounded crown of stout branches.

BONPLAND WILLOW *(Salix bonplandiana)* has lanceolate leaves, 4 to 6 inches long and 0.5 to 0.8 of an inch wide. They are a lustrous yellow-green above and silvery white below, with a yellowish midrib and usually toothed margins somewhat curled under. On larger trees, the dark-brown to black bark is ridged and fissured. Bonpland Willow grows to 30 feet tall and 1 foot in diameter, with a rounded crown of slender, erect branches that usually droop toward the ends. An interesting feature of this species is that it can be considered semi-evergreen; its leaves, instead of being early deciduous in the fall like other willows, drop irregularly from the branches during the winter.

COASTAL PLAIN WILLOW *(Salix caroliniana)* has lanceolate leaves, 2 to 4 inches long and 0.5 to 0.8 inch wide, with finely toothed margins. They are green above, paler and hairy below. On large trees, the bark is black, ridged, and scaly. Coastal Plain Willow grows as a shrub or small tree, to 30 feet tall and 1 foot in diameter.

YEWLEAF WILLOW *(Salix taxifolia)* has small, linear-lanceolate leaves, 0.5 to 1.3 inches long and 0.1 of an inch wide, usually with smooth margins. As they unfold, the leaves are white and hairy; later they become pale green. Yewleaf Willow grows 40 to 50 feet tall and 1.5 feet in diameter, with a broad, open crown of erect branches usually drooping toward the ends.

BEBB WILLOW *(Salix bebbiana)* has elliptical, oblong or lanceolate leaves, 1 to 3 inches long and 0.5 to 1 inch wide. They are often toothed above the middle. At first pale green, they later become dull and usually hairy, especially along the midrib and veins on the undersurface. A shrub or small bushy tree, to 25 feet tall and 6 to 8 inches in diameter, Bebb Willow has a rounded crown of slender, reddish-brown branches. The bark is greenish gray tinged with red.

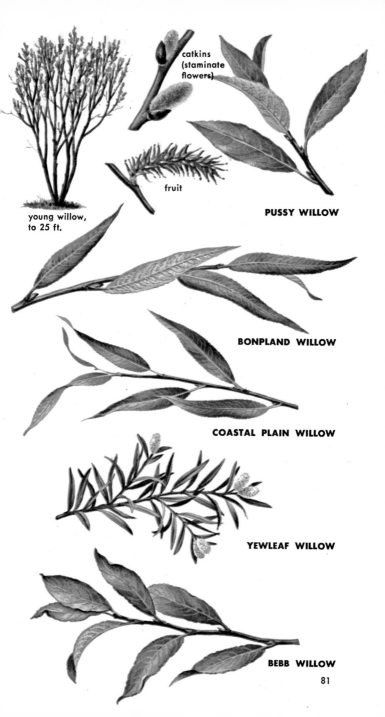

catkins
(staminate
flowers)

fruit

young willow,
to 25 ft.

PUSSY WILLOW

BONPLAND WILLOW

COASTAL PLAIN WILLOW

YEWLEAF WILLOW

BEBB WILLOW

81

FELTLEAF WILLOW (*Salix alaxensis*) leaves are narrowly elliptical to obovate, 2 to 4 inches long and 1 to 1.5 inches wide. Dull yellowish green above and white and hairy below, they have smooth margins, a yellow midrib, and may be somewhat wrinkled. Grows to 30 feet tall and 6 inches in diameter, with a crown of stout branches hairy during tree's early years.

HOOKER WILLOW (*Salix hookeriana*) leaves are 2 to 6 inches long and 1 to 1.5 inches wide. They have coarse marginal teeth, are bright green above, paler and hairy below, especially along the midrib. Usually a shrub; sometimes 25 to 30 feet tall, 6 to 8 inches in diameter, often with several stems. Bark light reddish brown.

SCOULER WILLOW (*Salix scouleriana*) leaves are dark yellow-green above, paler and usually hairy below. Widest above the middle, they are 1 to 4 inches long and 0.5 to 1.5 inches wide, with a yellowish-green midrib. One of the "pussy willows," the staminate flowers are furry and silky. Scouler Willow grows 50 feet tall and 12 to 14 inches in diameter or is a large shrub.

SOME COMMON INTRODUCED WILLOWS

WEEPING WILLOW (*Salix babylonica*) is native to China but is now widely planted throughout the world. This large handsome tree, 30 to 70 feet tall and 1 to 3 feet in diameter, has a broad, rounded crown of slender, pendulous branches. Bark on large trees heavily ridged, furrowed, and dark brown to black. Narrow, lanceolate leaves are 3 to 6 inches long, 0.5 to 1 inch wide; finely toothed margins. Smooth, glossy above; paler below.

WHITE WILLOW (*Salix alba*), introduced from Europe into eastern U.S., grows 50 to 80 feet tall and 1 to 3 feet in diameter. It has a crown of olive-green branches and furrowed, dull-brown bark. The finely toothed, lanceolate leaves are 2 to 4 inches long and 0.5 to 1.5 inches wide. They are pale green above and silvery white below with fine silky hairs on both sides.

CRACK WILLOW (*Salix fragilis*), native to Eurasia and introduced from Europe during Colonial days, grows 50 to 80 feet tall and 1 to 3 feet in diameter, with a broad crown of relatively upright branches; the glossy, yellow-green, brittle twigs snap off readily. Large trees have heavily ridged, dark-brown to black bark. The smooth, bright-green, lanceolate leaves are 4 to 6 inches long and 0.5 to 1.3 inches wide; finely toothed margins.

BASKET WILLOW (*Salix viminalis*) is a small shrubby tree, to 20 feet tall. Its slender green twigs were once important in basketry. The linear to narrowly lanceolate leaves are 2.5 to 3.5 inches long and up to 1 inch wide. They usually have smooth margins, are dark green above, and silky white with fine hairs below. Introduced from Europe, it is now common in eastern U.S.

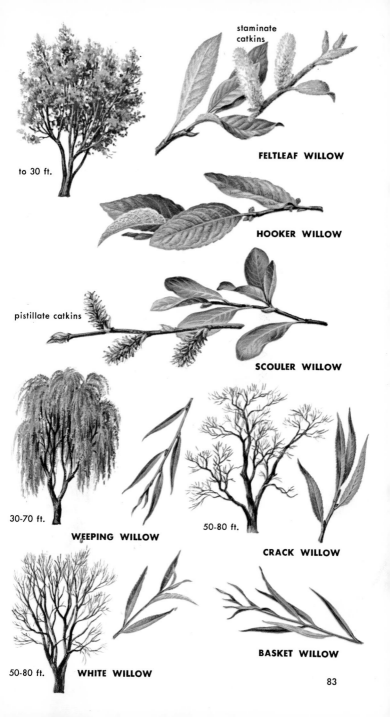

staminate catkins

FELTLEAF WILLOW

to 30 ft.

HOOKER WILLOW

pistillate catkins

SCOULER WILLOW

30-70 ft.

WEEPING WILLOW

50-80 ft.

CRACK WILLOW

50-80 ft. **WHITE WILLOW**

BASKET WILLOW

83

POPLARS AND ASPENS *(Populus)*

About 15 species of poplars, or cottonwoods, and aspens are native to North America. Both have broad, usually coarsely toothed, alternate leaves with long stems. Staminate and pistillate flowers are in aments, or catkins, on separate trees. The seeds are borne within small, green, flask-shaped capsules clustered along short, slender stems that hang from the branches in narrow, elongated clusters. When ripe, fruits split open and release the many tiny, dark-brown seeds. Each seed is attached to a tuft of cottony hairs and is blown by the wind. Twigs have long, pointed buds covered by several overlapping scales (p. 77); the buds extend at an angle from branches. Buds of some species are resinous and fragrant in early spring.

Poplars prefer moist soils and are often found along streams. Because they grow rapidly they are planted for quick shade or for wind protection. The soft wood of some species is used for veneers, boxes, matches, excelsior, and paper. The name poplar is also used for Yellow-poplar (p. 154) of the magnolia family.

EASTERN COTTONWOOD *(Populus deltoides)* leaves are roughly triangular, 3 to 6 inches long and 4 to 5 inches wide, with coarsely rounded marginal teeth. They are smooth and lustrous green above and paler below with a flattened stem, 1.5 to 3 inches long. The seed-bearing capsules are 3- to 4-valved, 0.3 of an inch long. Bark of mature trunks is dark gray and furrowed or ridged; on the upper branches and on young trees, smooth and greenish yellow. Eastern Cottonwood commonly attains a height of 75 to 100 feet and 3 to 4 feet in diameter.

PLAINS COTTONWOOD *(Populus sargentii)* has ovate leaves, 3 to 3.5 inches long and 3.5 to 4 inches wide, with coarsely rounded marginal teeth and flattened stems. Bark pale, ridged. Plains cottonwood grows to 80 feet tall and 3 feet in diameter. This species is the principal cottonwood along streams of the prairie country in west-central United States and Canada.

NARROWLEAF COTTONWOOD *(Populus angustifolia)* leaves are 2 to 3 inches long and 0.5 to 1 inch wide, bright yellow-green above and paler below, with toothed margins and nearly round stems. Capsules 2-valved. On young trees, bark yellowish green, becoming thick, dark brown, and furrowed on older trunks. Narrowleaf Cottonwood grows 50 to 60 feet tall and 1 to 1.5 feet in diameter.

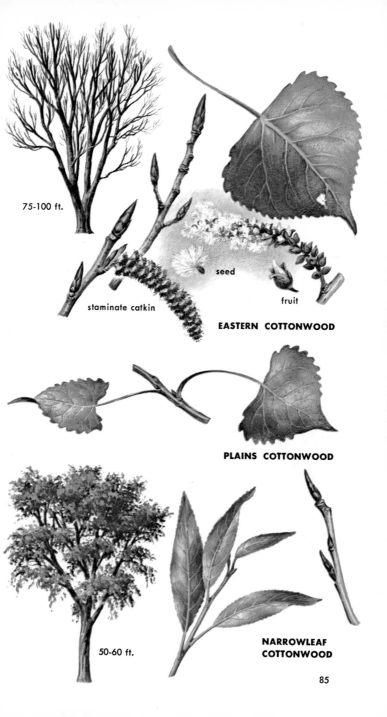

75-100 ft.

staminate catkin

seed

fruit

EASTERN COTTONWOOD

PLAINS COTTONWOOD

50-60 ft.

NARROWLEAF COTTONWOOD

85

BLACK COTTONWOOD *(Populus trichocarpa)* leaves are 5 to 6 inches long, 2 to 4 inches wide, tapering from a broad, rounded base. The marginal teeth are small and rounded; stems also round. They are dark green above, veiny and pale green, silvery white, or rusty brown below. The 3-valved capsules are hairy. Resinous buds are fragrant in early spring. Bark on old trees is dark to black and deeply furrowed; smooth and greenish gray on branches or on young trees. Black Cottonwood grows 80 to 125 feet tall and 2 to 4 feet in diameter. Its wood is used for paper pulp and also for veneer.

BALSAM POPLAR *(Populus balsamifera)* resembles Black Cottonwood but is smaller, 60 to 80 feet tall and 1 to 2 feet in diameter. Capsules are 2-valved and not hairy. Like those of Black Cottonwood, its buds are sticky, fragrant, and resinous in spring.

SWAMP COTTONWOOD *(Populus heterophylla)* has ovate leaves, 4 to 7 inches long and 3 to 6 inches wide. They have a gradually narrowed or rounded apex, a rounded to heart-shaped base, coarsely rounded marginal teeth, and round stems. They are dark green above and paler below, with a yellow midrib. The capsules are 2- to 3-valved. Bark of older trees is reddish brown, scaly, and somewhat shaggy. Swamp Cottonwood may attain a height of 70 to 90 feet and 2 to 3 feet in diameter. It has a narrow, rounded crown of stout branches.

PALMER COTTONWOOD *(Populus palmeri)* leaves are thin, ovate, 2.5 to 5 inches long and 1.5 to 2.5 inches wide, with small, incurved marginal teeth and slender, flattened stems. The seed-bearing capsules are 4-valved. Bark of old trunks is gray-brown and deeply fissured; on branches or on small trees, smooth and gray to reddish brown. Palmer Cottonwood grows 40 to 60 feet tall and 1 to 3 feet in diameter. It has an open, pyramidal crown.

FREMONT COTTONWOOD *(Populus fremontii)* leaves are roughly triangular, 2 to 2.5 inches long and 2.5 to 3 inches wide. They are shiny green with a thin, yellow midrib, a coarsely toothed margin, and yellow, flattened stem. Seed-bearing capsules are usually 3-, sometimes 4-valved. On older trees, bark is thick, deeply furrowed, dark reddish brown; on branches or on young trees, thin, smooth, and gray-brown. Grows 50 to 75 feet tall and 2 to 5 feet in diameter, with a broad crown.

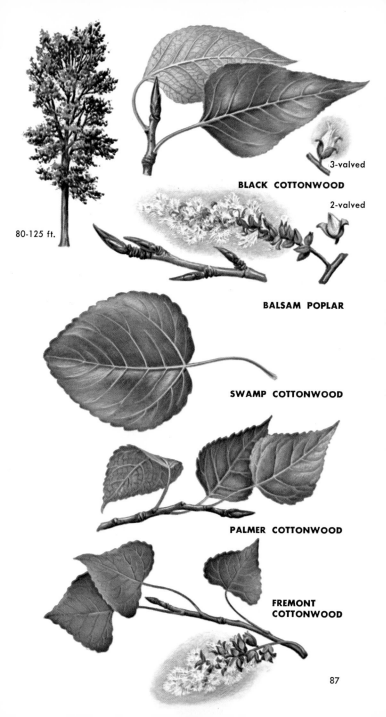

80-125 ft.

3-valved

BLACK COTTONWOOD

2-valved

BALSAM POPLAR

SWAMP COTTONWOOD

PALMER COTTONWOOD

FREMONT COTTONWOOD

87

QUAKING ASPEN (*Populus tremuloides*) leaves are nearly circular, 1 to 3 inches in diameter, with small, rounded marginal teeth and long, slender, flattened stems. They are lustrous green above, pale silvery below. The foliage quivers in the slightest breeze, hence the common name. In fall, the leaves turn brilliant gold or yellow. The smooth, greenish-white to cream-colored bark is marked by black, warty patches, and unlike most other poplars, buds are essentially nonresinous. Quaking Aspen grows 20 to 60 feet tall and 1 to 2 feet in diameter, with a narrow, rounded crown of slender branches.

BIGTOOTH ASPEN (*Populus grandidentata*) leaves are ovate to nearly round, 2 to 3.5 inches long and 2 to 2.5 inches wide, with coarse, rounded marginal teeth. Dark green above and paler below, they have a yellow midrib and a slender, flattened stem. The buds are minutely haired (Quaking Aspen buds smooth) and essentially nonresinous. On younger trees, the bark is dark green; on older trees, it is brown and furrowed. Bigtooth Aspen grows 30 to 60 feet tall and 1 to 2 feet in diameter, with a narrow, round-topped crown of rather stout branches.

SOME INTRODUCED POPLARS

WHITE POPLAR (*Populus alba*) leaves are usually 3- to 5-lobed, 2 to 5 inches long and 1.5 to 3.5 inches wide, with wavy or coarsely toothed margins; occasionally heart-shaped, with flattened base. Leaves are dark green above and woolly white below. On branches and on small trees, bark is greenish gray; on older trunks, black and furrowed. A medium-sized to large tree, 50 to 80 feet tall and 2 to 3 feet in diameter, White Poplar often has several trunks forming a broad, rounded crown. A native of Eurasia, White Poplar, with several varieties, is now widespread in the U.S.

LOMBARDY POPLAR (*Populus nigra* var. *italica*) has triangular to somewhat diamond-shaped leaves, 2 to 3.5 inches long and 1.5 to 3 inches wide. They have rounded marginal teeth and flattened stems. Bark thin and greenish gray on upper branches and on young trees; at base of larger trunks, black and furrowed. The slender, columnar crown of short, sharply ascending branches makes Lombardy Poplar easy to recognize from a distance. Grows 40 to 80 feet tall and 1 to 3 feet in diameter. Introduced from Europe, it is now planted throughout the United States, especially for windbreaks.

SIMON POPLAR (*Populus simonii*), a native of China, is planted as an ornamental in the U.S. There are several varieties. The leaves, 2 to 5 inches long and 1 to 3 inches wide, taper from the center to a rounded base and long-pointed apex. They are bright green above, paler or whitish below, with numerous small, rounded, marginal teeth. Simon Poplar has a narrow crown and slender, reddish-brown branchlets. It commonly attains a height of about 40 feet and may have a diameter of about 2 feet.

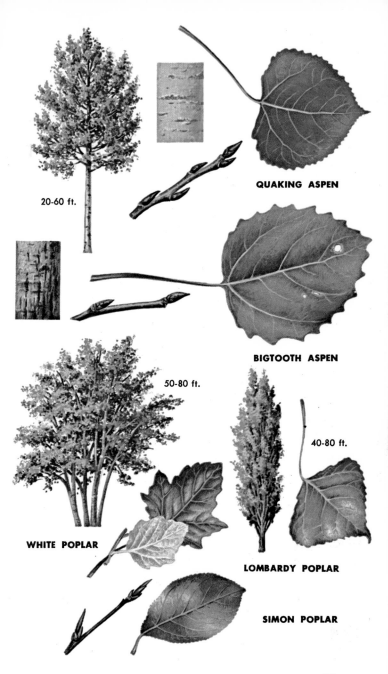

20-60 ft.

QUAKING ASPEN

BIGTOOTH ASPEN

50-80 ft.

40-80 ft.

WHITE POPLAR

LOMBARDY POPLAR

SIMON POPLAR

89

WAXMYRTLE FAMILY (Myricaceae)

Bayberries, or waxmyrtles (*Myrica*), are widely distributed in temperate and warm climates. Five species, all with alternate leaves, occur in the U.S. and Canada, usually in sterile, sandy soils; two are usually shrubs. Northern Bayberry (*M. pensylvanica*), found from Newfoundland south to North Carolina and Ohio, has tardily deciduous to evergreen foliage and white buds on twigs covered with gray hair. Evergreen Bayberry (*M. heterophylla*), of coastal plains from New Jersey to Louisiana, has evergreen foliage and twigs covered with black hair.

SOUTHERN BAYBERRY (*Myrica cerifera*) has short-stemmed, evergreen leaves, 1.5 to 4 inches long and 0.3 to 0.5 of an inch wide, usually widest and with coarse marginal teeth above the middle. Aromatic when crushed, they are yellow-green, spotted with small dark glands above and orange glands below. Staminate and pistillate flowers are in leaf axils of separate plants, in oblong catkins 0.2 to 0.7 of an inch long. Fruits are globose, light-green drupes, about 0.1 of an inch in diameter, thickly coated with pale-blue wax, sometimes used to make candles. Bark is thin, smooth, and gray-green. Grows to 40 feet tall and 8 inches in diameter, with a narrow, round-topped crown of slender, upright, or slightly spreading reddish branches.

ODORLESS BAYBERRY (*Myrica inodora*) leaves are dark lustrous green above and bright green below, with a glandular midrib slightly hairy below. Broader than leaves of Southern Bayberry, they usually have smooth curled-under margins and are not aromatic. Dioecious; the fruit, about 0.5 of an inch in diameter, is black and covered with white wax. The bark is ash gray to white. Odorless Bayberry is usually a shrub, but occasionally grows 15 to 20 feet tall.

PACIFIC BAYBERRY (*Myrica californica*) has oblong to oblanceolate, leathery, aromatic leaves, 2 to 4 inches long and 0.5 to 0.8 of an inch wide, with smooth or toothed, recurved margins; dark green above, yellow-green with black glandular dots below. Flowers resemble those of other bayberries, but both sexes are on the same plant (monoecious). The dark-purple fruit, 0.3 of an inch in diameter, is thinly coated with a granular gray wax. Branchlets are somewhat hairy. Pacific Bayberry is most commonly a shrub but is occasionally a small tree 20 to 30 feet tall.

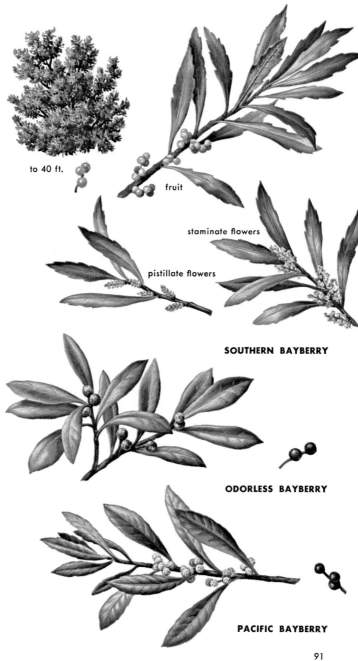

to 40 ft.

fruit

staminate flowers

pistillate flowers

SOUTHERN BAYBERRY

ODORLESS BAYBERRY

PACIFIC BAYBERRY

WALNUT FAMILY (Juglandaceae)

In addition to walnuts and hickories, most of which are native to North America, four wholly foreign groups of trees and shrubs belong to this family—*Pterocarya* (Wingnut, occasionally planted in the United States), *Engelhardtia*, *Platycarya*, and *Alfaroa*. Many species of the walnut family, valued for the wood's strength and resilience, are used in fine cabinet work.

WALNUTS (Juglans)

Walnuts have deciduous, alternate, pinnately compound leaves, the numerous oblong-lanceolate leaflets with toothed margins; in North American species, the leaflets midway along the stem are largest. Staminate and pistillate flowers are in different inflorescences on the same tree (monoecious); the staminate in tassel-like, unbranched catkins, the pistillate in few-flowered, erect, terminal spikes. Fruit, a drupaceous nut, is enclosed in a thick leathery husk, which does not split open when ripe. Pith of twigs is chambered. Six species are native to the United States. About 15 other members of this genus occur in South America, the West Indies, southern Europe, and Asia.

BLACK WALNUT (*Juglans nigra*) leaves are 12 to 24 inches long, with 15 to 23 almost sessile leaflets, smooth above and hairy below. The nearly spherical fruit, 1.5 to 2 inches in diameter, has a thick, semi-fleshy, yellowish-green husk enclosing the woody, corrugated nut and its sweet, oily seed. The husk contains a dark-brown dye. The stout twigs have 3-lobed leaf scars, blunt buds covered by a few hairy scales, and a buff-colored chambered pith. Bark of mature trees is furrowed and dark brown to black. Black Walnut grows 70 to 100 feet tall and 2 to 3 feet in diameter. It is valued for its beauty, its fruit, and its rich-brown, fine-grained wood.

BUTTERNUT (*Juglans cinerea*) leaves are 18 to 30 inches long, larger than those of Black Walnut, but have only 11 to 17 leaflets. Butternut leaflets are also more hairy on the underside. The oval fruit, 1.5 to 2.5 inches long, has a greenish-brown husk with a sticky surface. The husk contains a yellow or orange dye. Butternut twigs are hairy above the leaf scar, and have dark, chocolate-colored diaphragms dividing the pith chambers. On mature trees, the bark is gray and furrowed. Butternut grows 50 to 60 feet tall and 1 to 2 feet in diameter. Its wood is a much lighter brown than is the wood of Black Walnut.

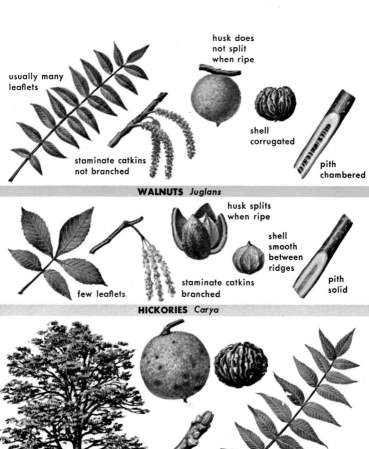

usually many leaflets

staminate catkins not branched

husk does not split when ripe

shell corrugated

pith chambered

WALNUTS *Juglans*

husk splits when ripe

shell smooth between ridges

staminate catkins branched

pith solid

few leaflets,

HICKORIES *Carya*

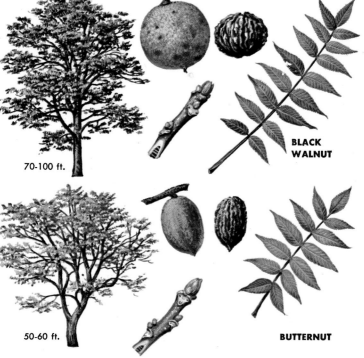

70-100 ft.

BLACK WALNUT

50-60 ft.

BUTTERNUT

CALIFORNIA WALNUT *(Juglans californica)* is a round-crowned, bushy tree, 15 to 50 feet tall and 1 to 2 feet in diameter, often with several stems. Leaves, 6 to 9 inches long, usually have 11 to 15 leaflets. Small, round fruits, 0.3 to 0.8 of an inch in diameter, have dark-colored, finely haired husks and nuts, with longitudinally grooved shells. California Walnut generally shows a preference for the moist soils along streams or in fertile bottomlands.

HINDS WALNUT *(Juglans hindsii)* grows 50 to 60 feet tall and 2 feet in diameter, with a single trunk and narrow, round-topped crown. The leaves are 9 to 12 inches long and have 15 to 19 leaflets with relatively coarse, wide-spaced marginal teeth. Leaflets are often slightly curved toward the ends. Round fruits, 1.3 to 2 inches in diameter, have thin, dark-brown, slightly hairy husks enclosing nuts, with longitudinally grooved shells. Usually occurs in moist soils.

LITTLE WALNUT *(Juglans microcarpa)* is a small, shrubby, often several-stemmed tree, 20 to 30 feet tall and 18 to 30 inches in diameter, with a rounded crown. Its leaves are 9 to 12 inches long, with 13 to 23 narrow, finely toothed, curved leaflets. The small fruits, about 0.5 to 0.8 of an inch in diameter, have thin, rusty-brown, slightly hairy husks and nuts with longitudinally ridged or grooved shells.

ARIZONA WALNUT *(Juglans major)* may grow 50 feet tall and 3 feet in diameter with a single trunk, but it is often shrubby. Leaves are 8 to 12 inches long, with 9 to 13 coarsely toothed leaflets. The round fruits, 1 to 1.5 inches in diameter, have thin, brown-haired husks and nuts with a deeply grooved shell.

AN INTRODUCED WALNUT

ENGLISH WALNUT *(Juglans regia)*, is native to southeastern Europe, India, and China. Its wood, known also as Circassian Walnut, is used for furniture and cabinet work. In the United States it is grown as an ornamental and for commercial nut production; there are many varieties. The leaves, 8 to 16 inches long, are pinnately compound with 7 to 9 leaflets. The leaflets differ from those of native American species in that they are oblong, with smooth rather than toothed margins and rounded rather than long-pointed tips, and the terminal leaflets are the largest. The round fruit, 1.5 to 2 inches in diameter, has a smooth green husk surrounding a thin-shelled nut that has rounded surface ridges. English Walnut may attain a height of 70 feet and a trunk diameter of 3 feet; it has a broad, rounded crown.

CALIFORNIA WALNUT

HINDS WALNUT

LITTLE WALNUT

ARIZONA WALNUT

to 70 ft.

ENGLISH WALNUT

HICKORIES (Carya)

Hickories are found mainly in eastern United States. One species grows in the Mexican highlands, two in eastern and southeastern Asia. Hickories are generally slow-growing trees with a long tap-root. Like walnuts, they have alternate, odd-pinnately compound leaves, but the leaflets are usually fewer and broader, with the terminal leaflets largest. Staminate flowers are in 3-branched catkins; the husk of the nut splits open when ripe and the pith of twigs is solid (p. 93). Pecan hickories, a subgroup, usually have more and narrower leaflets, and "winged" husks; the buds have valvate rather than overlapping scales.

Nuts of most hickories are edible, the Pecan grown commercially. Hickories are also grown as ornamentals and their strong, tough, resilient wood is used for tool handles, athletic equipment, and similar items. Green hickory wood is used to flavor meat in smoking or barbecuing.

SHAGBARK HICKORY *(Carya ovata)* leaves are 8 to 14 inches long, with 5 (occasionally 9) smooth, broadly lanceolate leaflets. The nut, nearly round and with a smooth, 4-ribbed, light-brown shell, is enclosed in a reddish-brown to black, 4-ribbed husk, about 1 to 2.5 inches in diameter and 0.3 to 0.5 inch thick. The husk splits into four parts when ripe. Mature trees have distinctive shaggy bark composed of thin, narrow scales, curved outward at ends. Young trees have smooth gray bark. Shagbark Hickory grows 70 to 90 feet tall and 1 to 2 feet in diameter, with a rather narrow crown except when growing in open situations.

SHELLBARK HICKORY *(Carya laciniosa)* resembles Shagbark Hickory, but the leaves are 15 to 22 inches long and the 5 to 9 leaflets (usually 7) are softly hairy below. In addition, the nuts are 4- to 6-ribbed. Shellbark Hickory grows 80 to 100 feet tall and 3 to 4 feet in diameter.

MOCKERNUT HICKORY *(Carya tomentosa)* has fragrant leaves, 8 to 12 inches long, with a hairy stalk and 7 to 9 relatively narrow leaflets, which are hairy below. The nut is ovoid, thick-shelled, and 4-ribbed, enclosed in a thick, reddish-brown, deeply 4-grooved husk, depressed at the apex. The husk splits nearly to the base when ripe. The kernel is sweet but is hard to extract. Mockernut Hickory grows to 80 feet tall and 2 feet in diameter; it is most common in the South, especially in drier soils.

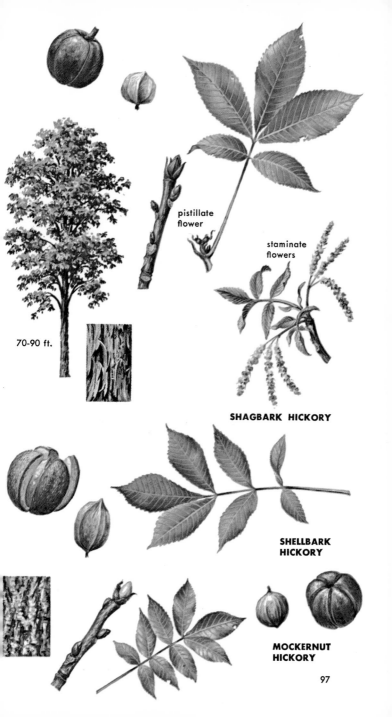

70-90 ft.

pistillate flower

staminate flowers

SHAGBARK HICKORY

SHELLBARK HICKORY

MOCKERNUT HICKORY

PIGNUT HICKORY (*Carya glabra*) leaves are 6 to 12 inches long, with 5 (occasionally 7) lanceolate leaflets. Nuts, not ribbed, are thick-shelled, enclosed in pear-shaped husks about 1.3 inches long. Husks, 0.1 of an inch thick, split only part way to the base when the nut is ripe. On mature trees, the scaly ridges of the bark form a rough, diamond-shaped pattern. Usually found in dry soils; grows 50 to 75 feet tall and 2 to 3 feet in diameter.

WATER HICKORY (*Carya aquatica*) leaves are 9 to 15 inches long and have reddish, hairy stems. The 7 to 13 narrow, curved leaflets are brownish and somewhat hairy below. The 4-ribbed, oblong, flattened nut has bitter "meat" and is enclosed in a thin, conspicuously 4-winged husk, 1.5 inches long and 1 to 1.3 inches in diameter, with yellow scales. Buds have valvate scales. Water Hickory is most common in moist to swampy soils, where it grows 60 to 80 feet tall and 1 to 2 feet in diameter. On mature trees, the light-brown bark is broken up into long scales.

BITTERNUT HICKORY (*Carya cordiformis*) leaves are 6 to 9 inches long, with 7 to 11 lanceolate leaflets, bright green above and paler below. Bitter, ovoid, thin-shelled, 4-ribbed nut, about 1 inch long, is enclosed in a thin, yellow-scaly husk, 4-winged above middle. Buds yellow, with valvate scales. Bark gray and smooth, except on large trunks. Bitternut Hickory grows 40 to 60 feet tall and 1 to 3 feet in diameter; usually in moist soils.

BLACK HICKORY (*Carya texana*) leaves are 8 to 12 inches long, with slender stems and usually 7 leaflets (occasionally 5). Leaflets dark green above, hairy below in axils of veins. Round to oblong, 4-ribbed, dark reddish-brown nut has a thin shell; enclosed in a thin, slightly 4-winged husk that splits to base. Buds have valvate scales. Bark black, deeply furrowed. To 50 feet tall and 2 feet in diameter.

NUTMEG HICKORY (*Carya myristicaeformis*) leaves are 7 to 14 inches long, with hairy stems and 7 to 9 leaflets, dark green above and silvery-hairy below. Bony nuts have a very thin, 4-winged husk, 1.5 inches long, covered with yellowish-brown hairs; splits nearly to base when ripe. The buds have valvate scales. Nutmeg Hickory's bark is scaly and reddish brown. The tree grows 100 feet tall and 2 feet in diameter.

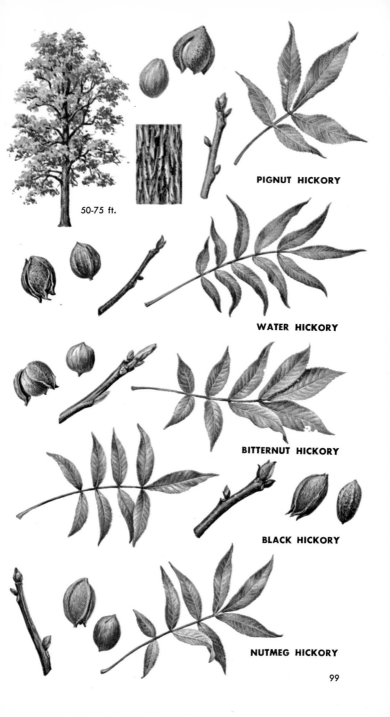

50-75 ft.

PIGNUT HICKORY

WATER HICKORY

BITTERNUT HICKORY

BLACK HICKORY

NUTMEG HICKORY

PECAN *(Carya illinoensis)* leaves are 12 to 20 inches long, with 9 to 17 narrow leaflets that are somewhat curved at their narrow, pointed ends. The oblong, reddish-brown nuts are 4-ribbed and 1 to 2.5 inches long, with a rather thin shell. The thin, dark-brown, prominently 4-winged husk splits to the base when the nut is ripe. The sharp-pointed buds have valvate scales with yellow hairs, and the twigs are somewhat hairy. On mature trees, the bark is light brown to gray and broken into narrow, vertical, scaly ridges. Largest of the hickories, the Pecan attains a height of 100 to 140 feet and a trunk diameter of 2 to 4 feet. It is most common and grows most rapidly on bottomlands in southeastern U.S. Not an important timber tree but valued commercially for nuts.

SWAMP HICKORY *(Carya leiodermis)* leaves are 12 to 14 inches long with slender, hairy stems. The 7 (occasionally 5) leaflets are smooth and dark green above; hairy below, especially along the midrib. The reddish-brown nut is enclosed in a thick, 4-ribbed husk, 1.5 to 1.8 inches long and 1.3 inches in diameter. It splits to the base when ripe. The pale, gray-brown bark is only slightly ridged. Swamp Hickory, most common in moist soils, may grow 50 to 70 feet tall, 1 to 2 feet in diameter. It has a round-topped crown, somewhat pendant branches, and reddish-brown branchlets.

OTHER NATIVE HICKORIES

SCRUB HICKORY *(Carya floridana)* **AND SAND HICKORY** *(C. pallida)* both grow to 75 feet tall, 2 feet in diameter. In early spring, leaf stems and underside of Scrub Hickory's 5 to 7 leaflets are brown, hairy. Nuts small, husks narrowed at base and depressed at apex. Sand Hickory has 7 to 9 long-pointed leaflets, silvery on underside; round nuts in oval husks. Both species are native to southeastern United States.

CORKWOOD FAMILY (Leitneriaceae)

CORKWOOD *(Leitneria floridana)*, the only species in its family, has extremely light wood. Leaves are deciduous, short-stemmed, smooth-margined. They are bright green above and somewhat hairy below, elliptic-lanceolate, and may be 4 to 6 inches long and 1.5 to 2.5 inches wide. Staminate and pistillate flowers on different trees; the leathery, brown, pointed-oval fruit, 0.8 of an inch long and 0.3 of an inch thick, is conspicuously net-veined. Corkwood grows about 20 feet tall and 5 inches in diameter.

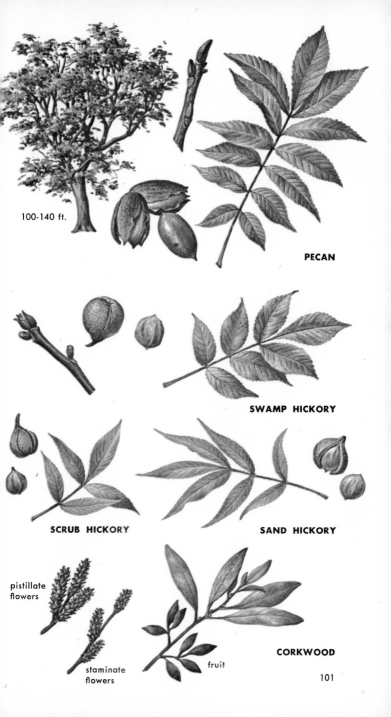

100-140 ft.

PECAN

SWAMP HICKORY

SCRUB HICKORY

SAND HICKORY

pistillate
flowers

staminate
flowers

fruit

CORKWOOD

101

BIRCH FAMILY (Betulaceae)

The birch family comprises about 100 species of trees and shrubs, found primarily in cooler parts of the Northern Hemisphere. The birches (Betula), alders (Alnus), hornbeams (Carpinus), hophornbeams (Ostrya), and hazels, or filberts (Corylus), are represented by native species in North America. A sixth genus (Ostryopsis) occurs in eastern Asia. All members of the birch family have alternate, deciduous leaves. Staminate and pistillate flowers are in different inflorescences on the same tree. Staminate catkins are developed the previous season (preformed) in all except hornbeams.

BIRCHES (Betula)

In early spring the preformed staminate catkins of birches become distinctively tassel-like, 1 to 4 inches long. Their conelike strobiles, about 1 to 1.5 inches long, disintegrate when ripe, scattering their numerous scales and tiny seeds. The leaves, which vary in shape, have prominent veins, noticeably toothed margins, and short stems. The bark, marked by conspicuous, horizontal lenticels, peels in some species into long, curled, horizontal strips.

Most of the some 40 species of birches are small to medium-sized trees. They grow rapidly, often forming extensive forests in the North, but are relatively short-lived. The hard, beautiful wood of some birches is used for veneers, cabinet work, and interior finish. Birches are also used for paper pulp, woodenware, and novelties. The twigs of some are distilled to get oil of wintergreen. Because of their beauty of form, foliage, and bark, several species of birches are grown as ornamentals; in addition, several horticultural varieties have been developed for this purpose. Ground Birch (Betula rotundifolia) is a low-growing Alaskan shrub important as a summer food for reindeer.

PAPER BIRCH (Betula papyrifera) leaves are oval to ovate, 2 to 3 inches long and 1.5 to 2 inches wide, with a rounded base, pointed tip, and doubly toothed margins. On branches or on the trunks of young trees, the bark is brown to bronze. On the trunks of mature trees, the bark is white, peeling into long, narrow, horizontal strips that are curled at the ends. The bark at the base of the trunk of older trees is black and fissured. Paper Birch grows to 80 feet tall and 2 feet in diameter, with a central trunk and an irregular, pyramidal to rounded crown. Areas destroyed by fire are quickly reseeded by the Paper Birch, which is found in several varieties throughout northern North America. The use of Paper Birch bark by Indians of the North Country in making canoes is legendary.

COMPARISONS OF FRUITS OF VARIOUS MEMBERS OF BIRCH FAMILY

Birch *(Betula)* ''cone,'' or strobile, disintegrates when mature.

Alder *(Alnus)* ''cone,'' or strobile, thick and woody; does not disintegrate.

Hornbeam *(Carpinus)* seed is attached to a 3-lobed leafy bract. The bracts hang in clusters.

Hophornbeam *(Ostrya)* produces a cluster of leafy bladders, each containing a single seed.

Hazelnut, or filbert *(Corylus),* is oval and enclosed in a leathery, leafy cluster, or husk.

to 80 ft.

staminate flower

strobile

PAPER BIRCH

YELLOW BIRCH (*Betula alleghaniensis*) leaves resemble those of the Paper Birch but are longer and narrower—3 to 4.5 inches long, 1.5 to 2 inches wide. They have a rounded to heart-shaped base, somewhat hairy stems, and tufts of fine hairs in axils of veins on underside. Strobiles are ovoid, erect, and shed scales slowly. (Paper Birch strobiles are cylindrical, pendant, and shed scales quickly.) Yellow Birch bark is yellowish to bronze and peels into narrow, curled strips; on large trees, occurs in reddish-brown plates. Bark flammable even when wet, hence useful in starting campfires; slender twigs have a wintergreen flavor. Resembles Paper Birch in size and form; also reseeds burned areas quickly.

WATER BIRCH (*Betula occidentalis*) has leaves similar to those of Paper Birch but smaller, 1 to 2 inches long and 0.8 to 1 inch wide. The dark-brown, lustrous bark does not readily separate into thin layers. Water Birch is a small, often shrubby tree, growing 20 to 25 feet tall and 1 foot in diameter, with a broad, open crown of somewhat slender, drooping branches. It commonly forms impenetrable thickets, especially along streams.

SWEET BIRCH (*Betula lenta*) leaves are ovate to oblong-ovate, 2.5 to 5 inches long and 1.5 to 3 inches wide, with a tapered apex, often heart-shaped base, singly toothed margin, and hairy stem. Tufts of fine hairs occur in axils of veins on underside. The strobiles are ovoid and erect, resembling those of Yellow Birch but with smooth rather than hairy scales. Bark of young trees is black or dark reddish brown, marked with horizontal lenticels; does not peel. Bark in scaly plates on old trunks. Twigs have a strong wintergreen flavor. Grows 60 feet tall and 2 feet in diameter; has a round-topped, spreading crown. Prefers good soil.

GRAY BIRCH (*Betula populifolia*) leaves are triangular, 2.5 to 3.5 inches long, with coarse, doubly toothed margins. On trunks of young trees or on branches of older trees, the bark is brownish; on trunks of mature trees, it is chalky white, with prominent horizontal lenticels and triangular black patches below branch insertions. Bark resembles that of the Paper Birch but does not peel readily. Grows to 30 feet tall and 1 foot in diameter, with an irregular, open crown. Gray Birch is able to establish itself quickly in poor soils and invades abandoned farms and cutover lands.

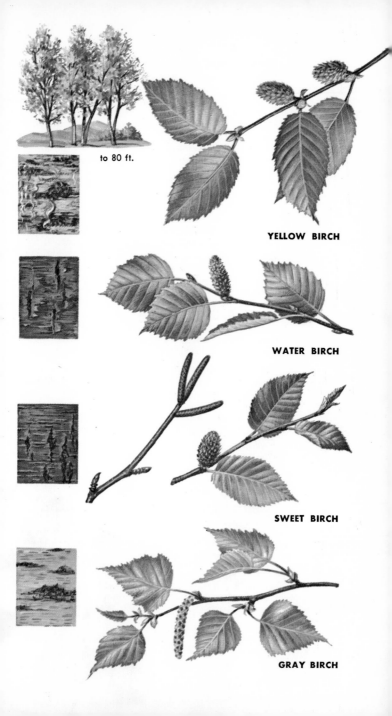

to 80 ft.

YELLOW BIRCH

WATER BIRCH

SWEET BIRCH

GRAY BIRCH

RIVER BIRCH (*Betula nigra*) leaves are irregularly oval, 1.5 to 3 inches long and 1 to 2 inches wide, with coarse, doubly toothed margins. They are hairy on the stems and on the underside of the stout midrib. Bark on young trees thin and pinkish to reddish brown; on older trunks, gray to black and scaly. A medium-sized tree, to 80 feet tall and 3 feet in diameter, the River Birch's trunk is commonly divided into several arching limbs, forming an irregular crown. Seeds mature in late spring when banks are exposed by receding flood waters, providing places for germination. River Birch is the only native birch at low elevations in southeastern United States; common along streams.

BLUELEAF BIRCH (*Betula caerulea-grandis*) is most commonly a shrub but sometimes a tree, growing to 30 feet tall and 10 inches in diameter, with a crown of slender, ascending branches. The bark, which does not peel, is white with a rosy hue. The bluish-green leaves, paler below, are 2 to 2.5 inches long and 1 to 1.5 inches wide, with a long-pointed tip and a wedge-shaped base. The margins are sharply double-toothed, and the veins and midrib on the underside are somewhat hairy. The cylindric strobiles, also hairy, are about 1 inch long, 0.3 of an inch in diameter.

YUKON BIRCH (*Betula eastwoodiae*) is a natural hybrid that grows to 20 feet tall and 6 inches in diameter. Bark chestnut brown, with white lenticels. Its elliptical to ovate leaves are 1 to 1.5 inches long and 0.8 to 1.5 inches wide, with an abruptly pointed apex and coarsely toothed margins, except along wedge-shaped base. The pendant strobiles are 0.8 of an inch long and less than 0.3 of an inch in diameter, their scales not hairy.

AN INTRODUCED BIRCH

EUROPEAN WHITE BIRCH (*Betula pendula*) leaves are ovate to somewhat diamond-shaped, 1 to 2.5 inches long and to 1.5 inches wide, with a rounded to wedge-shaped base and coarse, irregularly toothed margins. The white bark, marked with conspicuous horizontal lenticels and with black triangular patches below the branch insertions, is somewhat similar to Gray Birch bark but rougher and thicker. European White Birch grows to 60 feet tall and 2 feet in diameter, with either a central or a divided trunk. Its branches are spreading and ascending or pendant. In northern Europe, the European White Birch is an important commercial hardwood tree. Several varieties are planted as ornamentals in the United States. Among these are the Weeping Birch, which has a crown of slender, gracefully drooping branches; and the even more attractive Cut-leaved Birch, with deeply cut, lobed leaf margins in which the margins of the lobes are coarsely toothed.

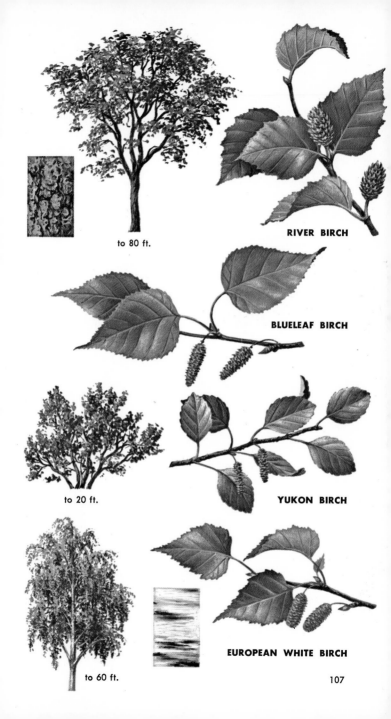

to 80 ft.

RIVER BIRCH

BLUELEAF BIRCH

to 20 ft.

YUKON BIRCH

to 60 ft.

EUROPEAN WHITE BIRCH

107

ALDERS *(Alnus)*

Alders have irregularly toothed, often shallowly lobed, oval to elliptical or oblong leaves, prominently veined. In spring, preformed staminate catkins (p. 102), 4- to 6-inches long, become tassel-like. Conelike strobiles, 0.5 to 1.3 inches long, do not disintegrate as do those of birches (p. 103). Stalked, reddish-brown buds are usually covered with several valvate scales. Alders grow rapidly and often form thickets in moist soils. They are relatively short-lived. Eight species native to the U.S. and Canada reach tree size. In addition to those described here, Speckled Alder *(A. rugosa)* and Hazel Alder *(A. serrulata)* are usually shrubs occasionally reaching tree size, along streams in eastern U.S. and Canada.

RED ALDER *(Alnus rubra)* leaves are ovate to elliptical, 3 to 6 inches long and 2 to 3 inches wide, dark green above and lighter with rusty-brown hairs below. Their coarsely doubly toothed margins are slightly curled under. Staminate catkins lengthen before leaves develop in spring, giving thickets a distinctive greenish-brown cast. Bark of young trees is smooth and blue-gray, with whitish blotches; on older trunks, darker and broken into flat plates. Inner bark is reddish brown. Usually grows 30 to 60 feet tall and 1 to 2 feet in diameter, with a central trunk and a domelike crown. On burned or logged-off land, becomes established quickly and adds humus and nitrogen to soil, preparing the way for the more valuable conifers. Favored for fireplace fuel, since it does not scatter sparks; also increasing in importance for furniture, veneers, and paper pulp.

WHITE ALDER *(Alnus rhombifolia)* resembles Red Alder but is smaller. Ovate leaves are small, light green, 2 to 4 inches long and 1.5 to 2.5 inches wide, and usually have single-toothed margins, which are not turned under. Pith chamber of twigs is distinctly triangular in cross section; Red Alder's is only roughly triangular.

SITKA ALDER *(Alnus sinuata)* has ovate leaves, 2 to 5 inches long and 1.5 to 4 inches wide, with sharply doubly toothed margins. The staminate catkins lengthen as the leaves develop in early spring, and the gray-green bark is smooth, except for warty lenticels. Though usually a sprawling shrub, it may grow to 30 feet tall and 6 inches in diameter.

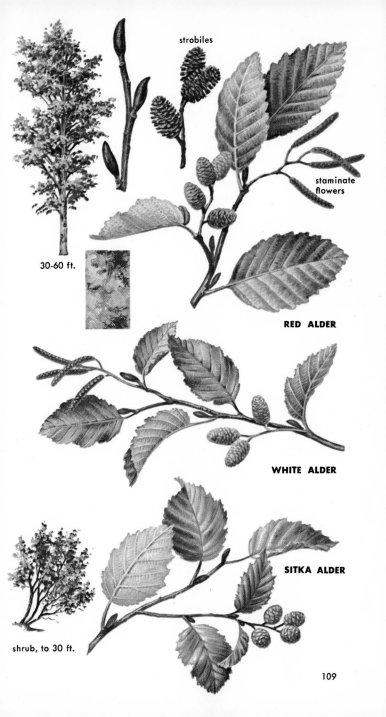

strobiles

staminate flowers

30-60 ft.

RED ALDER

WHITE ALDER

SITKA ALDER

shrub, to 30 ft.

THINLEAF ALDER *(Alnus tenuifolia)*, similar in size to Sitka Alder, has ovate to oblong leaves, 2 to 4 inches long and 1.5 to 2.5 inches wide, with shallowly lobed, doubly toothed margins. Leaves have a stout, orange-brown midrib and rusty-brown hairs below.

ARIZONA ALDER *(Alnus oblongifolia)*, about the same size as Sitka Alder, has elliptical leaves, 2 to 3 inches long and 1.5 to 2 inches wide, usually with doubly toothed margins. They are dark green above, paler and slightly hairy on yellow midrib and veins below. Staminate catkins lengthen in winter, dropping before leaves unfold. Bark smooth, gray to brown.

SEASIDE ALDER *(Alnus maritima)* has broadly elliptical leaves with small, incurved marginal teeth. They are lustrous green above, with stout, yellow midrib and stem. The flowers open in the fall, staminate catkins to 2.5 inches long and bulky pistillate strobiles to 1 inch long. Seeds ripen the following year. Bark smooth, gray to light brown. Seaside Alder has a narrow, round-topped crown of zigzag branches; grows to about 30 feet tall, 6 inches in diameter.

AN INTRODUCED ALDER

EUROPEAN ALDER *(Alnus glutinosa)* is a medium-sized tree, 50 to 70 feet tall and 1 to 2 feet in diameter. Most common of several foreign alders planted as ornamentals. Bark is dark and has many warty stripes. Leaves, broadly ovate or widest above middle and with coarse marginal teeth, are dark green above and paler below, with fine hairs especially along veins. Young leaves and twigs are gummy.

HAZELS, OR FILBERTS *(Corylus)*

Hazels, or Filberts, are shrubs and small trees with hairy, ovate to elliptical leaves, 3 to 5 inches long and 2 to 4 inches wide, with heart-shaped base and coarse, doubly toothed margins. Preformed staminate catkins resemble those of birches, but the buds are oval and the fruit is a nut surrounded by leafy bracts or enclosed by a leafy husk (p. 103). American Hazel *(C. americana)* and Beaked Hazel *(C. rostrata)* are native shrubs of eastern United States and Canada. California Hazel *(C. cornuta var. californica)*, a tall shrub with fruit resembling Beaked Hazel, occurs in the West. The Giant Filbert *(C. maxima)*, a small tree (to 25 feet) native to southeastern Europe, is occasionally planted in the United States as an ornamental. Varieties are grown commercially for edible nuts.

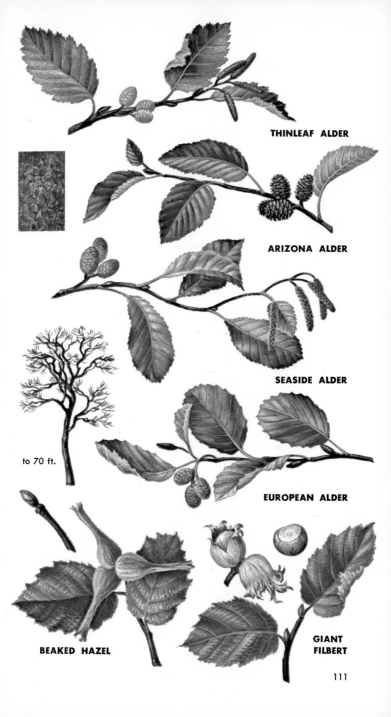

THINLEAF ALDER

ARIZONA ALDER

SEASIDE ALDER

to 70 ft.

EUROPEAN ALDER

BEAKED HAZEL

GIANT FILBERT

111

HOPHORNBEAMS *(Ostrya)*

Hophornbeams are small trees with birchlike leaves and preformed staminate catkins that become about 2 inches long. Hophornbeams are most distinctive for their pendant clusters of flattened, leafy, hoplike bladders, each with a small, nutlike seed attached inside at base. Two species are native to North America; other species occur in Europe and in Asia.

EASTERN HOPHORNBEAM *(Ostrya virginiana)* is often called Ironwood because of its very hard, heavy wood. Its oblong, lanceolate leaves, 3 to 5 inches long and 1.5 to 2 inches wide, are narrowed to a slender point and have doubly toothed margins. Leaves are dull yellow-green above and lighter below, with tufts of hairs in the axils of veins. The clusters of bladder-like, seed-bearing pods are 1.5 to 2 inches long. Reddish-brown bark is broken into thick, narrow scales that are loose at ends, giving trunk a shaggy appearance. A round-topped tree, 20 to 30 feet tall (rarely to 50 feet) and 1 to 1.5 feet in diameter. Usually grows in dry soils.

KNOWLTON HOPHORNBEAM *(Ostrya knowltonii)* is generally smaller than the above and may have several stems. Leaves elliptical. Knowlton Hophornbeam is often found in moist canyons.

HORNBEAMS *(Carpinus)*

Hornbeams are small trees with birchlike leaves. Staminate catkins, to 1.5 inches long in spring, are not preformed (p. 102). Recognized by their many pendant clusters of loose, leafy, 3-pointed bracts, each bearing a small, nutlike seed attached to the base. Of about 26 species, all found in the Northern Hemisphere, only one is native to North America. European Hornbeam *(C. betulus)* is occasionally planted in the United States as an ornamental or shade tree.

AMERICAN HORNBEAM *(Carpinus caroliniana)*, also called Blue Beech or Water Beech, has elliptical leaves, 2 to 4 inches long and 1 to 2 inches wide. They are dull green above and yellow-green below, with tufts of hairs in axils of the veins and doubly toothed margins. The light-green, leafy clusters of seed-bearing bracts are 3 to 6 inches long and conspicuous in late spring. A small tree with a round-topped crown, American Hornbeam has a short, fluted, or "muscular," trunk, and smooth, blue-gray bark. It grows to 40 feet tall and 1 to 2 feet in diameter. Most common in moist, rich soil bordering streams or swamps.

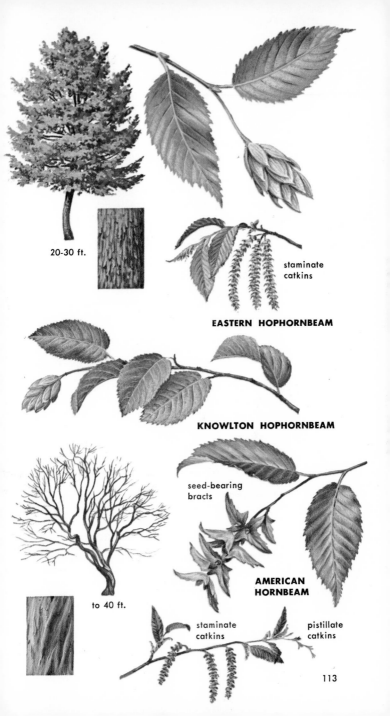

20-30 ft.

staminate
catkins

EASTERN HOPHORNBEAM

KNOWLTON HOPHORNBEAM

seed-bearing
bracts

**AMERICAN
HORNBEAM**

to 40 ft.

staminate
catkins

pistillate
catkins

BEECH FAMILY (Fagaceae)

One of the most important of families of trees, both commercially and aesthetically, the beech family is widespread in both the Northern and Southern hemispheres. Of the 600 species, nearly 100 are native to North America. Familiar members are the beeches, oaks, and chestnuts, prized for the quality of their wood and admired for their regal beauty. Less familiar are the chinkapins and tanoaks, most typical of southeastern Asia and adjacent islands but each including one tree species native to the Pacific Coast states. The beechlike, deciduous or evergreen trees of the genus *Nothofagus* occur in South America, Australia, and New Zealand. All members of the beech family have alternate leaves.

BEECHES *(Fagus)*

Beeches are handsome deciduous trees with short-stemmed, prominently veined elliptical leaves that have wide-spaced marginal teeth. Monoecious, the flowers appearing with the leaves—the staminate yellowish green, in long-stemmed heads; pistillate, in 2- to 4-flowered spikes. Triangular, edible nuts are borne in 2's or 3's in a husk covered by weak, unbranched spines. Bark is smooth and gray, even on large trunks. Long, spindle-shaped, scaly buds extend at sharp angle from slender twigs. Of 10 species in this genus, one is native to U.S. and Canada; others grow in Europe.

AMERICAN BEECH *(Fagus grandifolia)* leaves are 2 to 6 inches long and 1 to 2.5 inches wide, with small but prominent, incurved marginal teeth. They are smooth on both surfaces, except for hairy tufts in axils of veins on underside, and taper to a pointed apex. The smooth bark is blue-gray and commonly blotched. A medium-sized to large tree, 60 to 100 feet tall and 2 to 3 feet in diameter, with a short trunk and a broad, rounded crown. Grows best in soils with ample surface moisture, as the wide-spreading root system is shallow.

AN INTRODUCED BEECH

EUROPEAN BEECH *(Fagus sylvatica)*, a common and important European timber tree, is widely planted in the United States as an ornamental. Resembles American Beech but is smaller, has darker bark, and smaller, more elliptical leaves, 2 to 4 inches long and 1 to 2 inches wide, with smaller, rounded marginal teeth. Leaf margins and veins on underside are noticeably hairy, especially on young leaves. Purple Beech *(F. sylvatica* var. *atropunica)* has purplish-bronze or copper-colored foliage. Other varieties include one with pendant branches (var. *pendula)* and a cut-leaved form (var. *laciniata).*

Beech
Fagus

Chinkapin
Castanopsis

Chestnut
Castanea

Tanoak
Lithocarpus

acorn, matures
in 2nd season

Oak
Quercus

ngled nuts in bur
ith weak spines;
ature 1st season

rounded nuts in prickly
bur; mature 2nd season

rounded nuts in
prickly bur; mature
1st season

acorn; matures in
1st or 2nd season

COMPARISON OF NUTS IN THE BEECH FAMILY

pistillate

staminate   **AMERICAN BEECH**

**EUROPEAN
BEECH**

15-40 ft.

115

CHESTNUTS *(Castanea)*

Chestnuts are deciduous trees with short-stemmed, prominently veined leaves that have coarse, bristly marginal teeth. Small flowers, in slender, erect, unisexual or bisexual catkins (aments), appear after the leaves. Staminate catkins are long and drooping; bisexual catkins shorter, with pistillate flowers at base. Rounded, edible nuts are in husks (burs) covered with stiff, branched, prickly spines; husks split open when nuts mature. About 10 species occur in southern Europe, northern Africa, eastern Asia, and eastern North America.

AMERICAN CHESTNUT *(Castanea dentata)* leaves are oblong-lanceolate, 5 to 8 inches long and 2 inches wide, dull dark green above, paler below, and smooth on both surfaces. Slender, arching, staminate catkins, 6 to 8 inches long, are conspicuous near ends of the branches in spring; bisexual flowers are shorter. Prickly husks, about 2.5 inches in diameter, contain two or three somewhat flattened nuts, about 1 inch in diameter. Bark dark brown; smooth on young trees and broken into broad, flattened, scaly ridges on large trunks. Once one of the most valuable of American hardwoods, this species has been virtually destroyed by chestnut blight, an introduced fungus disease affecting the bark. Few uninfected trees exist, though stump sprouts persist. Grew nearly 100 feet tall and 4 feet in diameter, with a broad, rounded crown.

ALLEGHENY CHINKAPIN *(Castanea pumila)* resembles the American Chestnut but is smaller and usually occurs in dry soils. A shrub or a small tree, rarely to 50 feet tall and 2 feet in diameter. Its leaves, not as sharply tapered, are 3 to 5 inches long and 1.5 inches wide, covered with gray hairs on underside and on stem. Smaller nuts, 0.8 of an inch in diameter, are borne singly in husks 1 to 1.5 inches in diameter. Other similar southern trees include Ashe Chinkapin *(C. pumila* var. *ashei),* Ozark Chinkapin *(C. ozarkensis),* and Florida Chinkapin *(C. alnifolia* var. *floridana),* a treelike variety of a shrubby species.

INTRODUCED CHESTNUTS

SPANISH CHESTNUT *(Castanea sativa),* native to southern Europe, Asia, and northern Africa, is grown in North America as an ornamental. It grows 75 feet tall and 2 feet in diameter. Leaves are 6 to 9 inches long and about 2 inches wide, and the nuts are over 1 inch in diameter. Two Oriental species of chestnuts have also been introduced; both produce large nuts. Chinese Chestnut *(C. mollissima)* becomes 60 feet tall. Japanese Chestnut *(C. crenata)* is rarely more than 30 feet tall.

to 100 ft.

dead tree
and sprouts

twig

flowers

bur

nut

AMERICAN CHESTNUT

ALLEGHENY CHINKAPIN

SPANISH CHESTNUT

117

CHINKAPINS *(Castanopsis)*

This group of about 30 species of evergreen trees and shrubs is found primarily in southeastern Asia, but two species grow in western United States. One *(C. sempervirens)* is a shrub of coastal ranges and Sierra Nevada in California and southern Oregon.

GOLDEN CHINKAPIN *(Castanopsis chrysophylla)* has leathery, lanceolate or oblong-lanceolate, evergreen leaves, with smooth, curled margins. Dark glossy green above and golden yellow on underside, they are 2 to 5 inches long and 0.5 to 1.5 inches wide. Flowers, similar to those of chestnuts, are in erect, 2- to 2.5-inch aments. Staminate flowers are creamy white. The burs resemble chestnuts but are smaller and mature in two years; they contain either one or two edible, rounded nuts. On young trees, bark is smooth; on older trees, it is broken into reddish-brown plates. In northern California and southern Oregon, grows 50 to 100 feet tall and 1 to 3 feet in diameter, with a dense, conical crown.

TANOAKS *(Lithocarpus)*

Except for the one species native to California and southern Oregon, this group of about 100 species is confined to southeastern Asia. Tanoak flowers resemble those of the chestnuts, while the fruits are like those of the oaks.

TANOAK *(Lithocarpus densiflorus)* has leathery, evergreen leaves that are elliptical to oblong-lanceolate, 2 to 5 inches long and 1 to 2.5 inches wide, with wide-spaced marginal teeth and short, hairy stems. They are smooth and dark green above; the underside is at first covered with rusty-brown hairs, later becoming blue-gray and only slightly hairy. Young twigs are also hairy. Catkins are similar to those of the chestnut, though 3 to 4 inches long. The fruit, an acorn about 0.8 of an inch long, has a shallow cup covered by many hairy, linear scales. The acorns are bitter and require two years to mature. Bark of large trees is ridged and fissured. Formerly the bark was used for tanning, and because the tree was once considered to be an oak, the name Tanoak was applied. Under best conditions, Tanoak grows 60 to 100 feet tall and 1 to 3 feet in diameter, with a narrow, pyramidal crown of ascending branches.

50-100 ft.

flowers

nut

bur

GOLDEN CHINKAPIN

60-100 ft.

TANOAK

119

OAKS *(Quercus)*

Oaks are widely distributed in North America. Of about 60 species native to the area covered by this book (p. 3), 41 are described. (Varieties, hybrids, shrubs, and rare or localized species are omitted.) Some oaks are deciduous, others evergreen; some are either, depending on local conditions. Monoecious—the staminate flowers in pendant, clustered aments near ends of twigs; pistillate, solitary or in several-flowered spikes in new-leaf axils. Fruit an acorn. Buds clustered at tips of twigs. Leaves alternate.

North American oaks are divided into two groups: white oaks and red oaks. Most white oaks have leaves with rounded lobes or marginal teeth not tipped with bristles. Their acorns mature in one season, and the shells are hairless inside. Their meat is not bitter. Red oaks have pointed bristle-tipped lobes; bristle-tipped or spiny marginal teeth; or smooth margins, often with a spiny or bristle-tipped apex. Usually their acorns mature in two years, the shells are hairy inside, and the meat is bitter. Chestnut oaks form a subsection of the white oak group; the willow oaks and live oaks are subsections of the red oak group.

WHITE OAK GROUP

WHITE OAK *(Quercus alba)* leaves are deciduous, 5 to 9 inches long and 2 to 4 inches wide, with 7 to 9 rounded lobes divided by narrow, variable sinuses often extending nearly to the midrib. The oblong acorns, 0.5 to 0.8 of an inch long, are set in a bowl-like cup covered with warty scales. The gray bark is in narrow, vertical blocks of scaly plates. Grows 80 to 100 feet tall and 3 to 4 feet in diameter, with a wide-spreading crown.

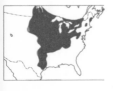

BUR OAK *(Quercus macrocarpa)* has deciduous leaves, 6 to 12 inches long and 3 to 6 inches wide, with 5 to 9 rounded lobes; only central sinuses extend nearly to midrib. The broadly ovoid acorn, 0.8 to 1.5 inches long, has a fringed cup covering lower half. Twigs often have corky "wings." Bark resembles White Oak's. Bur Oak prefers bottomland soils. Grows 70 to 80 feet tall, 2 to 3 feet in diameter.

OVERCUP OAK *(Quercus lyrata)* has deciduous leaves, 6 to 10 inches long and 1 to 4 inches wide, with 5 to 9 rounded lobes separated by broad, irregular sinuses. The broad, nearly round acorn, 0.5 to 1 inch long, is covered almost completely with a scaly cup. The bark is similar to White Oak's. Typical of wet bottomlands, Overcup Oak may grow 60 to 100 feet tall and 3 to 4 feet in diameter, usually smaller.

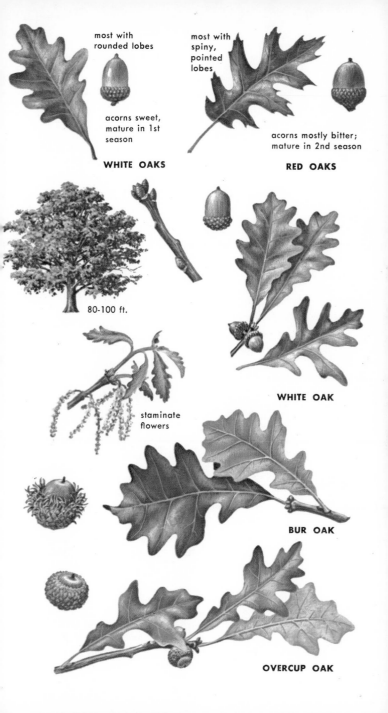

most with rounded lobes

WHITE OAKS

acorns sweet, mature in 1st season

most with spiny, pointed lobes

RED OAKS

acorns mostly bitter; mature in 2nd season

80-100 ft.

WHITE OAK

staminate flowers

BUR OAK

OVERCUP OAK

POST OAK *(Quercus stellata)* has leathery, deciduous leaves, 4 to 6 inches long and 3 to 4 inches wide, usually deeply 5-lobed, with center lobes squarish. Leaf margins are somewhat curled under, surfaces slightly hairy. A bowl-like, scaly cup covers lower third of the ovoid-oblong acorns, 0.5 to 0.8 of an inch long. Bark similar to White Oak's. Often found in dry soils. Grows 40 to 50 feet tall and 1 to 2 feet in diameter, usually with a crown of gnarled, twisted branches.

OREGON WHITE OAK *(Quercus garryana)* leaves are deciduous, 4 to 6 inches long and 2 to 5 inches wide. Sinuses separating the 5 to 7 (occasionally 9) rounded lobes extend about halfway to the midrib. The lower surface and petioles somewhat hairy, the margin slightly curled under. The ovoid to obovoid acorn, about 1 inch long, has a shallow cup with hairy scales loose at tip. Bark resembles White Oak's. Grows 50 to 70 feet tall and 2 to 3 feet in diameter, with rounded crown.

CALIFORNIA WHITE OAK *(Quercus lobata)* has deciduous leaves, 2 to 4 inches long and 1 to 2 inches wide, with 7 to 11 rounded lobes. The slim, conical acorn, 1 to 2.5 inches long, has a deep cup covering the lower third. At first green, acorns later turn brown; cup scales are knobby, with free tips. Largest of western oaks, it grows 80 to 120 feet tall and 3 to 5 feet in diameter, with a short trunk and a broad crown.

GAMBEL OAK *(Quercus gambelii)* leaves are deciduous, 2 to 7 inches long and 1.5 to 3.5 inches wide, with 7 to 11 deep lobes. They are smooth on upper surface, hairy below. Broadly oval acorns, 1 inch long, are nearly half enclosed by a bowl-like cup with hairy scales. Bark similar to White Oak's. Grows 15 to 30 feet tall and 5 to 10 inches in diameter, with rounded crown.

CHAPMAN OAK *(Quercus chapmanii)* leaves, 2 to 3 inches long and 1 inch wide, are obovate or oblong with smooth or undulating margins. They are leathery, dark green above and silvery below, sometimes remaining until new foliage forms. Oval acorns, about 0.8 of an inch long, are half enclosed by a cup with pointed scales. Bark usually in dark-gray plates. A shrub or small tree of sandy soils, to 50 feet tall, 1 foot in diameter.

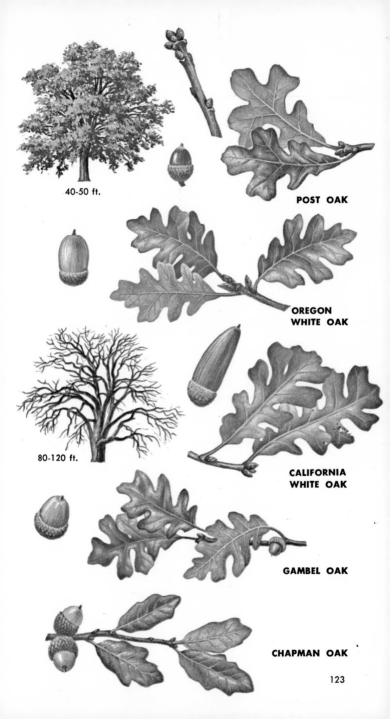

40-50 ft.

POST OAK

OREGON WHITE OAK

80-120 ft.

CALIFORNIA WHITE OAK

GAMBEL OAK

CHAPMAN OAK

123

CHESTNUT OAK *(Quercus prinus)* has obovate to nearly lanceolate, deciduous leaves, 4 to 8 inches long, 1.5 to 3 inches wide; margins with large, rounded teeth; undersurface often hairy. Oval acorns, 1 to 1.5 inches long, are lustrous and short-stemmed, their lower third covered with a thin cup with fused scales. Bark dark brown to black, deeply ridged, furrowed. Chestnut Oak grows 50 to 60 feet tall and 1 to 2 feet in diameter, preferring drier soils. Also called Rock Oak, as it is common in drier, often rocky soils.

SWAMP CHESTNUT OAK *(Quercus michauxii)* leaves are deciduous, obovate, 5 to 8 inches long, 3 to 4 inches wide; silvery or somewhat hairy on underside; marginal teeth coarse, rounded. Lower third of oblong acorns, 1 to 1.5 inches long, covered by a bowl-like cup with coarse, wedge-shaped scales. Bark gray to reddish, irregularly furrowed. Prefers moist bottomland soils, growing 60 to 80 feet tall, 2 to 3 feet in diameter, usually with its trunk clear of branches for some distance above the ground. Swamp Chestnut Oak is known also as Cow Oak, since cattle eat the acorns.

SWAMP WHITE OAK *(Quercus bicolor)* has obovate, deciduous leaves, 5 to 6 inches long and 2 to 4 inches wide. The margin is irregularly and shallowly lobed or has bluntly pointed teeth; lower surface is hairy. Long-stemmed (1-4 inches), oval acorns are usually in pairs. Each acorn is about 1 inch long and has a scaly, somewhat fringed cup enclosing lower third. Dark-brown to black bark is coarsely ridged, furrowed, or scaly on upper branches. Swamp White Oak generally grows in moist to swampy soils; it may be 50 to 70 feet tall and 1 to 3 feet in diameter.

CHINKAPIN OAK *(Quercus muehlenbergii)* leaves are deciduous, oblong-lanceolate, 4 to 7 inches long and 1 to 4 inches wide, with coarse, bluntly pointed marginal teeth and fine white hairs below. Acorns sessile, brown to black, ovoid, 0.5 to 0.8 of an inch long, the lower half in a bowl-shaped, scaly cup. Bark ash gray, rough and flaky. Grows 50 to 80 feet tall and 1 to 3 feet in diameter, usually in dry rocky soils. Dwarf Chinkapin Oak *(Q. prinoides)* grows in same area, has smaller obovate leaves, and is rarely tree size.

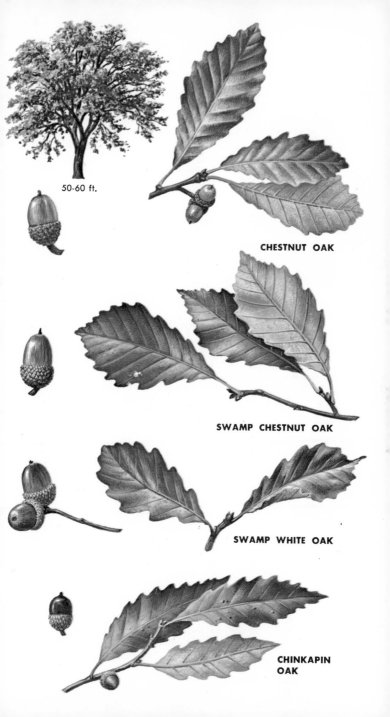

50-60 ft.

CHESTNUT OAK

SWAMP CHESTNUT OAK

SWAMP WHITE OAK

CHINKAPIN
OAK

RED OAK GROUP
(see pp. 120-121)

(see pp. 120-121)

NORTHERN RED OAK (*Quercus rubra*) has deciduous leaves, 5 to 8 inches long and 4 to 5 inches wide, with 7 to 11 pointed, toothed lobes separated by regular sinuses that extend halfway to the midrib. The leaves turn red in the fall. The oblong-ovoid acorns are 0.8 to 1 inch long, with a flat, saucer-like cup at their base. The dark-brown to black bark is ridged and furrowed. Grows 50 to 70 feet tall and 1 to 3 feet in diameter, with a rounded crown.

BLACK OAK (*Quercus velutina*) leaves resemble those of Northern Red Oak but have 5 to 7 lobes separated by variable sinuses and are coppery with axillary tufts of hair below. Ovoid acorns, 0.5 to 0.8 of an inch long, have deep, bowl-like, scaly cups. Bark is black, ridged, and furrowed. Grows 50 to 70 feet tall and 1 to 3 feet in diameter, with rounded crown.

SCARLET OAK (*Quercus coccinea*) has deciduous leaves about the same size as those of Northern Red Oak, but the 5 to 9 narrow, toothed, and pointed lobes are separated by deep, rounded sinuses that extend nearly to the midrib. In fall, the leaves turn red or scarlet. The oval acorns, 0.5 to 1 inch long, have a deep, bowl-like, scaly cup, and the apex is often marked with circular lines. Grows 50 to 75 feet tall and 1 to 3 feet in diameter, with an irregular, spreading crown.

PIN OAK (*Quercus palustris*) leaves are deciduous, 3 to 5 inches long and 2 to 5 inches wide. The 5 (occasionally 7 to 9) lobes are toothed and pointed, with deep, irregular sinuses extending nearly to the midrib. The leaves turn red in fall. The nearly round, brownish and hairless acorns are 0.5 of an inch long, have thin, scaly, shallow cup; the branches have short, stubby twigs. Prefers bottomland soils. Grows 50 to 75 feet tall and 1 to 3 feet in diameter, with smooth to ridged, gray-brown bark.

NORTHERN PIN OAK (*Quercus ellipsoidalis*) is similar to Pin Oak, except the slim, tapered acorns, about 1 inch long, are in a deep, scaly cup. Also, Northern Pin Oak grows on dry and higher ground.

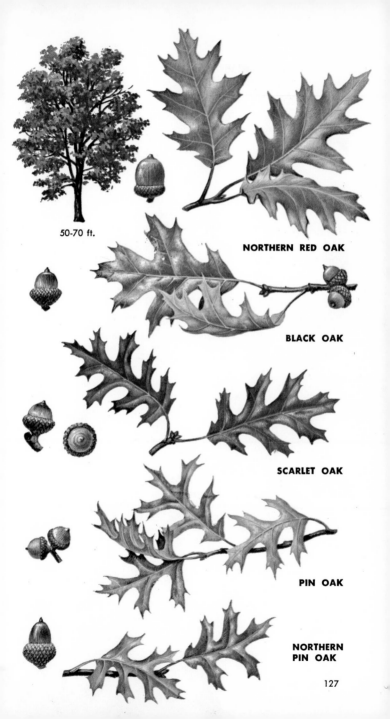

50-70 ft.

NORTHERN RED OAK

BLACK OAK

SCARLET OAK

PIN OAK

NORTHERN
PIN OAK

127

SOUTHERN RED OAK *(Quercus falcata)* has deciduous leaves, 5 to 9 inches long and 4 to 5 inches wide, with a rusty or hairy underside. They are deeply 3- to 7-lobed, the terminal lobe much longer and narrower than the others. Rounded acorns, 0.5 of an inch long, have a scaly cup over lower third. Grows 60 to 80 feet tall and 1 to 3 feet in diameter, with a large, rounded crown and dark-brown to black, roughly ridged bark. Usually found in poor upland soils.

SHUMARD OAK *(Quercus shumardii)* has deciduous leaves, 6 to 8 inches long and 4 to 5 inches wide, with 7 to 9 toothed lobes. Acorns are oblong-ovoid and 0.8 to 1.3 inches long, with a thick, shallow, saucer-like, scaly cup. Attaining a height of more than 100 feet and a trunk diameter of 2 to 5 feet, this is one of the largest of the "red oaks." Bark on the usually clear trunk is gray, ridged, and furrowed, the crown wide-spreading. Grows commonly in moist bottomland soils.

NUTTALL OAK *(Quercus nuttallii)* has deciduous leaves, 4 to 8 inches long and 2 to 5 inches wide, with 5 to 7 broad lobes separated by deep sinuses. Oblong-ovoid acorns, 0.8 to 1 inch long, have a thick, deep, scaly cup. Grows 60 to 80 feet tall and 1 to 3 feet in diameter, most commonly in moist bottomland soils.

BLACKJACK OAK *(Quercus marilandica)* has leathery, deciduous leaves, 3 to 7 inches long, variable in shape but widest and shallowly 3-lobed at the apex. Their undersurface is brown and hairy. The small, oblong acorns, 0.8 of an inch long, are about half covered with a thick, scaly, bowl-shaped cup, and the black bark is in thick, rough plates. Blackjack Oak grows 20 to 30 feet tall and 1 foot in diameter. It is a ragged tree of poorer soils.

TURKEY OAK *(Quercus laevis)* has deciduous leaves, 3 to 12 inches long and 1 to 6 inches wide, with 3 to 7 narrow, curved, and often toothed lobes. Lower third of the ovoid acorns, about 1 inch long, are in a thin, bowl-shaped cup. Turkey Oak has gray to black, scaly and ridged bark. Grows 20 to 30 feet tall and 1 to 2 feet in diameter, with stout branches and an irregular, rounded crown. Common in sandy soils.

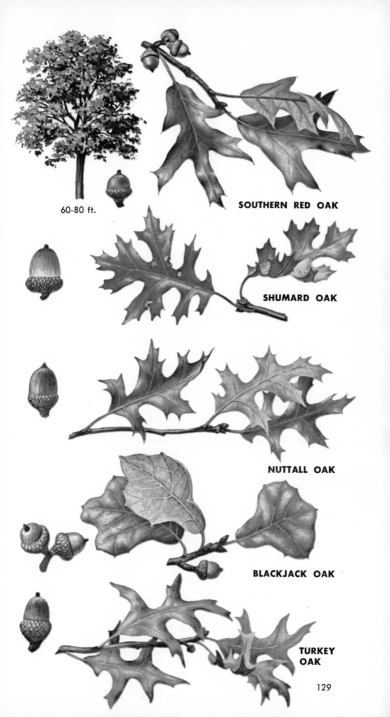

60-80 ft.

SOUTHERN RED OAK

SHUMARD OAK

NUTTALL OAK

BLACKJACK OAK

TURKEY OAK

129

CALIFORNIA BLACK OAK (*Quercus kelloggii*) has deciduous leaves, 3 to 6 inches long and 2 to 3 inches wide, with 5 to 7 toothed lobes. The ellipsoidal, inch-long acorn, once a staple food of California Indians, has a deep, bowl-like, roughly scaly cup covering lower third. Usually with a short trunk and rounded crown, California Black Oak has black, heavily ridged bark. Grows 50 to 100 feet tall, 1 to 3 feet in diameter; most common on drier soils.

BLUE OAK (*Quercus douglasii*) has oblong to oval, deciduous leaves, 3 inches long, the margins smooth or with 4 or 5 lobes. The ellipsoidal acorn, about 1 inch long, has a shallow cup. Unlike many "red oaks," the meat of the Blue Oak's acorn is not bitter, the shell is hairless inside, and it matures in one season. The gray-brown bark is scaly. Blue Oak grows 50 to 75 feet tall and 1 to 3 feet in diameter, with a rounded to irregular crown.

BEAR OAK (*Quercus ilicifolia*) leaves are deciduous, 2 to 5 inches long and 1 to 3 inches wide, with wide, shallow sinuses and 3 to 7 (usually 5) toothed lobes. The underside of the leaves is silvery-haired. A scaly cup surrounds lower half of broadly ovoid acorn, 0.5 of an inch long. Grows 15 to 20 feet tall, 6 inches in diameter, with slender branches and round-topped crown; usually in dry, sandy soil.

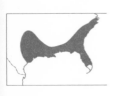

BLUEJACK OAK (*Quercus incana*) leaves are blue-green, oblong-lanceolate, 2 to 5 inches long and 0.5 to 1.5 inches wide, with smooth margins (occasionally 3-lobed at apex), and white-hairy below. They are tardily deciduous; very young leaves pink and pubescent. Acorns are ovoid, 0.5 of an inch long, hairy at apex, striated, with a thin, scaly cup. Bark reddish brown to black, broken into small blocks. A shrub or small tree of dry soils, Bluejack Oak grows to 20 feet tall and 6 inches in diameter.

MYRTLE OAK (*Quercus myrtifolia*) leaves are evergreen, 0.5 to 2 inches long and 0.3 to 1 inch wide, widest above the middle; tips sharp or rounded, base gradually narrowed. The margins are smooth and turned under. Acorns are dark lustrous brown, nearly round, 0.3 to 0.5 inch long, striated, with a scaly cup on the lower third. A shrub or small tree of sandy coastal soils, to 40 feet tall and 5 inches in diameter.

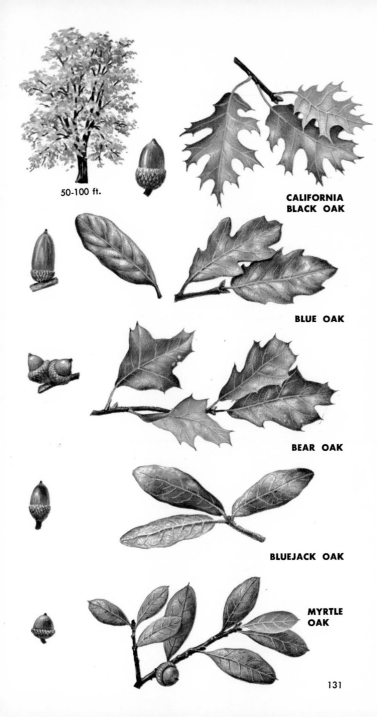

50-100 ft.

CALIFORNIA BLACK OAK

BLUE OAK

BEAR OAK

BLUEJACK OAK

MYRTLE OAK

131

WILLOW OAK *(Quercus phellos)* has willow-like, deciduous leaves, 2 to 5 inches long and 0.5 to 1 inch wide, with smooth margins and a bristle-tipped apex. They are light green above, dull and paler below. The small, roundish acorns, 0.5 inch long, have a thin, scaly, saucer-like cup. Typical of bottomland soils, Willow Oak grows 80 to 100 feet tall and 2 to 4 feet in diameter, with gray to black, irregularly furrowed bark, a short trunk, and a broad, rounded crown. It may also be nearly evergreen in the South.

WATER OAK *(Quercus nigra)* has deciduous leaves, 2 to 4 inches long and 1 to 2 inches wide, which remain on tree well into winter. They are variable in shape but usually taper from a broad, shallowly 3-lobed apex, and have smooth to shallowly lobed margins. Small, ovoid, black acorns, 0.5 inch long, are set in a shallow, scaly cup. Bark mottled gray-black, broken into scaly ridges. A bottomland species; grows 60 to 70 feet tall and 2 to 3 feet in diameter, usually with a rounded crown.

SHINGLE OAK *(Quercus imbricaria)* has laurel-like, oblong-lanceolate to oblong-obovate, deciduous leaves, with smooth, wavy, and slightly curled margins. They are 4 to 6 inches long and 1 to 2 inches wide, brown-hairy below. The acorns, 0.5 to 0.8 of an inch long, are oval, the lower third enclosed in a thin, scaly cup. Common in moist soils near streams, Shingle Oak has gray-brown, broadly ridged bark. It grows 40 to 60 feet tall and 1 to 3 feet in diameter. The common name was applied during pioneer days, when its wood was widely used for split shingles. It is known also as Northern Laurel Oak.

LAUREL OAK *(Quercus laurifolia)* is semi-evergreen, the leaves of the current year remaining on the tree through the winter. Elliptical and occasionally irregularly lobed, they are 2 to 4 inches long and 0.5 to 1 inch wide, with a pointed apex, smooth margin, and a prominent yellow midrib. The ovoid, dark-brown to black acorn, 0.5 of an inch long, has a saucer-like cup with hairy scales. The bark is brown to black, smooth or broadly ridged. Usually in moist soils bordering streams, Laurel Oak grows 80 to 100 feet tall and 3 to 4 feet in diameter. It has a broad, rounded crown.

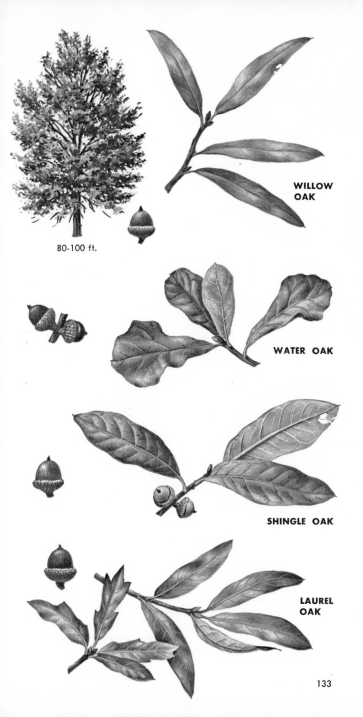

WILLOW
OAK

80-100 ft.

WATER OAK

SHINGLE OAK

LAUREL
OAK

133

LIVE OAK (*Quercus virginiana*) has elliptical to ob-ovate, evergreen leaves, 2 to 5 inches long and 1 to 2.5 inches wide. They usually have smooth margins, a rounded apex, and often are hairy below. The 0.8-inch-long acorn is brown to black and ellipsoidal, its lower third enclosed in a deep, tapering, scaly cup. Unlike many "red oaks," acorns of the Live Oak mature in one season and the meat is not bitter. Bark is dark reddish brown, scaly, and fissured. Grows 40 to 50 feet tall and 3 to 4 feet in diameter, with a short trunk and huge, wide-spreading crown. It is one of the more majestic trees of the coastal region of the Deep South, and its branches are often heavily festooned with Spanish Moss.

CANYON LIVE OAK (*Quercus chrysolepis*) has ever-green leaves, 1 to 4 inches long and 0.5 to 2 inches wide. Oblong to elliptical, some of the leaves have smooth margins and a rounded apex; others are holly-like. The ovoid acorn, 1.5 inches long, has a thick, scaly cup covered with a golden-yellow "wool." Bark is black, ridged, and scaly. Typical of rocky canyon sites, it is medium-sized to large, with a short, crooked trunk and massive limbs that form a broad, irregular crown. Canyon Live Oak grows 60 to 80 feet tall, 1 to 5 feet in diameter. Because of its striking acorns, it is also known as Golden Cup Oak.

INTERIOR LIVE OAK (*Quercus wislizenii*) leaves are evergreen, 1 to 1.5 inches long and 0.5 to 0.8 of an inch wide. Elliptical to broadly lanceolate and with smooth or holly-like margins, they remain on the tree through the second season. Acorns, about half en-closed in a deep, bowl-like, scaly cup, are an inch long. Bark black and furrowed. Grows 50 to 80 feet tall and 2 to 3 feet in diameter, with short trunk and large branches forming a broad, rounded crown.

CALIFORNIA LIVE OAK (*Quercus agrifolia*) resem-bles Interior Live Oak, but its evergreen leaves are often somewhat larger and remain on the tree only through one year. Acorns are chestnut brown, conical 0.8 to 1.5 inches long, with a bowl-like cup having thin, somewhat hairy scales covering the lower third mature in one season. California Live Oak grows 60 to 90 feet tall and 2 to 3 feet in diameter, with a short trunk and large branches forming a broad, rounded wide-spreading crown.

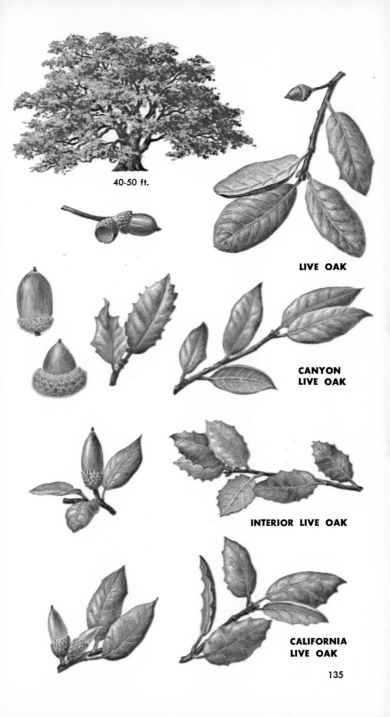

40-50 ft.

LIVE OAK

CANYON
LIVE OAK

INTERIOR LIVE OAK

CALIFORNIA
LIVE OAK

EMORY OAK *(Quercus emoryi)* leaves are evergreen, 2.5 inches long and oblong-lanceolate, with smooth or spiny-toothed margins. The oblong acorns, 0.8 of an inch long, mature in one season. The base is set in a deep cup covered with hairy scales. The inner shell is hairy. The meat is not bitter. Bark is black, in rectangular blocks like an alligator's hide. A shrub or small tree, 20 to 60 feet tall and 1 to 3 feet in diameter.

ARIZONA WHITE OAK *(Quercus arizonica)* has broadly oval leaves, 2.5 inches long, with smooth or spiny-toothed margins. The acorns, 1 inch long, have lower half enclosed in a hairy-scaled, bowl-like cup; they mature in one season and inner shell is hairless. Grows 20 to 60 feet tall, 1 to 3 feet in diameter, with rounded crown and plated bark. In spite of its common name this evergreen tree is classed with "red oaks."

ENGELMANN OAK *(Quercus engelmannii)* leaves are evergreen, 1 to 3 inches long and 2 inches wide, with smooth, shallowly lobed or toothed margins. The oblong acorns are 0.8 of an inch long, the lower half covered by a tapering cup with hairy scales. Bark gray-brown, in scaly ridges, its thick branches forming a broad, irregular crown. Engelmann Oak grows 20 to 50 feet tall and 1 to 3 feet in diameter.

MEXICAN BLUE OAK *(Quercus oblongifolia)* leaves are evergreen, 2 inches long, their margins curled and either smooth or with small teeth. The lower third of the ovoid acorns, 0.5 of an inch long, is enclosed in a bowl-like, scaly cup fringed on margin. Ash-gray bark is in scaly plates. A shrub or small tree, grows 10 to 30 feet tall and 1 foot in diameter.

SILVERLEAF OAK *(Quercus hypoleucoides)* has lance-shaped, evergreen leaves, 2 to 4 inches long and 0.5 to 1 inch wide, which are white-hairy on the underside. A few coarse teeth occur near the tapered apex, otherwise the rolled-under margin is smooth. Acorns are conical, 0.5 to 0.8 of an inch long, dark green to chestnut brown; a deep cup covering the lower third has thick, often silvery-haired scales. The bark is black, deeply ridged, and furrowed. Silverleaf Oak is a shrub or small tree, to 60 feet tall, usually found in moist, shaded canyons.

20-60 ft.

EMORY OAK

ARIZONA WHITE OAK

ENGELMANN OAK

MEXICAN BLUE OAK

SILVERLEAF OAK

137

ELM FAMILY (Ulmaceae)

Over 150 species of trees and shrubs, all with simple, alternate leaves, comprise the elm family, worldwide in distribution but mainly in temperate regions.

Elms *(Ulmus)* have distinctive wafer-like fruits (samaras). Leaves of native species are deciduous, pinnately veined, and short-stemmed, with doubly toothed margins; usually rough-textured and lopsided at base. Small, perfect flowers lack petals; borne on slender, jointed stems in several types of clusters. Flowers of some species develop in early spring before leaves unfold; others flower in autumn. Siberian Elm *(U. pumila)* is planted for windbreaks in central and western United States and also now grows wild.

Hackberries *(Celtis),* with five native species and several varieties, have deciduous, usually long-pointed leaves, with singly toothed or smooth margins. Small clusters of perfect or imperfect flowers develop with the leaves, and small fruits consist of a hard seed in a thin leathery covering (drupe).

Other members of the elm family in North America are the Planer tree *(Planera aquatica)* of southeastern United States and several species of the tropical genus *Trema* occurring in southern Florida.

AMERICAN ELM *(Ulmus americana)* has elliptical to oblong-ovate leaves, 4 to 6 inches long and 1 to inches wide. Greenish, wafer-like fruits, 0.5 inch long usually mature as the leaves unfold; papery wing surrounding the flat seed is oblong, the tip deeply notched and the edges hairy. On mature trees, bark is dark gray, in flat-topped ridges separated by roughly diamond-shaped areas. Grows 80 to 120 feet tall and 2 to 4 feet in diameter, its vase-shaped form recognizable even at a distance. Unfortunately many American Elms have been destroyed by the Dutch elm disease, an introduced fungus spread by a bark beetle.

SLIPPERY ELM *(Ulmus rubra)* leaves are similar to American Elm's but are rougher and also somewhat larger, 5 to 7 inches long and 2 to 3 inches wide. The greenish fruits, 0.8 of an inch long, are only slightly notched at the apex; the surface of the wing is smooth but the seed cavity is hairy. On mature trees the gray to reddish-brown bark is in flat-topped, nearly vertical ridges, and the inner bark, especially of twigs, contains a sticky, aromatic substance that once was chewed for relief of throat ailments. Slippery Elm grows 60 to 80 feet tall and 1 to 3 feet in diameter, resembling the American Elm's vase-shaped form.

leaf margin
doubly toothed

fruit a samara

ELMS *Ulmus*

leaf more pointed;
margin singly toothed
or smooth

fruit a drupe

HACKBERRIES *Celtis*

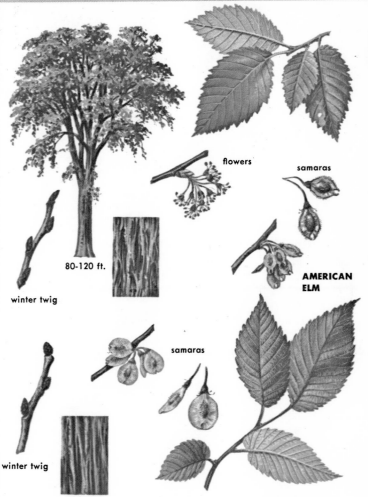

flowers

samaras

80-120 ft.

winter twig

**AMERICAN
ELM**

samaras

winter twig

SLIPPERY ELM

ROCK ELM *(Ulmus thomasii)* leaves resemble those of American Elm but are smaller, 2.5 to 4.5 inches long and 1.5 to 2.5 inches wide. The fruits, 0.8 to 1 inch long, have an indistinct seed cavity and are irregularly oval, with a rounded rather than notched apex and with a hairy margin. Twigs often have corky wings. Bark of mature trees is similar to American Elm's. Grows 60 to 80 feet tall and 1 to 3 feet in diameter, with a central trunk and oval crown.

WINGED ELM *(Ulmus alata)* leaves are oblong, 1.5 to 3 inches long and 1 to 1.5 inches wide, with base wedge-shaped or unequally rounded. Hairy, reddish fruits, 0.3 of an inch long, have narrow wings and a distinctive 2-pronged apex. Twigs have corky wings, often 0.5 of an inch wide. Bark is reddish brown, in flat-topped, vertical ridges. A small tree, 40 to 50 feet tall and 3 feet in diameter, with a narrow, oblong crown. Most common in dry soils.

CEDAR ELM *(Ulmus crassifolia)* leaves are 1 to 2 inches long and 0.5 to 1 inch wide. Flowers develop in late summer. The fruits are 0.5 of an inch long, deeply notched, and white-hairy; they mature in fall. Bark is gray to reddish brown and scaly; the twigs often have two narrow, corky wings. Grows 60 to 80 feet tall and 2 to 3 feet in diameter. September Elm *(U. serotina)*, also a southern species, flowers in late summer. Fruits white-haired, notched; twigs with corky wings. Leaves 3 to 4 inches long and 1 to 2 inches wide.

SOME INTRODUCED ELMS

ENGLISH ELM *(Ulmus campestris)* is a large, deciduous tree, 40 to 100 feet tall and 1 to 3 feet in diameter. It has a wide-spreading crown, corky wings on the branches, and oval leaves 2 to 3.5 inches long and 1 to 2.5 inches wide. English Elm's oval fruits are deeply notched at the apex.

CHINESE ELM *(Ulmus parvifolia)* is 20 to 60 feet tall, with a broad crown of slender, drooping branches. Leathery elliptical to ovate leaves, 0.8 to 2.5 inches long and to 1 inch wide, are singly toothed and slightly lopsided at base. May be evergreen in warm regions. Bark usually smooth.

WYCH ELM *(Ulmus glabra)* grows 40 to 100 feet tall, 2 to 3 feet in diameter. Its bark is smoother than English Elm's; the oval leaves are 3 to 6 inches long, 2 to 4 inches wide. The fruits have a slightly notched apex.

CAMPERDOWN ELM *(Ulmus glabra camperdownii)* is a grafted variety of the Wych Elm, also known as Umbrella Elm because of its crown of long, drooping branches. Leaves are larger and more lopsided than Wych Elm's.

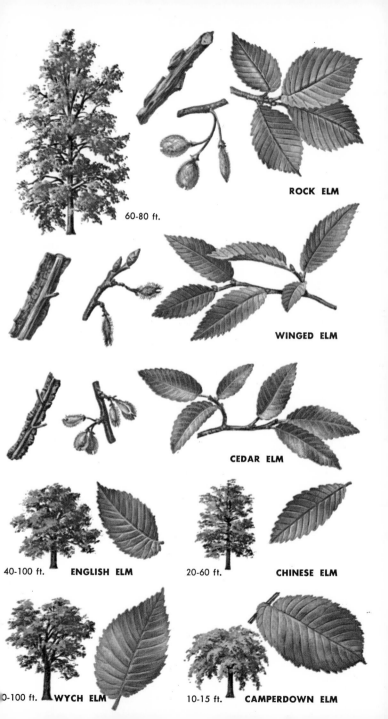

60-80 ft.

ROCK ELM

WINGED ELM

CEDAR ELM

40-100 ft.   **ENGLISH ELM**   20-60 ft.   **CHINESE ELM**

0-100 ft.   **WYCH ELM**   10-15 ft.   **CAMPERDOWN ELM**

HACKBERRY (*Celtis occidentalis*) has ovate to ovate-lanceolate leaves, 2.3 to 4 inches long and 1.5 to 2 inches wide. The margins are singly toothed and the tapering apex slightly curved; the base is obliquely rounded. Dark-red to purple fruits, 0.3 of an inch in diameter, are borne on slender stems, 0.5 of an inch long. The warty, gray to brown bark is an excellent identification feature. Usually grows 30 to 40 feet tall and 1 to 2 feet in diameter; occasionally much larger. It has a narrow, round-topped crown.

SUGARBERRY (*Celtis laevigata*) and 3 other species resemble Common Hackberry. Sugarberry has oblong-lanceolate, smooth-margined leaves, 2 to 5 inches long; fruit orange or yellow. Georgia Hackberry (*C. tenuifolia*) leaves are ovate, about 2 inches long, with smooth or toothed margins; fruit orange-red. Lindheimer Hackberry (*C. lindheimeri*) has oblong-ovate leaves, 1 to 3 inches long, with smooth or toothed margins; fruit reddish brown. Netleaf Hackberry (*C. reticulata*) has ovate leaves, 1 to 3 inches long, the margins smooth or occasionally toothed; fruit red.

PLANERTREE (*Planera aquatica*) has ovate-oblong, deciduous leaves, 2 to 2.5 inches long and 0.5 to 1 inch wide, with single-toothed margins, a pointed apex, and wedge-shaped base. Clusters of small, greenish, perfect, and unisexual flowers appear in spring. The brown, nutlike fruit, 0.5 of an inch long, is covered by soft, irregular projections. The outer bark is gray-brown and scaly; inner bark, exposed when scales peel, is reddish brown. Planertree grows 30 to 40 feet tall and 10 to 20 inches in diameter, forming a broad, low crown. Common in swamps and along streams.

FLORIDA TREMA (*Trema micrantha*) leaves are evergreen, 3 to 4 inches long and 1 to 2.5 inches wide, with a short, hairy stem, fine, singly toothed margins, a rounded, heart-shaped, or oblique base, and abruptly pointed apex. Dark green and finely haired above; white-woolly below. Clusters of small, unisexual flowers appear in spring. Fruit is a yellowish-orange drupe, 0.3 of an inch in diameter. The dark-brown bark is warty. Usually a shrub, occasionally grows 20 to 30 feet tall and 1 to 2 feet in diameter, with a single trunk and rounded crown.

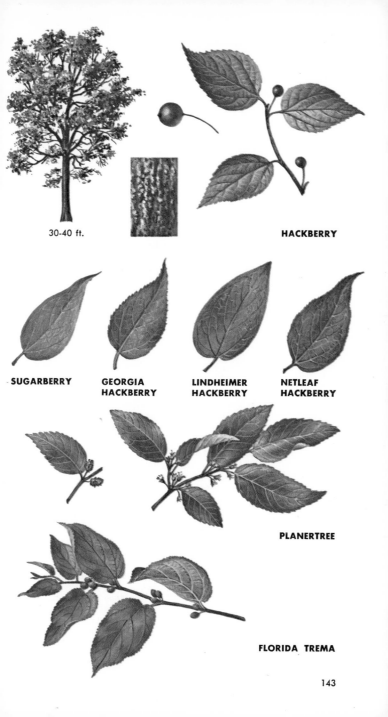

30-40 ft.

HACKBERRY

SUGARBERRY

GEORGIA HACKBERRY

LINDHEIMER HACKBERRY

NETLEAF HACKBERRY

PLANERTREE

FLORIDA TREMA

143

MULBERRY FAMILY (Moraceae)

About 1,000 species of deciduous and evergreen trees, shrubs, and herbs form the mulberry family. All have simple, alternate leaves. Some, like the mulberries (Morus), certain figs (Ficus), and Breadfruit (Artocarpus), bear valuable fruits. Commercial figs grown in warmer parts of the United States are varieties of a deciduous species (Ficus carica) native to the Mediterranean region. The India rubber-plant (Ficus elastica) and the rubber tree of the American tropics (Castilla elastica) yield a latex that has been a minor source of rubber. In Japan, mulberry leaves are food for silkworms. Hop (Humulus) and Hemp (Cannabis), both herbs, are the only members of the family that do not produce a milky sap, or latex.

MULBERRIES (Morus)

RED MULBERRY (Morus rubra) leaves are deciduous, 3 to 5 inches long and 2 to 3 inches wide, hairy below, and with coarse marginal teeth. Though usually broadly ovate, they often have 2 or 3 lobes. The leaves turn yellow in the fall. Staminate and pistillate flowers commonly occur on different trees in pendant, greenish spikes. Staminate spikes are narrow, 2 to 2.5 inches long; pistillate are oblong, about 1 inch long. Juicy, edible, multiple fruit, 1 to 1.3 inches long, resembles an elongated blackberry; red at first, purple when ripe. Bark on mature trees is in dark reddish-brown, scaly plates. In fertile, moist soils, grows 50 to 70 feet tall and 2 to 3 feet in diameter, with a dense, round-topped crown.

TEXAS MULBERRY (Morus microphylla) is similar to Red Mulberry but smaller (10 to 20 feet tall, 1 foot in diameter). The leaves are 1.5 inches long and 0.8 of an inch wide, and the fruit is black and subglobose, about 0.5 of an inch long when ripe.

SOME INTRODUCED MULBERRIES

WHITE MULBERRY (Morus alba) leaves are smooth on the underside, and the fruit is white. An introduced native of the Orient, it is now common in eastern U.S.

BLACK MULBERRY (Morus nigra) leaves are rarely lobed. Cultivated for the large fruit, which are black when ripe. Native of Asia.

PAPER MULBERRY (Broussonetia papyrifera) leaves resemble Red Mulberry's. Dioecious—staminate flowers in greenish aments 2 to 3 inches long, the pistillate in globose heads 0.8 of an inch in diameter. Fruit red, in globose heads. Native of Orient where bark is used in papermaking. An ornamental in eastern U.S.; also grows wild.

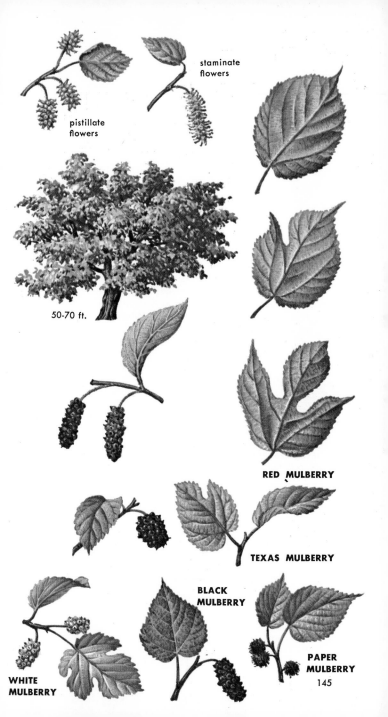

pistillate flowers

staminate flowers

50-70 ft.

RED MULBERRY

TEXAS MULBERRY

BLACK MULBERRY

WHITE MULBERRY

PAPER MULBERRY

145

FIGS (Ficus)

FLORIDA STRANGLER FIG (Ficus aurea) leaves are evergreen, smooth-margined, leathery, and elliptical to oblong. They are 2 to 5 inches long and 1 to 3 inches wide. The small flowers, separated by reddish-purple, chaffy scales, are borne in nearly closed receptacles, either attached directly to the branch or on very short stems; they are yellow at first, later turning red. The fruit consists of small drupelets embedded in a fleshy, yellow to reddish-purple receptacle, about 0.5 to 0.8 of an inch in diameter. On young trees, the bark is smooth and ash-gray, sometimes becoming scaly on large trunks. Florida Strangler Fig grows 40 to 50 feet tall and 1 to 3 feet in diameter. Usually the seeds germinate in bark crevices of other trees. They send out aerial roots that eventually reach the ground and develop an independent root system. Commonly several aerial roots may wrap around or "strangle" the host tree. Branches that touch the ground may also take root, forming a compound tree of many trunks much like the Banyan of India. The less common Short-leaf Fig (F. laevigata) of the Florida Keys, Bahamas, and Cuba is similar in growth habits but has broader leaves with heart-shaped bases, larger fruit (to 1 inch), and longer stems on flowers and fruit.

SOME INTRODUCED FIGS

COMMON FIG (Ficus carica) is a deciduous shrub or small tree, to 30 feet tall, with a low, wide, rounded crown. The leaves, 4 to 8 inches long and nearly as broad, are palmately 3- to 5-lobed. Margins of lobes are wavy. There are many varieties, grown commercially in warmer parts of the U.S. for fruit. Also planted as an ornamental in areas of moderate climate.

FIDDLE-LEAF FIG (Ficus lyrata) is also a house plant but is not as popular as the India Rubber-plant. Grown outdoors in warmer parts of the U.S., it may reach a height of 30 feet. Differs from other common species of Ficus in having irregular, violin-shaped leaves with conspicuous whitish veins. In its native West Africa, the Fiddle-leaf Fig grows 70 feet tall.

INDIA RUBBER-PLANT (Ficus elastica) is a popular house plant. When grown outdoors in warmer parts of the U.S. it may become 100 feet tall. The dark, glossy, evergreen leaves are pinnately veined and 6 to 12 inches long, with smooth margins and an abruptly pointed apex. The fruits of the India Rubber-plant are greenish yellow when ripe. The tree is native to tropical Asia.

BENJAMIN FIG (Ficus benjamina), also known as Weeping Laurel, has slender, drooping branches. Grows to 30 feet tall. The thin, shiny-green, prominently veined, ovate-elliptical leaves are 2 to 4.5 inches long, with smooth margins and an abruptly pointed apex. Globose fruit is yellowish to reddish. Native to tropical Asia. Grown as a potted plant, or outdoors in warm parts of U.S.

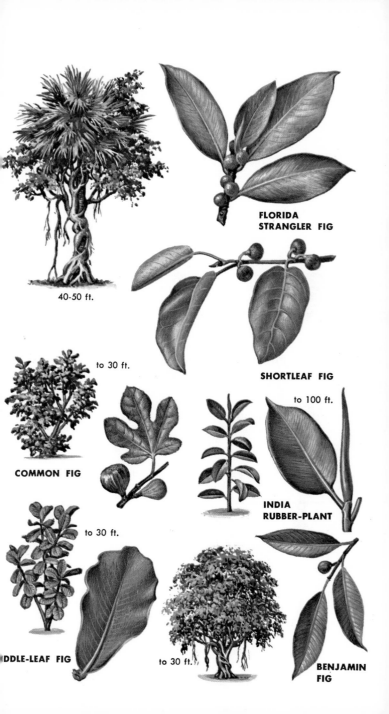

40-50 ft.

FLORIDA STRANGLER FIG

to 30 ft.

SHORTLEAF FIG

to 100 ft.

COMMON FIG

INDIA RUBBER-PLANT

to 30 ft.

DDLE-LEAF FIG

to 30 ft.

BENJAMIN FIG

OSAGE-ORANGE (*Maclura pomifera*) has ovate to ovate-lanceolate, deciduous leaves, 3 to 5 inches long and 2 to 3 inches wide, with smooth margins. Leaves turn bright yellow in fall. Flowers, staminate (in racemes) and pistillate (in heads), are borne in leaf axils on separate trees after leaves appear. Inedible, rough, multiple fruit, 3 to 5 inches in diameter, exudes milky juice when bruised. Bark breaks into broad, rounded, scaly ridges; twigs often thorny. Grows 10 to 50 feet tall, 1 to 2 feet in diameter. Hedge plantings have extended range over much of U.S.

OLAX (TALLOWWOOD) FAMILY (Olacaceae)

TALLOWWOOD (*Ximenia americana*) leaves are evergreen, alternate, leathery, oblong to elliptical, 1 to 2.5 inches long and 0.5 to 1 inch wide. Apex spiny or notched, margin curled under. Short-stalked clusters of two to four fragrant, yellowish-white flowers, each with four curled, hairy petals, occur in leaf axils. Yellowish-red, plumlike fruits, about 1.3 inches long, have thin, astringent flesh. Bark smooth and dark reddish brown, twigs spiny, wood fragrant. Grows 30 feet tall, 1.5 feet in diameter.

BUCKWHEAT FAMILY (Polygonaceae)

SEAGRAPE (*Coccoloba uvifera*) has leathery, evergreen leaves, 4 to 5 inches long and 5 to 6 inches wide, smaller at growing tip. Flowers white, produced singly or in fascicles and in racemes 5 to 15 inches long. Grapelike fruits greenish white to purple. To 25 feet tall and 1.5 feet in diameter; bark smooth, gray to mottled brown. On sandy shores.

DOVEPLUM (*Coccoloba diversifolia*), or Pigeon Seagrape, has leathery, evergreen leaves, 3 to 4 inches long and 1.5 to 2.5 inches wide. Fascicles of white flowers in racemes 2 to 3 inches long; fruit dark red. Reddish-brown bark smooth, occasionally scaly. Grows 70 feet tall, 2 feet in diameter; rounded crown. In sandy soils.

FOUR-O'CLOCK FAMILY (Nyctaginaceae)

LONGLEAF BLOLLY (*Torrubia longifolia*) has evergreen leaves, 1 to 2 inches long, 0.5 to 1 inch wide. Small, greenish-yellow flowers, in loose clusters; fruits red, ribbed, 0.8 of an inch long. Bark reddish brown, scaly. A shrub or small tree, to 40 feet tall, 1.5 feet in diameter. Two similar shrubby species in same area.

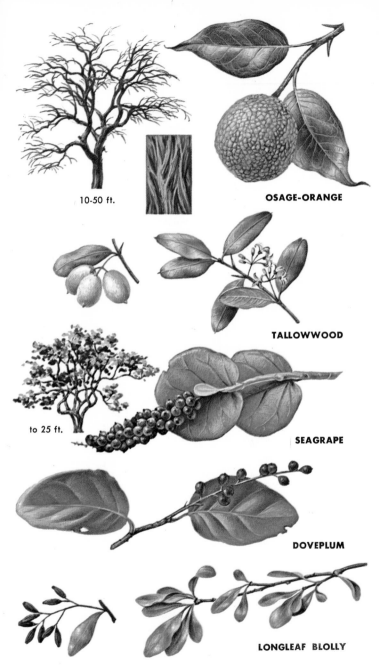

10-50 ft.

OSAGE-ORANGE

TALLOWWOOD

to 25 ft.

SEAGRAPE

DOVEPLUM

LONGLEAF BLOLLY

MAGNOLIA FAMILY (Magnoliaceae)

This is a family of about 100 species of trees and shrubs that grow in the warmer parts of North America and eastern Asia. Trees in two of the 10 genera, *Magnolia and Liriodendron,* grow in the United States. Two species of Anis-trees *(Illicium),* usually shrubs but rarely trees, grow in northern Florida and on Gulf Coast.

Magnolias have unique scarlet to rust-brown aggregate fruit composed of numerous podlike follicles, each containing 1 or 2 crimson seeds that hang by slender threads when ripe. The alternate leaves, deciduous or evergreen, have short stems and smooth, usually wavy margins. A single scale covers each bud, and stipule scars encircle the twigs. Asiatic magnolias grown as ornamentals include Star Magnolia *(M. stellata),* Kobus Magnolia *(M. kobus),* and Saucer Magnolia *(M. soulangeana).*

SOUTHERN MAGNOLIA *(Magnolia grandiflora)* leaves are evergreen, leathery, oval to ovate, 5 to 10 inches long, 2 to 3 inches wide; dark, glossy green above, lighter and brown-hairy below, with short, pointed apex. Fragrant flowers, 6 to 9 inches in diameter, have 3 sepals and 6 to 12 showy white petals. Aggregate fruit, 3 to 4 inches long and about 2 inches in diameter, red to rust-brown, hairy. Bark is brownish gray and scaly. Grows 25 to 80 feet tall, 2 to 3 feet in diameter, with a pyramidal or a round-topped crown.

SWEETBAY *(Magnolia virginiana)* leaves are deciduous in the North, but in the South remain on tree until new foliage forms. They are 4 to 6 inches long and 1 to 3 inches wide, with a blunt-pointed apex; shiny green above, whitish below. Fragrant, cup-shaped flowers are 2 to 3 inches in diameter, with 3 sepals and 9 to 12 creamy-white, concave petals. Dark red aggregate fruit is 2 inches long and about 0.5 of an inch in diameter; not hairy. Bark light brown, scaly. Usually 10 to 30 feet tall, 1 to 1.5 feet in diameter.

CUCUMBERTREE *(Magnolia acuminata)* leaves are deciduous, 6 to 10 inches long and 3 to 5 inches wide, with a pointed apex; yellow-green above, paler below. Flowers, about 2 inches long, have 3 sepals and 6 greenish-yellow petals (canary yellow or orange in rare variety). Red to brown, hairless, aggregate fruit is 2 to 3 inches long, 1 inch in diameter. Bark of mature trees gray-brown, scaly. Cucumbertree grows 40 to 90 feet tall and 3 to 4 feet in diameter, with straight trunk and pyramidal crown.

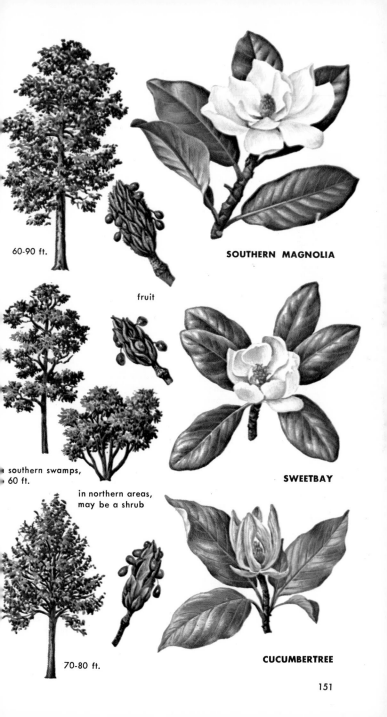

60-90 ft.

SOUTHERN MAGNOLIA

fruit

southern swamps,
60 ft.

in northern areas,
may be a shrub

SWEETBAY

70-80 ft.

CUCUMBERTREE

151

UMBRELLA MAGNOLIA *(Magnolia tripetala)* has deciduous, broadly elliptical leaves, 18 to 20 inches long and 8 to 10 inches wide, clustered near the ends of the branches. The flowers, 6 to 10 inches in diameter, with 3 sepals and 6 or 9 narrow, concave, creamy-white petals, have an unpleasant odor. Rose-colored, hairless, aggregate fruit is 2.5 to 4 inches long. A large shrub or small tree, 10 to 35 feet tall and 1 to 1.5 feet in diameter, Umbrella Magnolia is typical of moist places.

BIGLEAF MAGNOLIA *(Magnolia macrophylla)* has huge, deciduous leaves, 20 to 30 inches long and 8 to 10 inches wide, often widest above the middle; apex rounded or bluntly pointed, the narrowed base shallowly lobed. Fragrant, cup-shaped flowers are 10 to 12 inches in diameter, with 3 sepals, which later turn dull yellow, and 6 creamy-white petals, with rose at base. Ovoid, aggregate fruit, 2.5 to 3 inches long, is rose-colored and hairy. Grows 30 to 50 feet tall and 1 to 1.5 feet in diameter, with a round-topped crown of wide-spreading branches. The bark is gray and often scaly on older trees.

ASHE MAGNOLIA *(Magnolia ashei)* resembles Bigleaf Magnolia but has shorter, broader leaves, smaller flowers, and longer (to 5 inches), more cylindrical fruit. Rarely grows to small tree size.

FRASER MAGNOLIA *(Magnolia fraseri)* leaves are deciduous, 10 to 12 inches long, 6 to 7 inches wide; widest above the middle, with bluntly pointed apex and conspicuous, earlike lobes at the narrowed base. Fragrant flowers, 8 to 10 inches in diameter, have 3 sepals (falling soon after opening of flower) and 6 or 9 pale-yellow petals. Rose-red, hairless, oblong, aggregate fruit is 4 to 5 inches long and 1.5 to 2 inches in diameter. Grows 30 to 40 feet tall and 1 to 1.5 feet in diameter. Bark brown, scaly, or warty.

PYRAMID MAGNOLIA *(Magnolia pyramidata)* leaves are similar to Fraser Magnolia's but smaller, 5 to 9 inches long and 3 to 5 inches wide. Flowers, 3 to 4 inches in diameter, have 3 sepals and 6 or 9 creamy-white petals. Rose-colored, oblong, aggregate fruit is 2 to 2.5 inches long and 1 to 1.5 inches in diameter. Grows 20 to 30 feet tall, 1 to 2 feet in diameter.

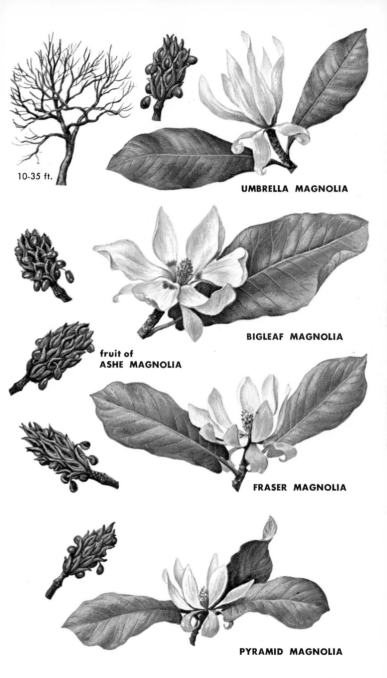

10-35 ft.

UMBRELLA MAGNOLIA

BIGLEAF MAGNOLIA

fruit of
ASHE MAGNOLIA

FRASER MAGNOLIA

PYRAMID MAGNOLIA

YELLOW-POPLAR *(Liriodendron tulipifera)*, also called Tuliptree, has long-stemmed, 4-lobed, deciduous leaves, with a tulip-like outline. They are 4 to 6 inches long, bright green above and paler below. The tulip-shaped flowers, 1.5 to 2 inches in diameter, have 6 greenish-yellow petals with orange at base. They do not appear until well after the leaves develop. Fruit is a conelike aggregate of single-winged samaras, which fall apart when mature. Buds have two valvate scales, and stipule scars encircle the twigs. Mature trees have gray-brown, ridged, and furrowed bark. One of the largest of eastern hardwoods, grows 80 to 150 feet tall and 4 to 6 feet in diameter, usually with a straight, clear trunk and pyramidal crown.

CUSTARD-APPLE (ANNONA) FAMILY
(Annonaceae)

This is a large (70 genera and about 600 species), primarily tropical family of deciduous and evergreen trees and shrubs with two representatives in United States. Leaves simple, alternate.

PAWPAW *(Asimina triloba)* leaves are deciduous, 10 to 12 inches long and 4 to 6 inches wide, widest above the middle. The apex is pointed, the margins smooth. Flowers, about 2 inches in diameter, have 3 green sepals and 6 heavily veined, purple petals in two ranks. Fruit irregularly oblong, to 5 inches long and 1.5 inches thick, with a yellow to dark-brown rind enclosing the white to yellow flesh and flat, dark-brown seeds. Edible when ripe. Blotched, gray-brown bark is thin and smooth to warty. A large shrub or small tree, 20 to 30 feet tall and 6 to 15 inches in diameter.

POND-APPLE *(Annona glabra)* leaves are leathery, oblong to elliptical, 3 to 5 inches long and 1.5 to 2 inches wide, with smooth margins and a pointed apex. They are bright green above, paler below, and are shed late in the fall. The flowers, about an inch in diameter, have 6 dull yellowish-white petals. The fleshy, aromatic, yellowish-brown, compound fruit is somewhat heart-shaped, 3 to 5 inches long and 2 to 3.5 inches in diameter with light-green, insipid flesh. Bark is thin, reddish brown, sometimes scaly. Small to medium-sized, 40 to 50 feet tall and 1 to 2 feet in diameter. Trunk short, usually buttressed base, and a spreading crown of somewhat twisted branches.

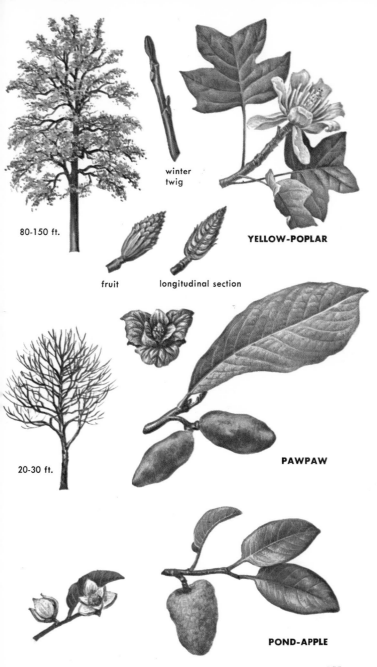

80-150 ft.

winter
twig

fruit   longitudinal section

YELLOW-POPLAR

20-30 ft.

PAWPAW

POND-APPLE

155

LAUREL FAMILY (Lauraceae)

Deciduous and evergreen trees and shrubs, usually with alternate leaves, are included in the more than 1,000 species of this primarily tropical family. Many have aromatic leaves, bark, twigs, and roots, providing cinnamon, camphor, and various oils used in drugs, soaps, and perfumes. Also included are the Avocado (*Persea americana*) and several important timber trees. Stinkwood (*Ocotea bullata*), of South Africa, and the Walnut Bean (*Endriandra palmerstonii*), of eastern Australia, furnish beautiful cabinet woods. Camphor-tree (*Cinnamomum camphora*), a source of commercial camphor, is grown as an ornamental in California and in southern United States, where it has escaped cultivation and grows wild. Greenheart (*Nectandra rodioei*) is used in marine construction; a related, native species, Jamaica Nectandra or Lancewood (*N. coriacea*), is common along the Florida coast.

SASSAFRAS (*Sassafras albidum*) has deciduous leaves, 4 to 6 inches long and 2 to 4 inches wide. Both elliptical or 2- to 3-lobed leaves may occur on same tree; turn yellow to red in fall. Dioecious; the small, yellow-green flowers in loose racemes appear with leaves in spring. Stalked, ovoid fruits, about 0.3 of an inch long, are blue with a hard seed enclosed in thin flesh. Aromatic leaves, bark, twigs, and roots yield oils used in soaps. Sassafras tea, a "spring tonic" of bygone years, is made by boiling roots or bark. Commonly grows 20 feet tall, rarely to 50 feet, with a diameter of nearly 3 feet. Often forms dense, shrubby thickets.

CALIFORNIA-LAUREL (*Umbellularia californica*) leaves are evergreen, lanceolate to elliptical, 2 to 5 inches long and 0.5 to 1.5 inches wide; aromatic when crushed. Loose axillary clusters of small, yellowish-green flowers appear in winter or early spring. Fruit greenish to purple, about 1 inch long. Bark greenish brown, smooth to scaly. Usually a shrub or small tree, rarely to 80 feet tall. Also called Oregon-myrtle.

REDBAY (*Persea borbonia*) has aromatic, evergreen leaves, 3 to 4 inches long and 1 to 1.5 inches wide. These are the bay leaves used as herbs. The creamy-white, bell-shaped flowers lack petals but have hairy sepals; they occur in loose axillary clusters. Blue to violet-black, ovoid fruit is 0.5 of an inch in diameter. Usually in moist soils near streams or swamps. To 60 feet tall.

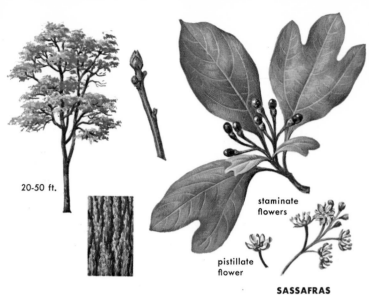

20-50 ft.

staminate
flowers

pistillate
flower

SASSAFRAS

to 80 ft. (rare)

CALIFORNIA-LAUREL

REDBAY

WITCH-HAZEL FAMILY (Hamamelidaceae)

About 100 species of deciduous trees and shrubs make up the witch-hazel family. Species are found in North America, South Africa, Madagascar, Australia, and Asia. One tree-sized species and a half dozen shrubs, several of which occasionally reach tree height, are native to eastern United States and southeastern Canada.

SWEETGUM (*Liquidambar styraciflua*) has distinctive star-shaped leaves, alternate, 5 to 7 inches wide and with 5 to 7 pointed lobes, with toothed margins. They are bright green, turning a brilliant red-and-gold in fall. Staminate and pistillate flowers are in separate, headlike clusters on same tree—the staminate in racemes, pistillate solitary. Fruit is a long-stemmed, woody, burlike head of capsules, 1.5 inches in diameter; each capsule contains two small seeds. Twigs often have corky wings. Grows 80 to 120 feet tall and 3 to 5 feet in diameter, with gray to brown, ridged and furrowed bark. Wood used for furniture, veneer, interior trim, and novelties.

WITCH-HAZEL (*Hamamelis virginiana*) leaves are alternate, 4 to 6 inches long and 2 to 3 inches wide, their greatest width above the middle. Leaves have deep, widely spaced, rounded marginal teeth and a lopsided base; dull green above and lighter below, with hairs along midrib and veins. Flowers with 4 narrow, yellow petals appear in fall or winter. They produce a 2-beaked, woody capsule, 0.5 of an inch long, which splits open when mature and forcefully ejects lustrous black seeds. A shrub or a small tree, to 30 feet tall and 12 inches in diameter, usually in moist soils near streams.

CAPER FAMILY (Capparidaceae)

JAMAICA CAPER (*Capparis cynophallophora*) leaves are evergreen, alternate, 2 to 3 inches long and 1 to 1.5 inches wide, with smooth margins and a rounded or notched apex. They are yellow-green above, with fine brownish scales below. Flowers, 1.3 inches across, have 4 scaly sepals, 4 petals (at first white, becoming purple), and a tuft of purple stamens 1 to 2 inches long with yellowish-orange anthers. Podlike fruit, 9 to 10 inches long, is constricted between seeds. To 20 feet tall, usually in sandy tidewater soils. Limber Caper (*C. flexuosa*) is similar, with lighter leaves; less commonly tree size.

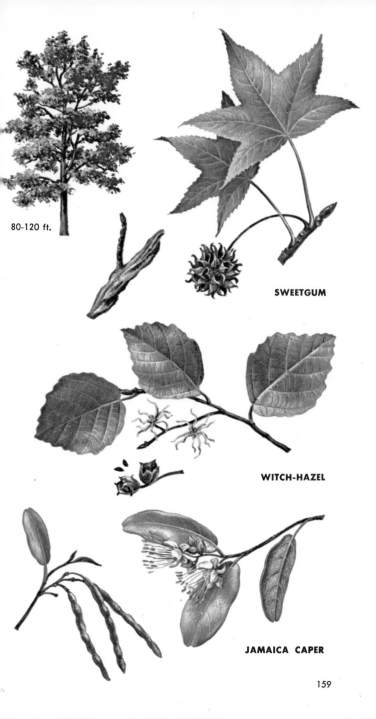

80-120 ft.

SWEETGUM

WITCH-HAZEL

JAMAICA CAPER

159

SYCAMORE FAMILY (Platanaceae)

This is a family of only one genus containing about six species, the sycamores, or planetrees. Three species are native to the United States. The other three are found in Mexico, Central America, southwestern Asia, and southeastern Europe. All have deciduous, alternate, palmately lobed leaves, usually with a hairy undersurface. Under the hollow, enlarged base of each leaf stem is a shiny-brown, conical bud covered by a single caplike scale. When the leaves fall, the buds are exposed, completely encircled by the leaf scar. Staminate and pistillate flowers are in separate globular heads on the same tree. The unique multiple fruit, commonly called buttonballs, consists of many tiny, elongated seeds with upright hairs at the base. The fruit breaks apart when ripe. Sycamore bark peels in thin, irregular patches giving the trunks a whitish-brown appearance. The twigs, encircled by stipule scars, have a distinctive zigzag form. Sycamores are typical of moist soils and are common along streams. They grow well in a variety of conditions, however, and are used as shade and street trees.

AMERICAN SYCAMORE (*Platanus occidentalis*) leaves are broadly ovate, 4 to 8 inches wide, and shallowly 3- to 5-lobed, the lobes with large marginal teeth. Globular heads of seeds, 1 to 1.5 inches in diameter, hang singly on slender stems 3 to 6 inches long. American Sycamore is a massive tree, frequently attaining a height of 100 feet and a diameter of 3 to 10 feet, with a wide-spreading crown.

CALIFORNIA SYCAMORE (*Platanus racemosa*) leaves are 6 to 10 inches wide, with 3 to 5 lobes that are longer than broad; margins toothed (occasionally smooth). Globular seed heads, to 1 inch in diameter, are in racemes of 3 to 7. California Sycamore grows 40 to 90 feet tall and 1 to 3 feet in diameter.

ARIZONA SYCAMORE (*Platanus wrightii*) is similar to California Sycamore, but its leaves are often 7-lobed and the globular seed heads are in racemes of 2 to 4.

INTRODUCED SYCAMORES

ORIENTAL PLANETREE (*Platanus orientalis*) resembles American Sycamore but has smaller, more deeply lobed leaves. Seed heads are in strings of 2 to 4. London Planetree (*P. acerifolia*), a hybrid between American Sycamore and Oriental Planetree, has leaves like American Sycamore; seed heads like Oriental Planetree's. Bark greenish brown.

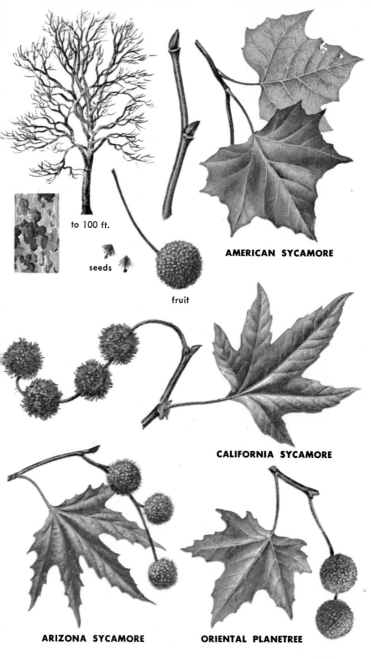

to 100 ft.

seeds

fruit

AMERICAN SYCAMORE

CALIFORNIA SYCAMORE

ARIZONA SYCAMORE

ORIENTAL PLANETREE

ROSE FAMILY (Rosaceae)

This large, diversified family contains more than 3,000 species of trees, shrubs, and herbaceous plants, most abundant in temperate regions. Their perfect flowers typically have 5 sepals and 5 petals. Among familiar members are apples, cherries, plums, peaches, pears, apricots, almonds, strawberries, raspberries, and blackberries. Important ornamentals include the roses, spireas, hawthorns, firethorns, and mountain-ashes.

APPLES (Malus)

About 25 species of apples are native to temperate regions of the Northern Hemisphere; five native North American species are included here. All are small trees or occasionally shrubs, their leaves deciduous, alternate, and toothed or less commonly lobed. Apple blossoms, usually fragrant, are white to pink and 1 to 1.5 inches in diameter. They are clustered in racemes on short, spurlike branches. The fruit (a pome) of native species is much smaller than the fruit of commercially grown varieties.

Numerous varieties of apples have been developed from *Malus pumila*, the common native apple of southeastern Europe and central Asia. This species was introduced into North America by early settlers and is now naturalized in many parts of the United States and Canada. Its toothed, ovate to elliptical leaves have white hairs on the underside and on the stems. Other species with showy flowers or attractive fruits are planted as ornamentals.

SOUTHERN CRAB APPLE *(Malus angustifolia)* leaves are elliptical to ovate, 1 to 3 inches long and 0.5 to 2 inches wide. They have toothed margins, a wedge-shaped base, and blunt to pointed apex. Fragrant, pinkish flowers, about 1 inch in diameter, are in clusters of 3 to 5. The apples are pale yellow-green, broader than long, and about 1 inch in diameter. A shrub or small tree, to 30 feet tall and 10 inches in diameter, with a broad, open crown of stiff branches.

SWEET CRAB APPLE *(Malus coronaria)* leaves are 2 to 3 inches long and 1.5 inches wide. Oval to ovate, with a rounded to abruptly pointed apex, usually a rounded base, and toothed margins. The fragrant, pinkish-white flowers, to 1.5 inches in diameter, are in clusters of 3 to 6. The yellow-green fruit is about an inch in diameter and broader than long. Grows as a shrub or small tree, often forming thickets in moist soils. The twigs are armed with sharp spines.

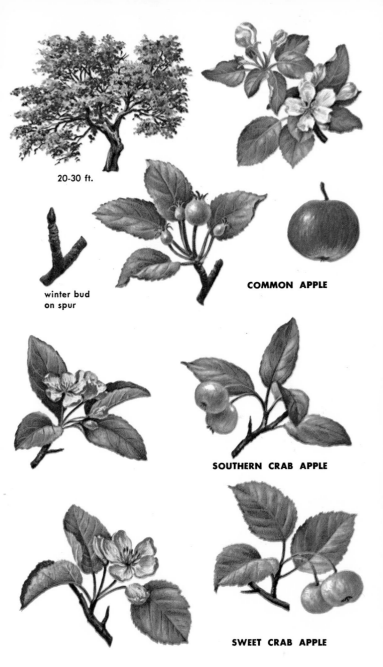

20-30 ft.

winter bud
on spur

COMMON APPLE

SOUTHERN CRAB APPLE

SWEET CRAB APPLE

163

BILTMORE CRAB APPLE *(Malus glabrata)* leaves are roughly triangular, 2.5 to 3.5 inches long, 2 to 2.5 inches wide, with 3 to 5 coarsely toothed, pointed lobes. Pink flowers, about 1.3 inches in diameter, are in clusters of 4 to 7. The fruit, about 1.5 inches in diameter, is ribbed at the apex. The twigs often have stout spines up to 1.5 inches long. A shrub or small tree to 25 feet tall, most common in mountain valleys.

PRAIRIE CRAB APPLE *(Malus ioensis)* leaves, usually hairy below, are 2 to 4 inches long, 1 to 1.5 inches wide. The rosy-white flowers, 1.5 to 2 inches in diameter, occur in clusters of 3 to 6 and the greenish-yellow fruit is about 1.3 inches in diameter. Grows as a shrub or a small bushy tree, to 30 feet tall.

OREGON CRAB APPLE *(Malus diversifolia)* leaves are ovate to elliptical, 1 to 4 inches long, 0.5 to 1.5 inches wide, occasionally 3-lobed; base wedge-shaped or rounded. White flowers, about 0.8 of an inch in diameter, occur in clusters of 4 to 10. Oblong, yellow-green to reddish-purple apples are 0.5 to 0.8 of an inch long. Oregon Crab Apple may form thickets in moist soil; it grows to 40 feet tall.

MOUNTAIN-ASHES *(Sorbus)*

About 80 species of small, deciduous trees and shrubs of cooler parts of the Northern Hemisphere are known as mountain-ashes; not related to ashes (p. 254). Mountain-ashes have pinnately compound, alternate leaves, flat-topped clusters (cymes) of small, white flowers that develop after leaves appear, and small, apple-like, red or orange fruits. In North America, only eastern species reach tree size.

AMERICAN MOUNTAIN-ASH *(Sorbus americana)* leaves are 6 to 8 inches long, with 13- to 17-toothed, lanceolate leaflets 2 to 4 inches long, 0.3 to 1 inch wide, toothed above middle; turn yellow in fall. To 30 feet tall; bark light gray-brown, smooth to scaly. The smaller Showy Mountain-ash *(S. decora)*, in the same area, has 7 to 13 broader leaflets, with larger flowers and fruits. Sitka Mountain-ash *(S. sitchensis)*, of northwestern North America, rarely reaches tree size.

EUROPEAN MOUNTAIN-ASH *(Sorbus aucuparia)* is similar to American Mountain-ash but has smaller, bluntly pointed leaflets, 0.8 to 2 inches long and 0.5 to 0.8 of an inch wide, often somewhat hairy below. Also called Rowan Tree, it occurs in several varieties and is planted widely as an ornamental in North America.

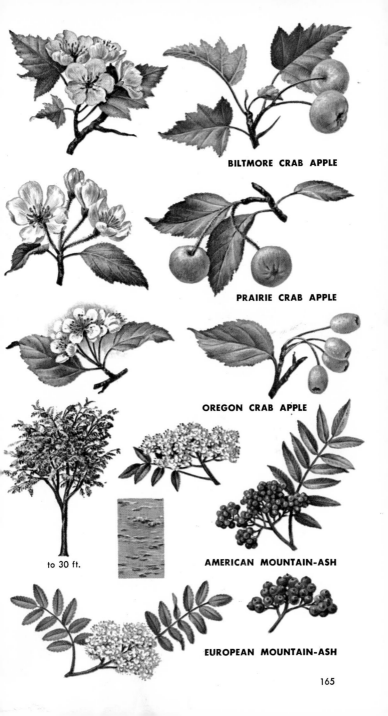

BILTMORE CRAB APPLE

PRAIRIE CRAB APPLE

OREGON CRAB APPLE

to 30 ft.

AMERICAN MOUNTAIN-ASH

EUROPEAN MOUNTAIN-ASH

165

CHERRIES AND PLUMS (*Prunus*)

Widely distributed in cool parts of the Northern Hemisphere, cherries and plums produce delicious fruits, are prized as ornamentals and, in some cases, are valuable for their beautiful wood. All have simple, alternate leaves, usually with serrate margins. The fruit is a drupe. Most cultivated cherries and plums came originally from Europe; ornamental flowering species from Asia. Several introduced species have escaped cultivation and are now naturalized in eastern North America. These include Mazzard Cherry (*P. avium*), Sour Cherry (*P. cerasus*), Garden Plum (*P. domestica*), Bullace Plum (*P. insititia*), Mahaleb Cherry (*P. mahaleb*), Peach (*P. persica*), and Sloe, or Blackthorn (*P. spinosa*). Apricots and almonds also belong to this genus. Desert Apricot (*P. fremontii*), of southern California, is a native apricot that is most commonly a shrub, rarely a tree.

BLACK CHERRY (*Prunus serotina*) has narrowly oval to oblong-lanceolate, deciduous leaves, 2 to 6 inches long and 1 to 1.5 inches wide, with fine marginal teeth. White flowers, about 0.3 of an inch in diameter, in racemes 4 to 6 inches long. Fruit 0.5 of an inch in diameter, black with dark-purple flesh. Satiny, reddish-brown wood prized for fine furniture. Grows 50 to 60 feet tall, 1 to 3 feet in diameter. Bark of young trees smooth, dark reddish brown to black, and marked with horizontal lenticels (raised, warty patches); scaly on large trees.

PIN CHERRY (*Prunus pensylvanica*) has oblong-lanceolate leaves, 3 to 4 inches long and 0.8 to 1.3 inches wide, with small marginal teeth. Creamy-white flowers about 0.5 of an inch in diameter and 4 to 5 per cluster (umbels or corymbs), appear with or after leaves. Bright-red cherries, 0.3 of an inch in diameter, have acid taste. Bark smooth, reddish brown, with horizontal lenticels; later in broad plates. Grows 15 to 25 feet tall, 18 to 20 inches in diameter.

COMMON CHOKECHERRY (*Prunus virginiana*) has broadly obovate leaves, 2 to 4 inches long and 1 to 2 inches wide; apex pointed; margins often doubly toothed. White flowers, 0.5 of an inch in diameter, in racemes 3 to 6 inches long. Astringent, dark-red cherries are 0.3 of an inch in diameter. Lustrous-brown bark, with pale lenticels, is ill-smelling; later becomes scaly. A bushy tree, Common Chokecherry grows to 25 feet tall and 8 inches in diameter.

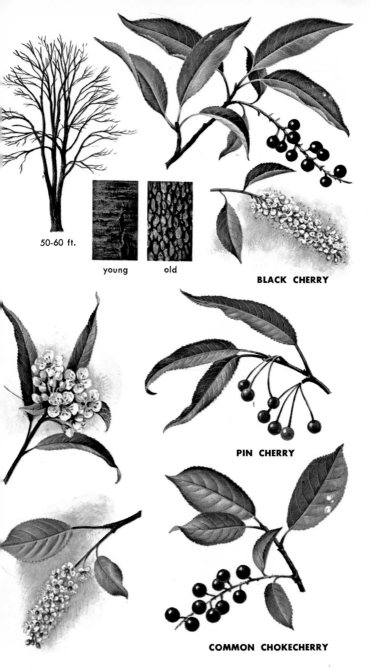

50-60 ft.

young   old

BLACK CHERRY

PIN CHERRY

COMMON CHOKECHERRY

BITTER CHERRY *(Prunus emarginata)* has elliptical or oblong-obovate leaves, 1 to 3 inches long and 0.5 to 1.5 inches wide, with toothed margins. White flowers 0.5 of an inch across, are in 6- to 12-flowered corymbs; appear when leaves are about half grown. Red to black cherries, about 0.5 of an inch in diameter have thin, astringent flesh. Bark brownish, with horizontal, orange lenticels. Bitter Cherry grows 30 to 40 feet tall and 1 to 1.5 feet in diameter, forming an oblong crown.

CATALINA CHERRY *(Prunus lyonii)* leaves are evergreen, ovate to lanceolate, 2 to 4 inches long and 0.5 to 2.5 inches wide; margins are smooth, thickened and wavy, occasionally sparingly toothed. White flowers, about 0.3 of an inch across, are in racemes 3 to 4 inches long. Dark-purple to black cherries, about 1 inch in diameter, have thick, delicious flesh. A bushy tree, 25 to 30 feet tall and 1 to 3 feet in diameter with a compact crown and reddish-brown bark.

MYRTLE LAURELCHERRY *(Prunus myrtifolia)* leaves are evergreen, elliptical to oblong-ovate, 2 to 4.5 inches long and 1 to 1.5 inches wide, with smooth margins. White flowers with yellow at base of the petals are 0.1 of an inch in diameter. They appear late in fall, in short racemes. Fruit is orange-brown, nearly round, 0.3 to 0.5 of an inch in diameter, with thin dry flesh. Myrtle Laurelcherry grows to 30 feet tall and 6 inches in diameter.

CAROLINA LAURELCHERRY *(Prunus caroliniana)* leaves are evergreen, oblong-lanceolate, 2 to 5 inches long and 0.8 to 1.5 inches wide; smooth or sparingly toothed margins. Short racemes of cream-white flowers appear in late winter or early spring. Oblong fruit about 0.5 of an inch in diameter, is nearly black, with thin, dry flesh. Gray bark is at first smooth, later roughened. Carolina Laurelcherry grows to 40 feet tall and 10 inches in diameter.

HOLLYLEAF CHERRY *(Prunus ilicifolia)* has ovate to ovate-lanceolate, evergreen leaves, 1 to 2 inches long and 1 to 1.5 inches wide, with coarsely toothed margins. White flowers, 0.3 of an inch in diameter, are in short racemes. Thin-fleshed fruit is nearly black and about 0.5 of an inch in diameter when they are ripe. Hollyleaf Cherry grows to 25 feet tall, with dark reddish-brown, fissured bark.

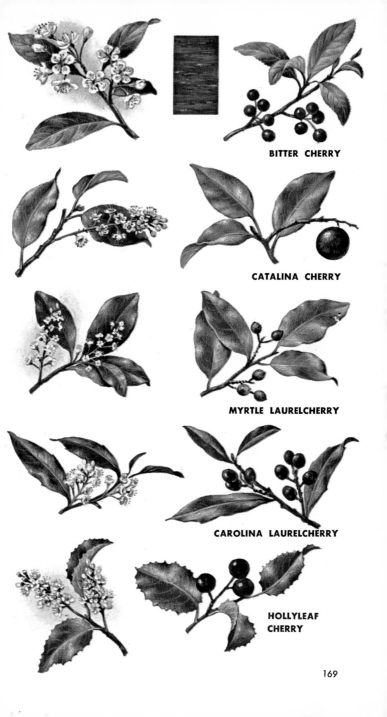

BITTER CHERRY

CATALINA CHERRY

MYRTLE LAURELCHERRY

CAROLINA LAURELCHERRY

HOLLYLEAF CHERRY

AMERICAN PLUM *(Prunus americana)* has oblong-ovate leaves, 3 to 4 inches long and 1.5 to 2 inches wide, with a long, tapering apex and toothed margins. The ill-smelling flowers, about 1 inch in diameter, are white with red sepals and occur in 2- to 5-flowered umbels; they appear before the leaves. The round, red fruit is about 1 inch in diameter and has tart, yellow flesh. On young trees the bark is thin, smooth, and brown; on mature trees, scaly. Grows 20 to 30 feet tall and 1 foot in diameter with a broad, spreading crown; commonly forms thickets in moist soil.

ALLEGHENY PLUM *(Prunus alleghaniensis)* leaves are narrowly lanceolate, 2 to 3.5 inches long and 0.8 to 1.3 inches wide, with small marginal teeth. The white flowers, 0.5 of an inch in diameter, are in 2- to 4-flowered umbels; they appear with the leaves. Globular plums, about 0.5 of an inch in diameter, are dark reddish purple with yellow flesh. A small tree to 20 feet tall, it has scaly, dark-brown bark.

FLATWOODS PLUM *(Prunus umbellata)* resembles Allegheny Plum, but slightly smaller leaves are oblong-lanceolate. Flowers, 1 inch in diameter, appear before leaves. The tart plums are usually purplish black, though sometimes yellow.

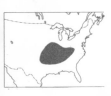

HORTULAN PLUM *(Prunus hortulana)* leaves are oblong-lanceolate, 4 to 6 inches long, with slender, orange stems. Flowers, to 1 inch across, have white petals with orange at the base; they appear after the leaves. Plums are red, occasionally yellowish, with thin flesh. Hortulan Plum is a small tree to 30 feet tall, with dark-brown bark.

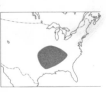

WILDGOOSE PLUM *(Prunus munsoniana)* has elliptical to lanceolate leaves, 2 to 4 inches long. Flowers are white, 0.5 to 0.8 of an inch across; the red plums, with yellow flesh, are about 0.8 of an inch long. To 20 feet tall and 6 inches in diameter, usually with smooth, brown bark; twigs occasionally thorny.

CHICKASAW PLUM *(Prunus angustifolia)* has lanceolate leaves, 1 to 2 inches long. White flowers, 0.3 of an inch across, appear before the leaves; the red to yellow plums are 0.5 of an inch in diameter. To 25 feet tall, often with spurlike, lateral twigs on branches.

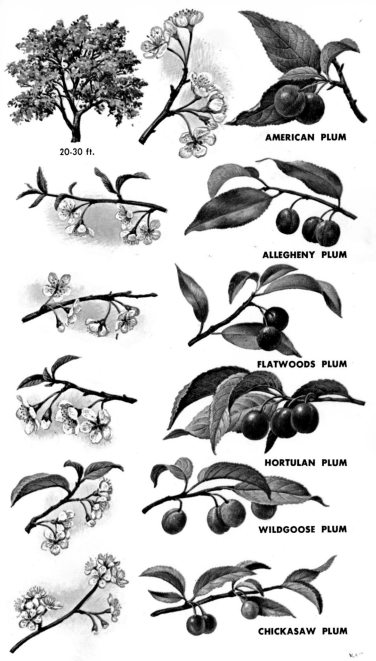

20-30 ft.

AMERICAN PLUM

ALLEGHENY PLUM

FLATWOODS PLUM

HORTULAN PLUM

WILDGOOSE PLUM

CHICKASAW PLUM

KLAMATH PLUM *(Prunus subcordata)* has elliptical to broadly ovate leaves, 1 to 3 inches long and 0.5 to 2 inches wide, with finely toothed margins. White flowers, 0.7 of an inch in diameter, are in 2- to 4-flowered umbels; bloom before leaves appear. The tart, dark-red or occasionally yellow plums are 0.8 to 1.3 inches long. Klamath Plum grows to 25 feet tall, with a rounded crown, gray-brown, scaly, and fissured bark. Branches are often spiny.

CANADA PLUM *(Prunus nigra)* leaves are oblong-ovate to obovate, 3 to 5 inches long and 1.5 to 3 inches wide, with an abrupt, narrow apex and marginal teeth. White flowers, about 1.3 inches in diameter, appear in 3- to 4-flowered umbels before or with the leaves. The yellow-fleshed, orange-red plums are 1 to 1.3 inches long. Grows 30 feet tall. Has a short trunk with gray-brown bark that peels off in layers.

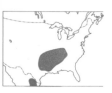

MEXICAN PLUM *(Prunus mexicana)* has ovate to elliptical leaves, 1.8 to 3.3 inches long. White flowers, about 1 inch in diameter and in 3- to 4-flowered umbels, bloom before leaves appear. Dark purple-red plums, to 1.5 inches long, have thick, sweet flesh. To 30 feet tall, with dark-gray, scaly to fissured bark.

SERVICEBERRIES *(Amelanchier)*

Widely distributed throughout temperate regions, these shrubs or small trees have deciduous, simple, alternate leaves, with either toothed or smooth margins; white flowers in racemes; the nearly round, usually succulent fruit is dark blue to black.

ALLEGHENY SERVICEBERRY *(Amelanchier laevis)* leaves are elliptical to ovate, 2 to 2.5 inches long and 1 to 1.5 inches wide, with apex abruptly pointed and toothed margins. Flowers, 0.5 to 0.8 of an inch long, appear when leaves are about half grown. Edible fruit, 0.3 inch in diameter. To 40 feet tall, 1 to 1.5 feet in diameter, with rounded crown; bark dark reddish brown. Downy Serviceberry *(A. arborea)*, more southern, has larger leaves, woolly below, and fruit is dry and tasteless. Pacific Serviceberry *(A. florida)* has oval to oblong-ovate leaves; juicy fruit. Similar species that may become small trees are Saskatoon Serviceberry *(A. alnifolia)*, Roundleaf Serviceberry *(A. sanguinea)*, Utah Serviceberry *(A. utahensis)*, and Inland Serviceberry *(A. interior)*.

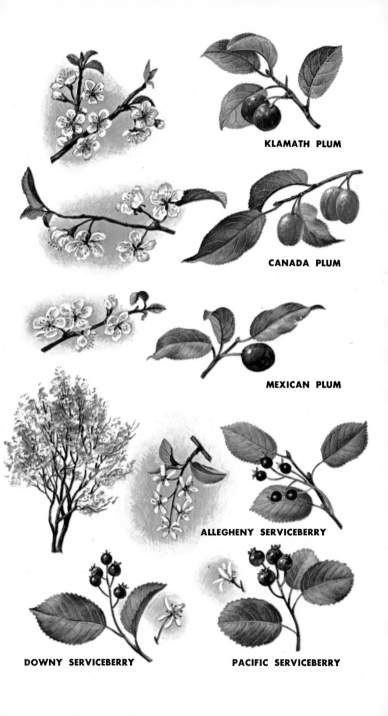

KLAMATH PLUM

CANADA PLUM

MEXICAN PLUM

ALLEGHENY SERVICEBERRY

DOWNY SERVICEBERRY

PACIFIC SERVICEBERRY

HAWTHORNS *(Crataegus)*

This very complex genus includes many species of shrubs or small, round-topped, usually thorny trees. They are most abundant in eastern North America, but nearly 100 species are found in the cooler parts of Europe and Asia. Hawthorns are easy to recognize as a group, but the species are difficult to identify. All have alternate, conspicuously toothed, sharply incised, or lobed leaves. They bear clusters of showy white, pink, or red flowers, each from 0.3 to 1 inch in diameter. The attractive, though dry and mealy, apple-like fruits, 0.3 to 0.8 of an inch in diameter, are usually red or orange but in some species are dark blue, black, or yellow. The smooth, greenish-brown bark of the branches and smaller trunks breaks up into thin, scaly plates with age. Trunks of mature trees are often fluted, or "muscular." The wood is hard and heavy but not commercially important. Hawthorns are popular as ornamentals, and a number of horticultural varieties have been developed. Twelve of the more than 100 native North American species of hawthorns are described and illustrated here.

BLACK HAWTHORN *(Crataegus douglasii)* leaves are ovate to obovate, about 1 to 2 inches long and 0.5 to 1.5 inches wide, and coarsely toothed near apex. Flowers are in broad clusters. Fruits shiny black.

FROSTED HAWTHORN *(Crataegus pruinosa)* leaves, 1 to 1.5 inches long and 1 inch wide, have either deeply cut margins or 3 to 4 pairs of shallow lobes. Few flowers in a cluster. Dark purple-red fruit, about 0.5 of an inch in diameter, is covered with small, dull dots.

SCARLET HAWTHORN *(Crataegus pedicellata)* leaves are broadly ovate to diamond-shaped, 3 to 4 inches long, and shallowly lobed. Many flowers per cluster. Fruits red with dark dots. Spines are 1 to 2 inches long.

COCKSPUR HAWTHORN *(Crataegus crus-galli)* leaves are 1 to 4 inches long and 0.3 to 1 inch wide, widest and toothed above the middle. Each of the many-flowered clusters produces oval, scarlet fruits about 0.5 of an inch long. The spines of Cockspur Hawthorn are 3 to 4 inches long.

DOWNY HAWTHORN *(Crataegus mollis)* leaves are 3 to 4 inches long and about as wide, broadest near their base. The margins are either sharply cut or shallowly lobed. Many flowers in each cluster. Fruits scarlet; spines may be 2 inches long.

20-40 ft.

BLACK HAWTHORN

FROSTED HAWTHORN

SCARLET HAWTHORN

COCKSPUR HAWTHORN

DOWNY HAWTHORN

175

LITTLEHIP HAWTHORN (*Crataegus spathulata*) leaves are spatula-shaped, often 3-lobed near apex. Many flowers in each cluster. Small, scarlet fruits are about 0.1 of an inch in diameter. Spines 1 to 1.5 inches long.

BLUEBERRY HAWTHORN (*Crataegus brachycantha*) leaves, 1 to 2 inches long, are usually widest near the rounded apex, with rounded marginal teeth. Flowers white, fading to orange. Fruit bright blue. Spines less than 1 inch long. Usually small but may grow to 50 feet tall.

BOYNTON HAWTHORN (*Crataegus boyntonii*) leaves are broadly ovate, toothed, and occasionally lobed near the apex. Flowers, in clusters of 4 to 10, produce yellowish-red fruits about 0.5 of an inch in diameter. The spines are 1.5 to 2 inches long.

TURKEY HAWTHORN (*Crataegus induta*) leaves are oblong-ovate, 3 to 4 inches long, with coarsely toothed to shallowly lobed margins. Flowers many per cluster. Oblong fruit, 0.8 to 2 inches in diameter, is red to reddish yellow with pale dots. Spines 2.5 inches long.

BARBERRYLEAF HAWTHORN (*Crataegus berberifolia*) leaves are oblong-obovate, to 2 inches long, hairy below. Flowers 4 to 5 in a cluster; fruits orange, about 0.5 of an inch in diameter. Spines 1 to 1.5 inches long.

PARSLEY HAWTHORN (*Crataegus marshallii*) leaves are broadly ovate to orbicular, with 5- to 7-toothed lobes. The many-flowered clusters produce oblong, scarlet fruits 0.3 of an inch long. The spines are 1 to 1.5 inches long.

WILLOW HAWTHORN (*Crataegus saligna*) leaves are narrowly oval, 1.5 to 2 inches long, and toothed toward apex; turn red in fall. Globose fruit, 0.8 of an inch in diameter, is first red, later turning black.

SOME INTRODUCED HAWTHORNS

ENGLISH HAWTHORN (*Crataegus oxyacantha*) leaves are broadly ovate, with 3 to 5 shallow lobes. Flowers red or white. Bright-red fruit contains two seeds. Native to Europe and northern Africa.

ONE-SEED HAWTHORN (*Crataegus monogyna*) resembles English Hawthorn, but leaves have 3 to 7 lobes, often with smooth margins. Fruits have one seed. Native to Europe, northern Africa, western Asia.

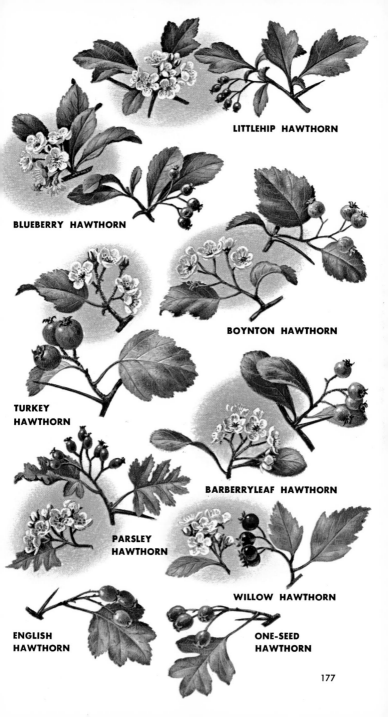

LITTLEHIP HAWTHORN

BLUEBERRY HAWTHORN

BOYNTON HAWTHORN

TURKEY
HAWTHORN

BARBERRYLEAF HAWTHORN

PARSLEY
HAWTHORN

WILLOW HAWTHORN

ENGLISH
HAWTHORN

ONE-SEED
HAWTHORN

177

CERCOCARPUS OR MOUNTAIN-MAHOGANY
(*Cercocarpus* spp.)

These shrubs or small trees are found in the dry, mountainous regions of western North America. Their leaves are simple, alternate, leathery, and either deciduous or evergreen, with either smooth or toothed margins. Flowers are solitary or clustered on short, lateral branchlets. They lack petals, and the greenish-white sepals form an elongated tube, expanded into a 5-lobed cup at the apex. Each flower produces a dry, leathery fruit that has a twisted, feathery plume at its apex. All have scaly bark and stiff branches.

BIRCHLEAF CERCOCARPUS (*Cercocarpus betuloides*) has obovate to oval leaves, 1 to 1.3 inches long and 0.3 to 0.5 of an inch wide, with rounded, toothed apex and wedge-shaped base. Dark green above; paler, often hairy below. Flowers 1 to 3 per cluster. A shrub or small tree to 25 feet tall; several varieties.

HAIRY CERCOCARPUS (*Cercocarpus breviflorus*) leaves are oblong to nearly elliptical, 0.5 to 1 inch long and 0.3 to 0.5 of an inch wide. They are gray-green, with rounded teeth near the apex, and hairy below. Flowers 1 to 3 per cluster. A shrub or small tree, to 15 feet tall and 5 inches in diameter, with erect branches forming an irregular, spreading crown.

CURLLEAF CERCOCARPUS (*Cercocarpus ledifolius*) has narrow, lanceolate leaves, 0.5 to 1 inch long and 0.3 to 0.8 of an inch wide, with smooth, curled-under margins. They are dark green above and hairy below. Flowers usually solitary. A shrub or small tree, to 25 feet tall and to 2 feet in diameter; branches stout, spreading.

MEMBERS OF MISCELLANEOUS GENERA IN THE ROSE FAMILY

CHRISTMASBERRY (*Photinia arbutifolia*) has alternate, oblong to elliptical, evergreen leaves, 3 to 4 inches long and 1 to 1.5 inches wide, with prominent marginal teeth. The white flowers occur in terminal clusters, 4 to 6 inches across. They develop somewhat pear-shaped, scarlet (rarely yellow) fruit, about 0.3 of an inch long. They ripen from October to December. Christmasberry grows as a shrub or small tree, to 30 feet tall and 1.5 feet in diameter, with gray bark and a narrow, round-topped crown of erect branches.

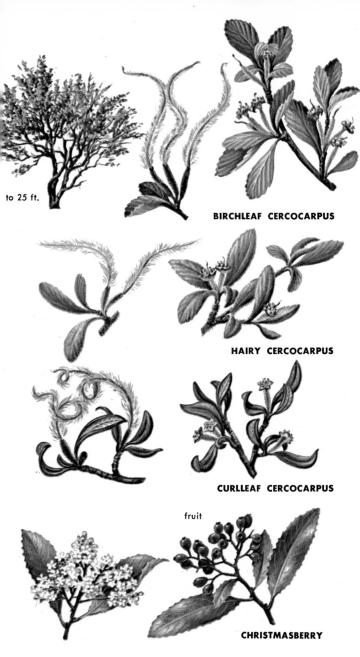

to 25 ft.

BIRCHLEAF CERCOCARPUS

HAIRY CERCOCARPUS

CURLLEAF CERCOCARPUS

fruit

CHRISTMASBERRY

ICACO COCO-PLUM (*Chrysobalanus icaco*) leaves, 1 to 3.5 inches long and 1 to 2.3 inches wide, are alternate, broadly elliptical to obovate leathery, evergreen, and smooth-margined. White flowers are in clusters 1 to 2 inches long. Fruit, 1.5 to 1.8 inches in diameter, is pink, yellow, or creamy, with thick, white, juicy flesh. The reddish-brown bark is scaly. Usually a shrub, often forming thickets in moist soils, but may grow to small-tree size (10 to 12 feet), with erect branches. The similar Smallfruit Coco-plum (*C. icaco* var. *pellocarpus*) occurs farther south.

LYONTREE (*Lyonothamnus floribundus*) has opposite, evergreen leaves, often of two types: simple and lanceolate, 4 to 8 inches long and 0.5 of an inch wide, with smooth or toothed margins; or pinnately compound, 3 to 6 inches long, with 3 to 7 leaflets. White flowers, 0.3 of an inch across, are in terminal clusters 4 to 8 inches broad, each flower producing a conical, woody carpel about 0.3 of an inch long. The dark reddish-brown bark peels into thin, papery strips. A small tree, often with several stems, but occasionally with a single trunk; to 40 feet tall and 10 inches in diameter. Grows in dry soils.

TORREY VAUQUELINIA (*Vauquelinia californica*) has leathery, usually alternate, lanceolate leaves, 1.5 to 3 inches long and 0.3 to 0.5 of an inch wide, with toothed margins and hairy below. Remain on the tree through the first winter after they form. White flowers, about 0.3 of an inch in diameter, occur in terminal clusters 2 to 3 inches across. Each produces a hairy, woody, ovoid capsule about 0.3 of an inch long. Grows in dry or rocky soils, as a shrub or a small tree, with scaly, reddish-brown bark. To 20 feet tall, 6 inches in diameter.

CLIFFROSE (*Cowania mexicana*) has wedge-shaped leaves less than 1 inch long, divided into 3 to 5 narrow lobes. Leathery, hairy below, and covered with resinous specks, they usually persist through the first winter. The white to pale-yellow flowers, about 1 inch in diameter, develop into a dry fruit with feathery plumes about 2 inches long. Usually a shrub but occasionally a small tree, to 25 feet tall and 8 inches in diameter, with stiff, erect branches. It has gray, scaly bark and grows in dry, rocky soils.

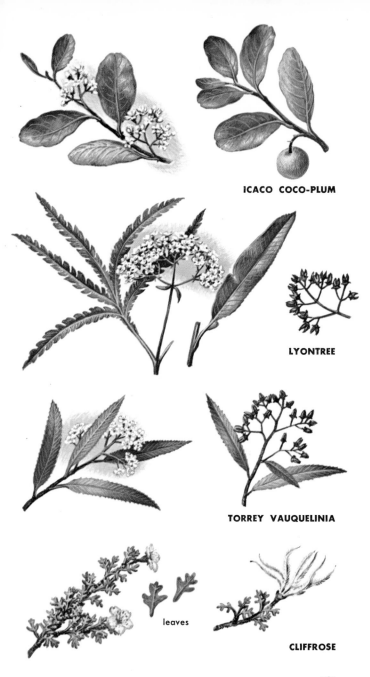

ICACO COCO-PLUM

LYONTREE

TORREY VAUQUELINIA

leaves

CLIFFROSE

181

LEGUME FAMILY (Leguminosae)

This family contains more than 500 genera and about 13,000 species of herbs, vines, shrubs, and trees found throughout the world. Many species have thorny branches. Leaves are alternate, compound in most. Some shed their leaves; others are evergreen. All produce a legume, or pod. Clover, alfalfa, peas, and beans are important legume crops. Other species are well-known ornamentals. Some, especially tropical trees, yield wood, dyes, and similar products. Nitrogen-fixing bacteria in root nodules of legumes aid in enriching the soil.

Silktree *(Albizia julibrissin)*, a native of southern Asia, is grown as an ornamental in California and southeastern United States where it now also grows wild. Lebbek or Woman's Tongue *(A. lebbek)*, a similar tree, is common in southern Florida, as are Flamboyant-tree, or Royal Poinciana *(Delonix regia)*, a native of Madagascar; Flower-fence, or Dwarf Poinciana *(Poinciana pulcherrima)*, of unknown origin; and Tamarind *(Tamarindus indica)*, of the Old World tropics. Paradise Poinciana *(P. gilliesii)*, of South America, is naturalized in parts of the Southwest.

BLACKBEADS *(Pithecellobium spp.)* are shrubs or small trees, to 30 feet tall. Bipinnately compound leaves are evergreen or tardily deciduous; twigs spiny. Catclaw Blackbead *(P. unguis-cati)* has one pair of leaflets on its two pinnae; flowers in globular heads; pods contorted. Huajillo *(P. pallens)* has many small leaflets on 8 to 10 pinnae; flowers in globular heads, pods straight and flat. Ebony Blackbead *(P. flexicaule)* has several leaflets on 4 to 6 pinnae, light-yellow flowers in spikes; pods thick and hairy.

BAHAMA LYSILOMA *(Lysiloma bahamensis)* leaves are evergreen, with 2 to 6 pairs of pinnae having numerous oblong leaflets 0.3 to 0.5 of an inch long. Small, greenish-white flowers, in globose heads, produce reddish-brown, pointed pods, 4 to 5 inches long, with dark-brown, oval seeds about 0.5 of an inch long. Branches not spiny. Bahama Lysiloma grows to 60 feet tall, 3 feet in diameter.

LEADTREES *(Leucaena spp.)*, shrubs or small trees, have bipinnate, evergreen leaves with numerous small leaflets; white flowers in globose heads and many-seeded pods; twigs not spiny. Native species include Littleleaf Leadtree *(L. retusa)*, Gregg Leadtree *(L. greggii)*, and Great Leadtree *(L. pulverulenta)*. Leadtree *(L. glauca)* is an introduced species in Florida.

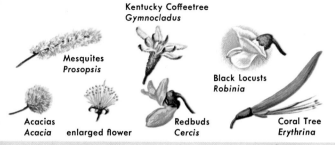

Mesquites
Prosopis

Kentucky Coffeetree
Gymnocladus

Black Locusts
Robinia

Acacias
Acacia

enlarged flower

Redbuds
Cercis

Coral Tree
Erythrina

DIFFERENCES IN FLOWERS OF SOME NATIVE LEGUMES

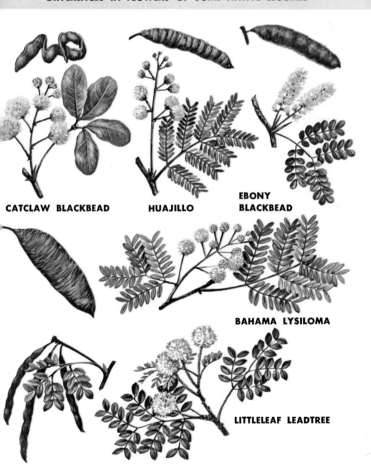

CATCLAW BLACKBEAD **HUAJILLO** **EBONY BLACKBEAD**

BAHAMA LYSILOMA

LITTLELEAF LEADTREE

CATCLAW ACACIA (*Acacia greggii*) leaves are gray-green, with 1 to 3 pairs of pinnae, each with 4 to 6 pairs of oval leaflets to 0.3 of an inch long. Cylindrical spikes of small, creamy-yellow, fragrant flowers are 1 to 2.5 inches long. Fruit a flattened pod, 1 to 6 inches long, 0.8 of an inch wide, often curled and constricted between seeds. Branches bear short, curved spines, 0.3 of an inch long; bark brown and scaly. A shrub or small tree, to 18 feet tall.

SWEET ACACIA (*Acacia farnesiana*) has bright-green deciduous leaves with 2 to 8 pairs of pinnae, each having 10 to 25 pairs of pointed leaflets about 0.2 of an inch long. Small, yellow, fragrant flowers are in globular heads about 0.8 of an inch in diameter. Thickened, lustrous reddish-purple pods, 2 to 3 inches long and 0.5 to 0.8 of an inch in diameter, contain ovoid seeds embedded in pulp. Grows to 30 feet tall and 1.5 feet in diameter, with a round, wide-spreading crown, reddish-brown bark, and straight, stiff spines about 1.5 inches long.

TWISTED ACACIA (*Acacia tortuosa*) has light-green leaves divided into 3 to 4 pairs of pinnae, with 10 to 15 pairs of small, linear, pointed leaflets. Small, bright-yellow, fragrant flowers in globular heads, 0.5 to 0.8 of an inch in diameter. Fruit a reddish-brown, slightly compressed pod, 3 to 5 inches long and 0.3 of an inch wide, constricted between seeds. Branches bear slender spines, 0.8 of an inch long. Grows to 20 feet tall, 6 inches in diameter; round, widespread crown and dark-brown to black, furrowed bark. Emory Acacia (*A. emoryana*), found in the same region, has flowers in short spikes and has larger pods.

WRIGHT ACACIA (*Acacia wrightii*) leaves are bright-green and somewhat hairy. They are divided into 1 to 3 pairs of pinnae, each with 2 to 5 pairs of leaflets 0.3 to 0.8 of an inch long. Small, light-yellow, fragrant flowers are borne in cylindrical spikes about 1.5 inches long. Fruit is a compressed pod, 2 to 4 inches long and 1 to 1.5 inches wide, with narrow, oval seeds about 0.3 of an inch long. A few stout, curved, chestnut-brown spines, 0.3 of an inch long, occur on the branches. Grows to 30 feet tall and 1 foot in diameter, with a wide crown and scaly, furrowed bark.

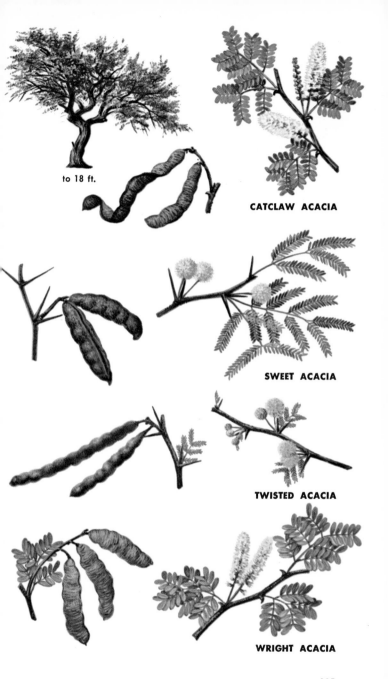

to 18 ft.

CATCLAW ACACIA

SWEET ACACIA

TWISTED ACACIA

WRIGHT ACACIA

185

MESQUITE (*Prosopis juliflora*) and its three varieties have deciduous leaves divided into 2, or occasionally 4, pinnae, each with many small leaflets. Greenish-white, fragrant flowers are in slender, cylindrical spikes 1.5 to 4 inches long. Narrow pods, 4 to 9 inches long and 0.3 to 0.5 of an inch in diameter, are constricted between seeds. Spines 0.5 to 2 inches long. Grows 20 to 50 feet tall, 1 to 3 feet in diameter.

SCREWBEAN MESQUITE (*Prosopis pubescens*) has hairy, deciduous leaves divided into 2, or occasionally 4, pinnae, each with 10 to 16 small leaflets. Small greenish-white flowers in cylindrical spikes 2 to 3 inches long. The distinctive spiraled pod is 1 to 2 inches long. This mesquite grows to 20 feet tall, 1 foot in diameter; branches twisted, spiny.

EASTERN REDBUD (*Cercis canadensis*) leaves are deciduous, broadly ovate to heart-shaped, 3 to 5 inches wide, with a pointed tip and smooth margins. Turn yellow in fall. Flowers pinkish to lavender, 0.5 of an inch long, in loose clusters of 4 to 8; appear before leaves. Pinkish, flattened pods, 2.5 to 3.5 inches long, have several seeds about 0.3 of an inch long. Bark reddish brown, scaly. Usually small, occasionally to 50 feet with a broad, rounded crown.

CALIFORNIA REDBUD (*Cercis occidentalis*) leaves are round or notched at apex, 2 to 4 inches broad with a heart-shaped base and smooth margins. Lavender flowers, 0.5 of an inch long, appear before leaves. Pods are dull red, 1.5 to 3 inches long and 0.5 to 0.8 of an inch wide. Though usually a shrub, California Redbud is sometimes a small tree, to 20 feet tall.

KENTUCKY COFFEETREE (*Gymnocladus dioicus*) has bipinnately compound leaves, 1 to 3 feet long, with 5 to 9 pinnae, each bearing 6 to 14 pointed, oval leaflets 2 to 2.5 inches long and about 1 inch wide. Terminal racemose clusters of staminate and pistillate flowers are on separate trees; the former 3 to 4 inches long, the latter 10 to 12 inches long. Purplish-brown pods, 4 to 10 inches long and 1 to 2 inches wide, have 6 to 8 round, flattened, reddish-brown seeds, about 0.8 of an inch in diameter, embedded in pulp. Grows 75 to 100 feet tall and 2 to 3 feet in diameter. Furrowed bark is dark gray to brown; branches lack spines.

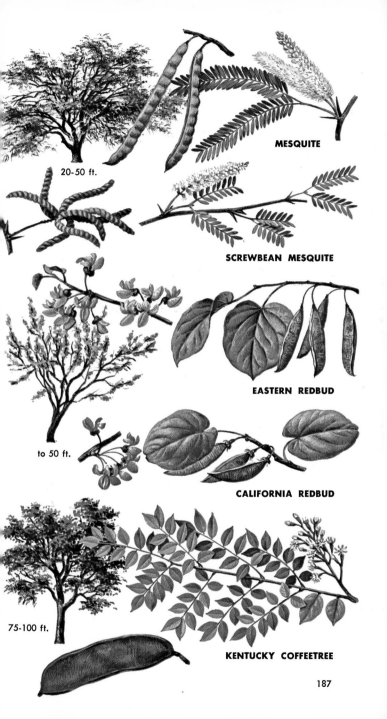

MESQUITE

20-50 ft.

SCREWBEAN MESQUITE

EASTERN REDBUD

to 50 ft.

CALIFORNIA REDBUD

75-100 ft.

KENTUCKY COFFEETREE

HONEYLOCUST (*Gleditsia triacanthos*) has pinnately or bipinnately compound leaves, 7 to 8 inches long. Elliptical to ovate leaflets, about 1 to 2 inches long and 0.3 to 0.5 of an inch wide, with smooth or remotely round-toothed margins; bipinnate leaflets smaller. Flowers greenish white, in racemes. Pods dark reddish brown, twisted, flattened, 7 to 18 inches long and 1 inch wide, with dark-brown, oval seeds, 0.3 of an inch long, in succulent pulp. Branches, and often trunk, armed with simple to 3-branched spines 2 to 3 inches long. Bark dark gray-brown, in narrow, flat-topped plates. In moist, fertile soils, Honeylocust grows 75 to 80 feet tall and 2 to 3 feet in diameter. It has a broad, flat-topped crown.

TEXAS HONEYLOCUST (*Gleditsia texana*) is considered to be a natural hybrid between Honeylocust and Waterlocust. Leaves and leaflets are smaller than Honeylocust's. Racemes of staminate flowers, 3 to 4 inches long, are orange-yellow; the shorter, many-seeded pods (4 to 5 inches long, 1 inch wide) lack pulp; twigs not spiny. Bark resembles Honeylocust's. Grows 100 to 120 feet tall and 2.5 feet in diameter. The crown is narrow and spreading.

WATERLOCUST (*Gleditsia aquatica*) leaves are 5 to 8 inches long and pinnate or bipinnately compound. The ovate-oblong leaflets are 1 inch long and to 0.5 of an inch wide. Flowers, in racemes 3 to 4 inches long, have greenish petals and sepals with soft, orange-brown hairs. Pods are oval, pointed at the apex, chestnut brown, 1 to 2 inches long and 1 inch wide. They lack pulp and contain 1 to 3 flat, nearly round seeds about 0.5 of an inch across. Twigs spiny; bark gray to reddish brown, in small, platelike scales. Waterlocust grows to 60 feet tall and 2.5 feet in diameter, with an irregular, flat-topped crown. It is most common in swampy places.

JERUSALEM-THORN (*Parkinsonia aculeata*) leaves are short-stemmed, bipinnately compound, with 1 to 3 pairs of wiry, flattened, evergreen pinnae 8 to 20 inches long, and many narrowly oblong, gray-green, deciduous leaflets about 0.1 of an inch long. Flowers golden yellow, in 3- to 6-inch racemes. Pods linear-cylindric, 2 to 6 inches long, constricted between seeds. Both the twigs and the base of the leaves are spiny. Jerusalem-thorn grows 15 to 20 feet tall.

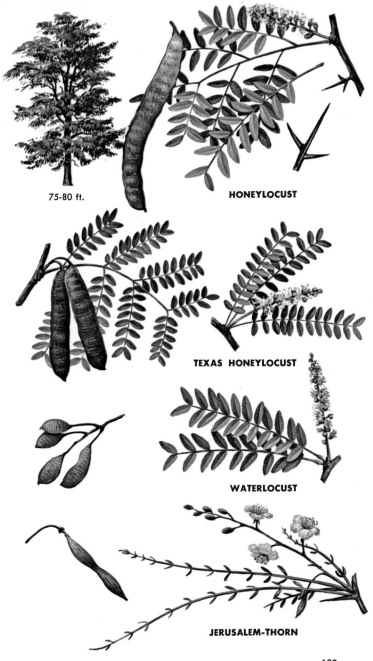

75-80 ft.

HONEYLOCUST

TEXAS HONEYLOCUST

WATERLOCUST

JERUSALEM-THORN

189

YELLOWWOOD *(Cladrastis lutea)* has pinnately compound leaves, 8 to 12 inches long, with 5 to 11 obovate leaflets 3 to 4 inches long and 1 to 2 inches wide. They turn yellow in fall. White flowers are in terminal panicles, 12 to 14 inches long. Pods are flat, 2 to 4 inches long, with 4 to 6 seeds. Smooth bark is dark gray to brown. Grows to 60 feet tall, 2 feet in diameter.

TEXAS SOPHORA *(Sophora affinis)* leaves are deciduous, 6 to 9 inches long, and pinnately compound. Each of the 13 to 19 elliptical leaflets is 1 to 1.5 inches long and about 0.5 of an inch wide. Flowers, white tinged with pink, are in racemes 3 to 5 inches long. Black pods are cylindrical, often hairy, 0.5 to 3 inches long and constricted between oval seeds. Grows to 20 feet tall and 10 inches in diameter, with spreading, round-topped crown and dark-brown, scaly bark.

MESCALBEAN *(Sophora secundiflora)* leaves are evergreen, hairy, pinnately compound, and 4 to 6 inches long. The 7 to 9 elliptical leaflets are 1 to 2.5 inches long and 0.5 to 1.5 inches wide. Fragrant, violet, pea-like flowers, about 1 inch long, occur in racemes 2 to 3 inches long. Cylindrical, hairy pods, 1 to 7 inches long and 0.5 of an inch in diameter, are constricted between scarlet seeds that contain poisonous alkaloid (sophrium). A shrub or small tree, to 30 feet tall, with a narrow crown.

BLUE PALOVERDE *(Cercidium floridum)* has scattered, bipinnately compound leaves, 1 to 1.5 inches long, with 2 pinnae, each with 2 to 3 pairs of dull-green, oblong leaflets 0.3 of an inch long. Yellow flowers, 0.8 of an inch across, are in racemes to 2 inches long. Flat, yellowish-brown pods are 3 to 4 inches long. The twigs are spiny. Smooth bark is bluish gray, becoming scaly and brown. Grows to 25 feet tall.

YELLOW PALOVERDE *(Cercidium microphyllum)* branches end in sharp spines. Leaves, to 1 inch long, have 2 pinnae, each with 4 to 7 pairs of tiny, elliptical leaflets, which are shed early. Small, yellow flowers are in racemes. Cylindrical pods, 2 to 3 inches long, are constricted between seeds. Bark is yellow-green to gray. A shrub or small tree, to 25 feet tall.

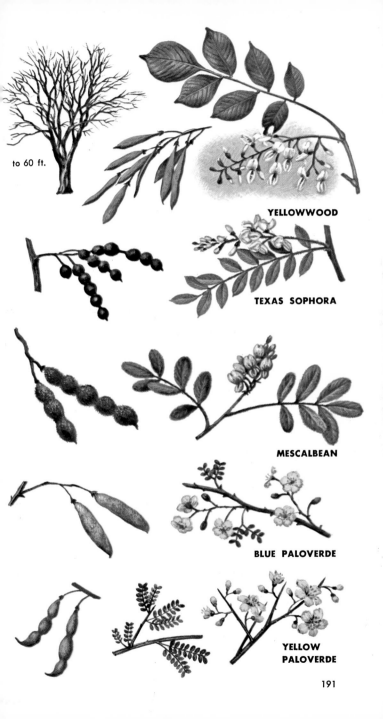

to 60 ft.

YELLOWWOOD

TEXAS SOPHORA

MESCALBEAN

BLUE PALOVERDE

YELLOW PALOVERDE

BLACK LOCUST *(Robinia pseudoacacia)* has pinnately compound leaves, 8 to 14 inches long; 7 to 19 smooth-margined leaflets 1 to 2 inches long, 0.5 to 0.8 of an inch wide. Fragrant, white flowers in drooping racemes. Flat, brown to black pods, 2 to 4 inches long, 0.5 of an inch wide; the 4 to 8 seeds are kidney-shaped, orange-brown. Spines, 0.5 to 0.8 inch, on twigs. Bark nearly black, in "corded" ridges. To 80 feet tall, 2 to 4 feet in diameter.

CLAMMY LOCUST *(Robinia viscosa)* leaves are 7 to 12 inches long, pinnately compound; 13 to 21 oval leaflets, 1.5 to 2 inches long, 0.8 of an inch wide, hairy below. Rose-colored, odorless flowers in drooping racemes. Pods, 2 to 3.5 inches long, contain several reddish-brown, mottled seeds. Twigs sparingly thorny. Pods, leaf stems, and branchlets covered with sticky, clammy hairs. Shrubby to 40 feet tall; bark reddish brown, generally smooth. New-Mexican Locust *(R. neomexicana)* is a common, generally shrubby species of the Southwest.

SMOKETHORN *(Dalea spinosa)* has simple, wedge-shaped leaves, 0.8 to 1 inch long, 0.1 to 0.5 of an inch wide, densely hairy, early deciduous. Leaves, twigs, flowers, and pods dotted with glands. Spiny twigs gray with dense hairs when young. Purple flowers, 0.5 of an inch long, in racemes 1 to 1.5 inches long. Ovoid pod contains 1 or 2 seeds. Bark gray-brown, scaly. Smokethorn grows to 20 feet tall.

FLORIDA FISHPOISON-TREE *(Piscidia piscipula)* has pinnately compound leaves, 4 to 9 inches long, the 5 to 11 leaflets 1.5 to 3 inches long, hairy below and along stems. Flowers white, tinged with red, in panicles; appear in spring before leaves. Winged pods, 3 to 4 inches long and constricted. The bark is olive-gray and scaly. This tree grows to 50 feet tall.

EASTERN CORALBEAN *(Erythrina herbacea)* has evergreen leaves 6 to 8 inches long, with three shallowly lobed leaflets 2.5 to 3.5 inches long, 1.5 to 2.3 inches wide. Elongated, scarlet flowers, 2 to 2.5 inches long, in racemes 8 to 13 inches long. Pods are 4 to 6 inches long, constricted between scarlet seeds. Branchlets have stout, curved spines. A shrub or small tree, to 25 feet tall. Southwestern Coralbean *(E. flabelliformis)*, ranging from Mexico into southwestern U.S., is occasionally tree size.

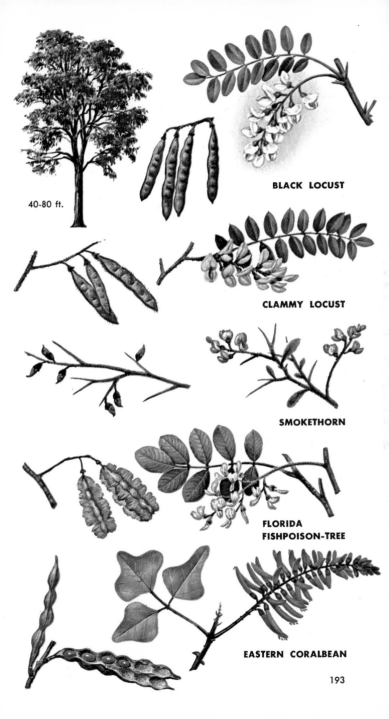

40-80 ft.

BLACK LOCUST

CLAMMY LOCUST

SMOKETHORN

**FLORIDA
FISHPOISON-TREE**

EASTERN CORALBEAN

193

RUE FAMILY (Rutaceae)

More than 1,000 species of trees, shrubs, and herbs native to the tropics and warm temperate zones belong to this family. It is best represented in Australia and South Africa, but a number of small trees of this family grow in North America. Several species of *Citrus* have escaped cultivation and are naturalized in Florida.

HERCULES-CLUB *(Zanthoxylum clava-herculis)*, also called Toothache-tree, has alternate, odd-pinnately compound, tardily deciduous leaves, 5 to 8 inches long. The 7 to 19 leaflets, 1 to 2.5 inches long, are bright green above, paler and somewhat hairy below; margins toothed; stems spiny. Greenish staminate and pistillate flowers on separate trees clustered (in cymes) at ends of branches. Brown, wrinkled capsule, 0.8 of an inch long, splits open to release a black seed on a slender thread. Spines, 0.5 of an inch long, arm stout, gray to brown twigs. A small tree, rarely to 40 feet, with a short trunk; light-gray bark often studded with stout spines.

YELLOWHEART *(Zanthoxylum flavum)* has alternate, odd-pinnately compound, evergreen leaves, 6 to 9 inches long. The 5 to 11 leathery, ovate to lanceolate to elliptical leaflets are 1.5 to 2 inches long, with smooth or finely toothed margins and dotted with translucent glands. Both flowers and fruits are similar to those of Hercules-club, but twigs are not spiny. Smooth, light-gray bark becomes fissured with age. Grows to 20 feet tall.

LIME PRICKLY-ASH *(Zanthoxylum fagara)* leaves are evergreen, alternate, odd-pinnately compound, 3 to 4 inches long, with 7 to 9 glandular-dotted leaflets finely toothed above middle. Leaf stems are winged; brownish twigs spiny. Yellow-green staminate and pistillate flowers in axillary clusters (cymes) on separate trees. Warty, brown capsule contains one black seed. A shrub or small tree, to 30 feet tall, with thin, gray, "warty" bark.

COMMON PRICKLY-ASH *(Zanthoxylum americanum)* foliage resembles Hercules-club, but margins of leaflets (5-11) are smooth or have only small, rounded teeth. Small, greenish flowers are in sessile, axillary clusters. Bark gray to bluish. It is usually a spiny shrub but occasionally is a small tree, to 25 feet tall.

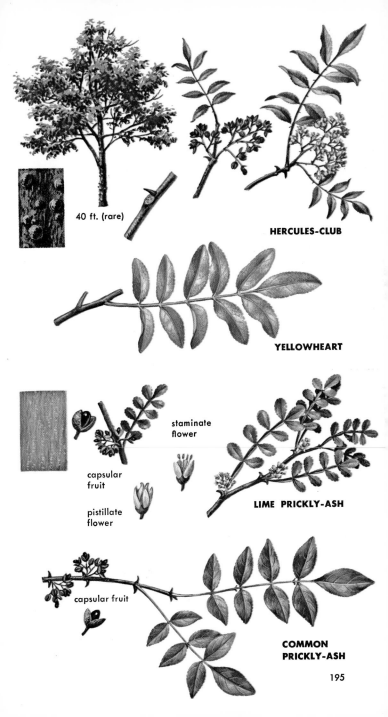

40 ft. (rare)

HERCULES-CLUB

YELLOWHEART

staminate
flower

capsular
fruit

pistillate
flower

LIME PRICKLY-ASH

capsular fruit

**COMMON
PRICKLY-ASH**

COMMON HOPTREE *(Ptelea trifoliata)* has alternate, usually 3-foliate, deciduous leaves, 4 to 6 inches long; leaflets, 2 to 4 inches long, have smooth to finely toothed margins. Polygamous, greenish-white flowers in terminal clusters (cymes). Buff-colored, wafer-like fruit (samara), about 1 inch in diameter, has a broad, veined wing. Twigs slender, giving off rank odor when broken. Bark thin, gray, warty. Crown broad, rounded; to 25 feet tall, 1 foot in diameter. Pale Hoptree *(P. pallida)* and Narrowleaf Hoptree *(P. angustifolia)*, most commonly shrubs, grow in southwestern United States and also in Mexico.

SEA AMYRIS *(Amyris elemifera)* has opposite, evergreen leaves, with 3 broadly lance-shaped leaflets, each 1 to 2.5 inches long; margins smooth or with small, rounded teeth. Flowers white, in terminal clusters (panicles). Fruit black, cherry-like, palatable, about 0.5 of an inch in diameter. Bark thin, graybrown, becoming furrowed. To 50 feet tall, 1 foot in diameter. Balsam Amyris *(A. balsamifera)* ranges from Florida southward.

BURSERA FAMILY (Burseraceae)

GUMBO-LIMBO *(Bursera simaruba)* has alternate, odd-pinnately compound leaves, 6 to 8 inches long, clustered at ends of branches. The 3 to 9 leathery leaflets are 2 to 3 inches long. Small, greenish-white flowers in racemes 2 to 5 inches long. Red, leathery, 3-angled fruits, about 0.3 of an inch long, split into 3 parts, releasing single seed. Bark thin, smooth, reddish brown; light wood sometimes used for fishing floats. To 60 feet tall, 3 feet in diameter. Elephanttree *(B. microphylla)* and the smaller Fragrant Bursera *(B. fagaroides)* are shrubs or small trees of southwestern U.S. Flowers and fruits are similar to Gumbo-limbo's; leaves have winged petioles and 5 to 30 leaflets about 0.8 to 1.5 inches long.

CALTROP FAMILY (Zygophyllaceae)

HOLYWOOD LIGNUMVITAE *(Guaiacum sanctum)* has opposite, even-pinnately compound, evergreen leaves, with 3 to 4 pairs of opposite, leathery, smooth-margined leaflets about 1 inch long. Blue flowers, about 0.8 of an inch across, in 2- to 4-flowered, terminal clusters. Orange, obovoid, fleshy capsule, about 0.8 of an inch long, contains scarlet-coated black seeds. Bark chalky; wood heavy. To 30 feet tall.

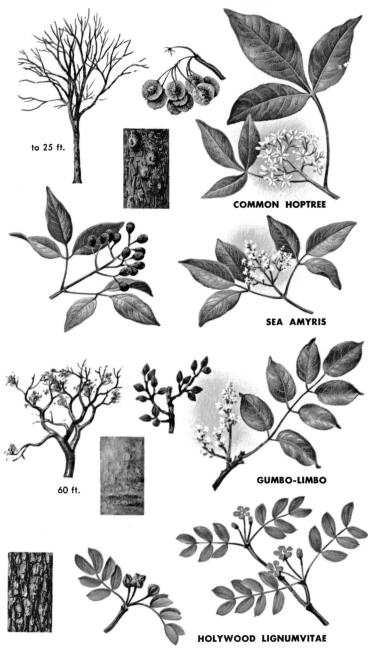

to 25 ft.

COMMON HOPTREE

SEA AMYRIS

60 ft.

GUMBO-LIMBO

HOLYWOOD LIGNUMVITAE

AILANTHUS (QUASSIA) FAMILY
(Simaroubaceae)

PARADISE-TREE *(Simarouba glauca)* leaves are evergreen, pinnately compound, alternate, and to 10 inches long. Their 10 to 14 leathery, oblong to obovate leaflets are 2 to 3 inches long and either alternate or opposite; dark green above, lighter below. Yellow staminate and pistillate flowers, on separate trees, are in axillary or terminal clusters (panicles). Fruit, about 1 inch long, is red, becoming purple as it ripens. A small tree, to 50 feet tall and 2 feet in diameter, with brown, scaly bark.

BITTERBUSH *(Picramnia pentandra)* leaves are evergreen, alternate, odd-pinnately compound and 8 to 12 inches long, with 5 to 9 leathery, pointed leaflets 1 to 3 inches long. Greenish staminate and pistillate flowers on separate trees, in slender racemes, 6 to 8 inches long. Oval fruit is 1- to 2-seeded and about 0.5 of an inch long, lustrous black when ripe. Slender twigs are hairy. A shrub or small tree, Bitterbush grows to 20 feet tall and 6 inches in diameter. It has smooth, yellowish-brown bark.

MEXICAN ALVARADOA *(Alvaradoa amorphoides)* has alternate, pinnately compound, evergreen leaves, 4 to 12 inches long. The 21 to 41 leaflets, 0.5 to 0.8 of an inch long, taper from a broad, rounded apex. Staminate and pistillate flowers, on separate trees, are in slender racemes 3 to 8 inches long. Reddish fruit is lance-shaped and 2-winged with fringed margins, about 0.8 of an inch long. A shrub or small tree of dry soils, to 30 feet tall and 8 inches in diameter, with gray or reddish-tinged bark.

AN INTRODUCED MEMBER OF AILANTHUS FAMILY

AILANTHUS *(Ailanthus altissima),* also called Tree-of-Heaven, has alternate, odd-pinnately compound, deciduous leaves, 1 to 3 feet long. The 11 to 41 ovate to ovate-lanceolate leaflets are 3 to 5 inches long and 1 to 2 inches wide. They are toothed at the base and have a disagreeable odor when crushed. Staminate and pistillate flowers are on different trees; they are small, greenish, and in dense, terminal panicles. Staminate flowers also have an unpleasant odor. The fruit is an oblong, twisted samara, about 1.5 inches long, with a seed in the center of the wing. They are in large, dense clusters that hang on the tree through the winter. Bark is thin, dark gray, and somewhat roughened. A rapidly growing tree with stout, hairy twigs and a flat-topped crown of stout branches, Ailanthus thrives even in poor soils and may grow to 100 feet tall and 3 feet in diameter. Produces many suckers; often a weed tree. Native to eastern Asia but grown widely as an ornamental.

PARADISE-TREE

BITTERBUSH

MEXICAN ALVARADOA

AILANTHUS

to 100 ft.

199

MAHOGANY FAMILY (Meliaceae)

WEST INDIES MAHOGANY (*Swietenia mahagoni*) leaves are evergreen, alternate, even-pinnately compound, 4 to 7 inches long, the 6 to 8 leathery, ovate to lanceolate, opposite leaflets 3 to 4 inches long. Flowers cup-shaped, 0.1 of an inch long, the 5 petals greenish or white; in long, axillary panicles. Reddish-brown capsular fruit, 3 to 4 inches long, splits from base along 5 valves, releasing squarish, winged seeds about 0.8 of an inch long. Bark dark brown, scaly. To 60 feet tall, 2 feet in diameter; rare in U.S.

AN INTRODUCED MEMBER OF MAHOGANY FAMILY

CHINABERRY (*Melia azedarach*) has alternate, bipinnately compound, deciduous leaves, 1 to 2 feet long. The numerous bright-green, pointed leaflets 1 to 3 inches long, with toothed (or slightly lobed) margins. Purplish, showy, fragrant flowers, about 0.8 of an inch in diameter; in loose panicles, 4 to 8 inches long. Fleshy fruits, 0.5 to 0.8 of an inch in diameter, yellow when mature. Rapid-growing, short-lived tree native of Asia, grown as an ornamental in southern U.S.

SPURGE FAMILY (Euphorbiaceae)

The more than 7,000 species of herbs, shrubs, and trees in this family include the Para or Brazilian Rubber Tree (*Hevea brasiliensis*), Tapioca (*Manihot esculenta*), and other commercially valuable tropical plants, plus poinsettia, crotons, snow-on-the-mountain, and other ornamentals. Castor-bean Plant (*Ricinus communis*) plus Brazil Sapium (*Sapium glandulosum*) and the Chinese Tallowtree (*S. sebiferum*), both related to Mexican Jumping-bean (*S. biloculare*), have escaped cultivation and now grow in warm parts of North America. Many members of the family have a milky juice, poisonous in some.

GUIANAPLUM (*Drypetes lateriflora*) leaves are evergreen, alternate, smooth-margined, broadly elliptical, 2 to 4 inches long. Small, greenish, staminate and pistillate flowers in leaf axils on separate trees, the staminate clustered. Fruit a scarlet, nearly globose drupe about 0.3 of an inch in diameter. Bark light brown, smooth; usually scaly. A shrub or small tree, to 25 feet tall, 6 inches in diameter. Milkbark (*D. diversifolia*), found only in southern Florida, has white fruit.

OYSTERWOOD (*Gymnanthes lucida*) has leathery, alternate, evergreen leaves, 2 to 3 inches long; margins usually smooth. Staminate (clustered) and pistillate (usually solitary) flowers on adjoining axillary stalks. Fruit a dark, 3-lobed capsule, 0.3 of an inch in diameter. To 35 feet tall. Bark thin, scaly.

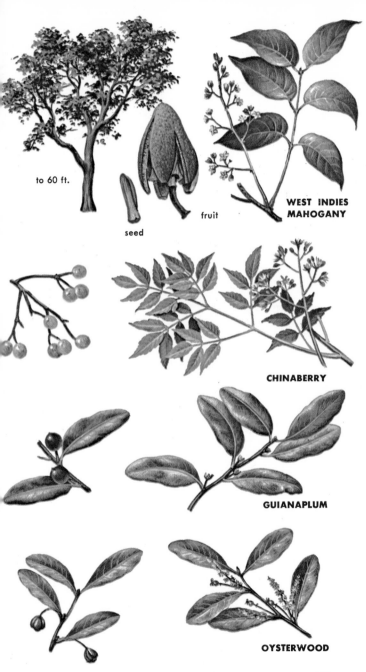

to 60 ft.

seed

fruit

WEST INDIES MAHOGANY

CHINABERRY

GUIANAPLUM

OYSTERWOOD

MANCHINEEL *(Hippomane mancinella)* has alternate broadly ovate leaves, 3 to 4 inches long, 1 to 2 inches wide; tips pointed, margins finely round-toothed. Flowers in terminal stalks 4 to 6 inches long; yellow-green staminate above, pistillate below. Fruits drupaceous yellow-green with red cheeks, 1.5 inches in diameter, with milky flesh. Bark white to dark brown, smooth, scaly on large trunks. A shrub or small tree, to 2 feet tall, 6 inches in diameter. Sap highly poisonous.

CASHEW (SUMAC) FAMILY (Anacardiaceae)

This family, represented in temperate and tropical regions, comprises about 600 species of trees, shrubs, and vines, with resinous, acrid, or caustic juice. In addition to the species listed here, the Mango *(Mangifera indica)* is grown in Florida and throughout the tropics and subtropics for its fruit. Peppertree *(Schinus molle),* from South America, is grown as an ornamental in California and in southern Florida, where it is now naturalized and grows wild. Cashew *(Anacardium occidentale)* and Pistachio *(Pistachia vera)* are grown mainly in the tropics for nuts.

AMERICAN SMOKETREE *(Cotinus obovatus)* has alternate, simple, oval to obovate, deciduous leaves, 4 to inches long, 2 to 3 inches wide; margins smooth, curled under; hair on veins below. Leaves turn orange or red. Dioecious; sparsely flowered terminal clusters, 5 to inches long. Fruit a dry, oblong, compressed, brown drupe, 0.3 of an inch long. Shrubby, to 35 feet tall.

FLORIDA POISONTREE *(Metopium toxiferum)* leaves are evergreen, alternate, odd-pinnately compound, to 10 inches long, the 5 (occ. 3) to 7 leaflets 3 to inches long, 2 to 3 inches wide, with slightly curled margins. Dioecious; the yellow-green flowers in loose clusters 6 to 12 inches long in leaf axils near tips of branches. Orange fruits (drupes) 0.8 of an inch long, resinous. Bark thin, reddish brown, mottled with dark gummy secretions; scaly on older trees. A shrub or small tree, to 35 feet tall. Poisonous to touch.

TEXAS PISTACHE *(Pistacia texana)* leaves are evergreen, alternate, pinnately compound, with slightly winged stems. The 9 to 19 leaflets, 0.8 of an inch long, widest above middle. Dioecious; small flowers without sepals or petals, in panicles to 2.5 inches long. Fruit a dark reddish-brown drupe, 0.2 of an inch long. A shrub or small tree, to 30 feet tall.

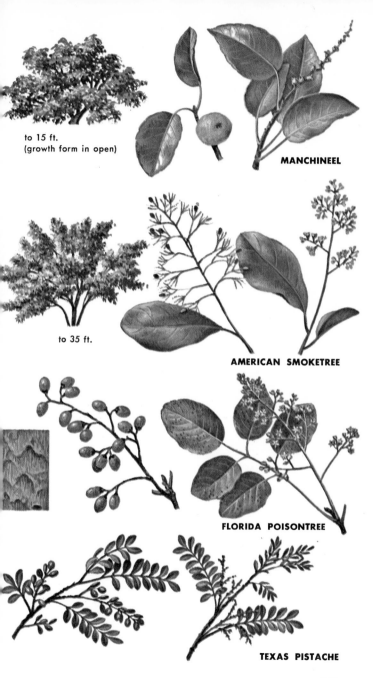

to 15 ft.
(growth form in open)

MANCHINEEL

to 35 ft.

AMERICAN SMOKETREE

FLORIDA POISONTREE

TEXAS PISTACHE

STAGHORN SUMAC *(Rhus typhina)* leaves are deciduous, alternate, odd-pinnately compound, and 12 to 24 inches long, with stout, hairy stems. The 11 to 31 lance-shaped leaflets are 2 to 5 inches long, with toothed margins; dull green above, paler and hairy on midrib below; scarlet in fall. Greenish staminate and pistillate flowers in dense panicles at ends of branches on separate trees. Fruits dry, red-hairy drupes, 0.1 of an inch in diameter. Stout, densely hairy twigs exude milky fluid when crushed. Bark of young trees thin, dark brown; on older trees, scaly. Shrub or small tree, to 35 feet tall. Smooth Sumac *(R. glabra),* similar but smaller, has smooth twigs. Lemonade Sumac *(R. integrifolia)* and Kearney Sumac *(R. kearneyi)* are among western species occasionally tree size.

SHINING SUMAC *(Rhus copallina)* leaves are similar to Staghorn Sumac's but have winged stems and fewer leaflets (9 to 21), usually not toothed. Flower clusters less dense, fruits smaller. Bark thin, reddish brown.

POISON-SUMAC *(Toxicodendron vernix)* leaves are 7 to 15 inches long, similar to those of *Rhus* but smaller and with fewer leaflets. Leaflets 3 to 4 inches long, with smooth margins. Clusters of greenish-yellow flowers produce ivory-white drupes about 0.3 of an inch in diameter. Thin, gray-brown bark smooth except for lenticels. Usually a shrub, rarely to 30 feet. Contains poisonous oil, like Poison Ivy of same genus.

CYRILLA FAMILY (Cyrillaceae)

SWAMP CYRILLA *(Cyrilla racemiflora)* leaves are simple, alternate, 2 to 3 inches long and 0.5 to 1 inch wide; tardily deciduous. Fragrant, white to pinkish flowers in racemes 4 to 6 inches long, near end of twigs. Dry, conical fruit about 0.1 of an inch long. Bark lustrous reddish brown. To 25 feet tall. Florida Cyrilla *(C. arida)* and Littleleaf Cyrilla *(C. parvifolia)* are two small, tree-size species found only in Florida.

BUCKWHEAT-TREE *(Cliftonia monophylla)* has simple, alternate, smooth-margined, evergreen leaves, 1 to 2 inches long and to 1 inch wide. Flowers white to pink, in slender, erect racemes. Fruit 4-winged, about 0.3 of an inch long. Bark reddish brown. A shrub or small tree, Buckwheat-tree grows to 35 feet tall and may form thickets in moist soils.

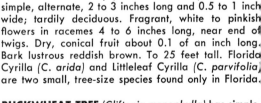

to 35 ft.

STAGHORN SUMAC

SHINING SUMAC

POISON-SUMAC

SWAMP CYRILLA

BUCKWHEAT-TREE

HOLLY FAMILY (Aquifoliaceae)

Hollies *(Ilex)* are the most familiar of three genera of trees and shrubs in this family, with nearly 300 species in temperate and tropical areas of both hemispheres. In addition to the species described here, six others that are most commonly shrubs are native to eastern United States. Those with leathery, spiny-toothed, evergreen leaves, and bright-red fruits are used in Christmas decorations. Others are deciduous, with smooth-margined leaves and fruits of a different color. In all hollies the leaves are alternate.

AMERICAN HOLLY *(Ilex opaca)* has leathery, evergreen leaves, 2 to 4 inches long and 1 to 2 inches wide, with a sharp-pointed tip and spiny-toothed (occasionally smooth) margins. Greenish-white staminate and pistillate flowers borne on separate trees. Fleshy berry-like, bright-red fruits, 0.3 of an inch in diameter contain several ribbed nutlets. Bark thin, gray, often warty. Grows to 50 feet tall, with short branches forming a narrow, pyramidal crown.

TAWNYBERRY HOLLY *(Ilex krugiana)* leaves are evergreen, 2.5 to 4 inches long and 1 to 1.5 inches wide. They have a long-pointed apex and smooth margins. Flowers are similar to American Holly's, and fruits, about 0.1 of an inch long, are purple-brown. Grows as a shrub or a small tree, to 30 feet tall and 6 inches in diameter. On twigs or trunks of young trees, bark is smooth and whitish; on mature trees scaly and brown.

DAHOON *(Ilex cassine)* leaves are evergreen, oblanceolate to oblong-ovate, 1.5 to 3 inches long and 0.5 to 1 inch wide, with margins smooth or slightly toothed above the middle. Flowers, similar to American Holly's, produce bright-red, occasionally yellowish fruits, 0.3 of an inch in diameter. The gray bark marked with numerous lenticels. Dahoon grows to 30 feet tall and 1.5 feet in diameter. It is often common in moist soils.

YAUPON *(Ilex vomitoria)* resembles Dahoon, but has smaller, elliptical, toothed leaves. The scarlet fruits are produced in greater abundance. Bark scaly and brown. Yaupon grows as a shrub or small tree, to 20 feet tall and 6 inches in diameter, often forming dense thickets. The leaves of Yaupon have been used in preparing a purgative.

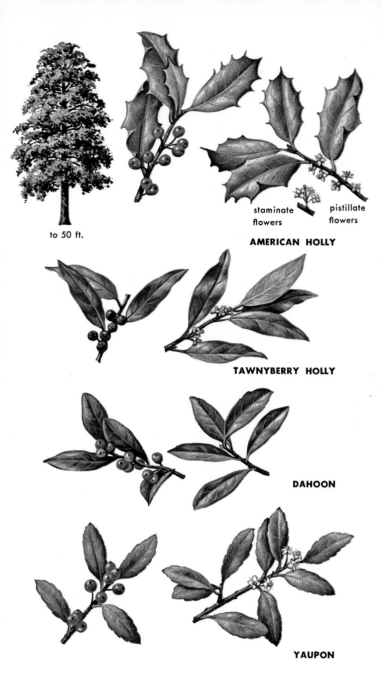

staminate flowers

pistillate flowers

AMERICAN HOLLY

to 50 ft.

TAWNYBERRY HOLLY

DAHOON

YAUPON

207

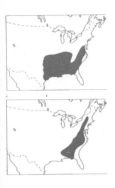

POSSUMHAW *(Ilex decidua)* has ovate-lanceolate, deciduous leaves, 2 to 3 inches long and 0.5 to 1 inch wide, with finely toothed margins. Flowers are similar to American Holly's, and the fruits, 0.3 of an inch in diameter, are reddish orange. Thin, smooth bark is greenish gray to brown. Usually a shrub but occasionally grows to 25 feet tall; common in moist soils.

MOUNTAIN WINTERBERRY *(Ilex montana)* resembles Possumhaw, but the leaves are 2 to 5 inches long and 0.5 to 2.5 inches wide, with larger, glandular, marginal teeth. Red fruits 0.5 of an inch in diameter.

AN INTRODUCED HOLLY

ENGLISH HOLLY *(Ilex aquifolium)*, of Europe and Asia, is widely planted as an ornamental. Resembles American Holly, but English Holly has smaller leaves and a greater abundance of fruit.

BITTERSWEET FAMILY (Celastraceae)

EASTERN WAHOO *(Euonymus atropurpureus)* has opposite, ovate to elliptical, deciduous leaves, 2 to 5 inches long and 1 to 2 inches wide, with finely toothed margins. Perfect flowers are 0.5 of an inch wide, with 4 dark-purple petals, in 7- to 15-flowered, axillary clusters. Fruit, 0.5 of an inch in diameter, a deeply 4-lobed purplish-red capsule with red seeds. Bark thin, gray, scaly. To 25 feet. The similar Western Wahoo *(E. occidentalis)* is most commonly a shrub.

WEST INDIES FALSEBOX *(Gyminda latifolia)* leaves are leathery, evergreen, 1 to 2 inches long and 0.8 to 1 inch wide, opposite, obovate, with smooth or finely toothed margins. Staminate and pistillate flowers, in short-stalked, axillary clusters (cymes) on separate trees, have 4 white petals. Black to dark-blue, oval, drupaceous fruits are about 0.3 of an inch long. Bark thin, scaly, light brown, often mottled with red. A shrub or small tree, to 25 feet tall.

CANOTIA *(Canotia holacantha)* is a leafless shrub or small tree, to 18 feet tall and 1 foot in diameter, with rough, gray-brown bark and many upright, yellowish-green branches and twigs ending in spiny tips. Greenish-white flowers, 0.3 of an inch across, are in clusters of 3 to 7 along the twigs. The fruit is a woody, ovoid, pointed capsule to 1 inch long. Typical of dry slopes and mesas.

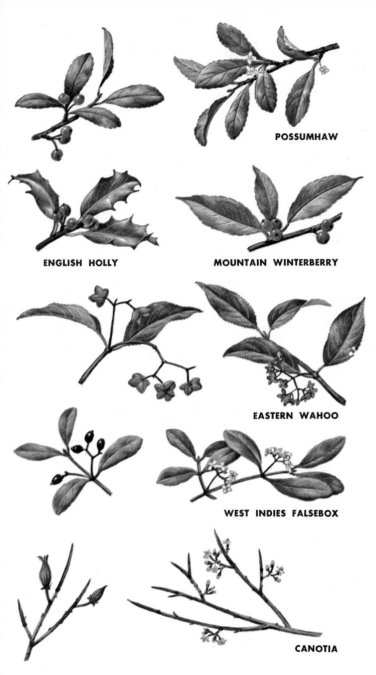

POSSUMHAW

ENGLISH HOLLY

MOUNTAIN WINTERBERRY

EASTERN WAHOO

WEST INDIES FALSEBOX

CANOTIA

209

MAPLE FAMILY (Aceraceae)

Maples (Acer) are among the most distinctive trees and shrubs in North America. Their winged seeds are in pairs (rarely in 3's) and their deciduous leaves are opposite on the branches. In most species the leaves are simple and palmately lobed. An exception is the Boxelder (Acer negundo), which has odd-pinnately compound foliage. Boxelder also differs from other native maples in having staminate and pistillate flowers on separate trees.

Maples, with nearly 150 species, are most abundant in eastern Asia. About a dozen species are native to the United States and Canada, but a number of foreign species have been introduced as ornamentals. The maple family has one other genus (Dipteronia), native to China.

SUGAR MAPLE (Acer saccharum) leaves are 3 to 5 inches in diameter and usually 5-lobed, their margins with several large, pointed teeth and the sides of the center lobe roughly parallel. Clusters of yellow, long-stemmed polygamous flowers develop with leaves. Inch-long, U-shaped pair of winged seeds ripen in fall. On young trees the bark is smooth and gray-brown, becoming scaly and furrowed with maturity. Sugar Maple grows 75 to 100 feet tall and 2 to 4 feet in diameter. In crowded woods, it has a long, branchless trunk; in the open a shorter trunk and a large, rounded crown. Its hard wood is used for furniture, in cabinet work, for interior trim, and flooring. The sap is the source of maple sugar and syrup. Sugar Maples are popular for shade and ornamental plantings because of their colorful red-and-yellow fall foliage.

BLACK MAPLE (Acer nigrum) is similar to the Sugar Maple, but the leaves are usually 3-lobed. In addition, the sides of the leaves tend to bend downward, and the underside, especially along the yellow veins, is somewhat hairy. Like the Sugar Maple, it is tapped in early spring for its sugary sap, and its hard wood is commercially valued.

FLORIDA MAPLE (Acer barbatum) resembles Sugar Maple but is smaller, growing to 60 feet tall and 3 feet in diameter. Its blue-green, 3- to 5-lobed leaves are 1.5 to 3 inches in diameter and usually hairy below. The lobes have wavy margins and rounded rather than pointed tips. In Florida Maple, the base of the leaf stem is noticeably enlarged.

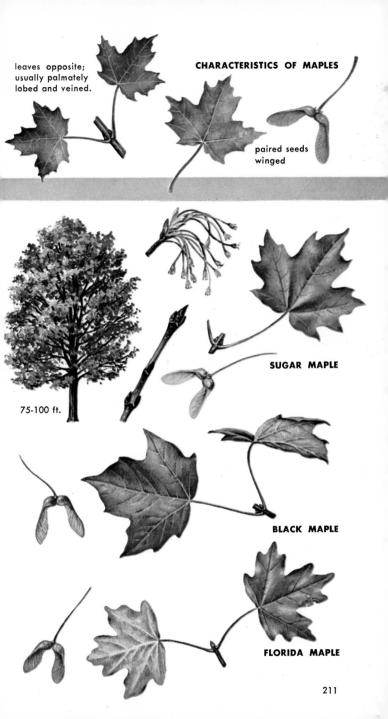

leaves opposite; usually palmately lobed and veined.

CHARACTERISTICS OF MAPLES

paired seeds winged

75-100 ft.

SUGAR MAPLE

BLACK MAPLE

FLORIDA MAPLE

211

RED MAPLE *(Acer rubrum)* leaves are 2 to 6 inches across, with 3, or occasionally 5, roughly triangular, coarsely toothed lobes; turn scarlet in autumn. Leaf stems usually reddish. Red to yellow polygamous flowers, in short-stemmed clusters, appear before the leaves. The paired seeds have slightly divergent wings, 0.8 of an inch long; they ripen in late spring. The twigs are reddish, with blunt reddish buds. The smooth, light-gray bark of young trees develops narrow, scaly plates with age. Red Maple reaches 75 to 80 feet in height and 1 to 2 feet in diameter. This tree grows rapidly, especially in moist to swampy soils. It is commonly planted as an ornamental.

SILVER MAPLE *(Acer saccharinum)* leaves are 6 to 7 inches across and deeply 5-lobed, with large marginal teeth; silvery below. Clusters of short-stemmed, greenish-yellow polygamous flowers appear before the leaves in early spring and produce paired seeds with widely spread wings, 1.5 to 2 inches long. The seeds ripen in spring. The bark of young trees is smooth and silver-gray; bark of old trees is characterized by long, narrow scales loose at their ends, giving the trunk a "shaggy" appearance. Silver Maple, typical of moist soils, grows rapidly. It reaches a height of 60 to 80 feet and a diameter of 2 to 4 feet, with a widespread crown of brittle branches. Although this maple is planted as an ornamental, its leaves do not become highly colored in fall.

BIGTOOTH MAPLE *(Acer grandidentatum)* leaves are 2 to 5 inches in diameter and 3-lobed, with blunt teeth on their margins. Leaves turn red or yellow in fall. The flowers, appearing with the leaves, resemble Sugar Maple's. The U-shaped, paired, winged seeds of Bigtooth Maple are about an inch long. The thin, gray to brown bark may be smooth or scaly. This tree grows to 50 feet tall and 1 foot in diameter, with a spreading, rounded crown. It is usually found in moist soils along canyon streams.

CHALK MAPLE *(Acer leucoderme)* leaves are 2 to 3.5 inches in diameter with 3 (occasionally 5) blunt lobes, their margins wavy or with widely spaced, blunt teeth. The leaves are hairy below and often turn red in fall. The flowers resemble those of Sugar Maple, but the paired seeds have widely spread wings, 0.5 to 1 inch long. Chalk Maple's bark is smooth and chalky white. This maple grows to 25 feet tall.

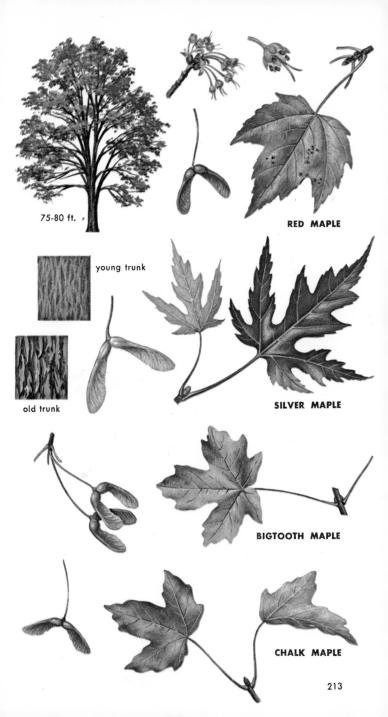

75-80 ft.

RED MAPLE

young trunk

old trunk

SILVER MAPLE

BIGTOOTH MAPLE

CHALK MAPLE

213

STRIPED MAPLE (*Acer pensylvanicum*) leaves are 5 to 6 inches long and 4 to 5 inches wide, with a rounded to heart-shaped base, and 3-lobed with doubly toothed margins. Turn yellow in fall. Bright-yellow flowers are borne in slender, drooping racemes 4 to 6 inches long, appearing when leaves are nearly grown; staminate and pistillate flowers are separate but on the same tree. Paired seeds have widely spread wings, about 0.8 to 1 inch long. Twigs and buds smooth. Bark smooth and green, with longitudinal, whitish stripes; later darker and warty. A shrub or small tree, to 40 feet tall, Striped Maple is common in cool, moist places.

MOUNTAIN MAPLE (*Acer spicatum*) leaves have 3 (occasionally 5) lobes with coarsely toothed margins. The yellow flowers are in erect racemes, with staminate above and pistillate below; they appear after the leaves and produce paired seeds with somewhat divergent wings, about 0.5 of an inch long; they are red in midsummer. Twigs and buds covered with fine "hairs." The thin bark is reddish brown. A shrub or small tree, to 30 feet tall. Mountain Maple is common in cool, moist places.

BIGLEAF MAPLE (*Acer macrophyllum*) leaves may be 12 inches in diameter, largest of any maple. The 5 deeply cut lobes have smooth margins, except for a few large, blunt teeth. In autumn, leaves turn yellow-brown. Pendant racemes of yellow, somewhat fragrant polygamous flowers appear with leaves. Paired seeds have slightly divergent wings, 1.5 to 2 inches long, with a densely brown-haired seed cavity; mature in fall. On young trees, bark is smooth, greenish brown; on old trees, black and deeply ridged. Grows to 100 feet tall, 4 feet in diameter. In open situations, trunk usually short, crown broad.

VINE MAPLE (*Acer circinatum*) leaves are 2 to 6 inches in diameter, with 7 to 9 pointed lobes having toothed margins. The leaves are usually tinged with red when they unfold; turn scarlet in fall. Loose clusters of purple-red polygamous flowers appear when leaves are about half grown. The paired, red seeds have widely divergent wings, 0.8 of an inch long. Ripen in fall. Usually a tall shrub with many supple stems; occasionally a small tree—to 40 feet tall and 1 foot in diameter. Bark smooth, greenish to reddish brown. Commonly forms dense thickets on logged-off land in Pacific Northwest. A favored browse food of deer.

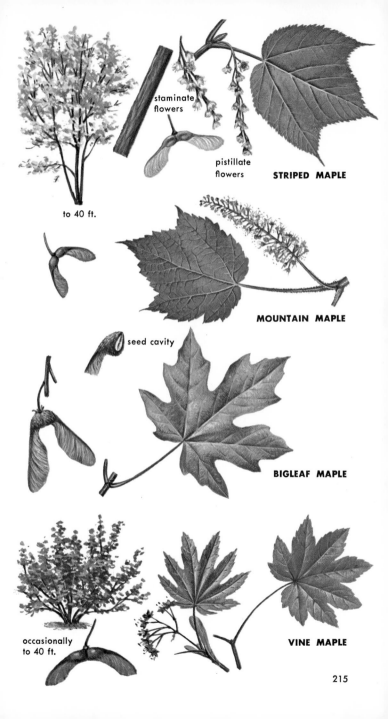

staminate flowers

pistillate flowers

STRIPED MAPLE

to 40 ft.

MOUNTAIN MAPLE

seed cavity

BIGLEAF MAPLE

occasionally to 40 ft.

VINE MAPLE

BOXELDER *(Acer negundo)*, with its several varieties, has pinnately compound leaves, 6 to 15 inches long, with 3 to 7 coarsely toothed or shallowly lobed leaflets. Greenish-yellow staminate and pistillate flowers are on separate trees, the staminate in drooping clusters and the pistillate in drooping racemes. V-shaped, winged seeds are 1.5 to 2 inches long, the clusters hanging on the branches through winter. On young trees, bark is gray-brown and slightly ridged; on old trees, heavily furrowed. Rapid-growing but short-lived, Boxelder reaches a height of 50 to 75 feet and a diameter of 2 to 4 feet. It prefers moist soils along streams, ponds, and lakes but is hardy on poor sites.

ROCKY MOUNTAIN MAPLE *(Acer glabrum)* resembles Vine Maple but has smaller leaves, 3 to 5 inches in diameter, with 3 to 5 lobes. The wings of its seeds are spread only slightly. Douglas Maple *(A. glabrum var. douglasii)* often grows with the more common Vine Maple in the Pacific Northwest.

SOME INTRODUCED MAPLES

NORWAY MAPLE *(Acer platanoides)* leaves resemble Sugar Maple's, but the stems exude a milky fluid when squeezed. Also, the clustered, long-stemmed, greenish-white flowers appear after the leaves, and the winged seeds, 1.5 to 2 inches long, are widely spread.

PLANETREE (SYCAMORE) MAPLE *(Acer pseudoplatanus)* grows to 90 feet tall, with a wide-spreading crown and scaly bark. Leaves are 3 to 7 inches in diameter, 5-lobed, and coarsely toothed. Greenish-yellow flowers, in pendant panicles 3 to 6 inches long, appear after leaves. Paired seeds have wings 1.3 to 2 inches long, spread widely to form a right angle.

FULLMOON MAPLE *(Acer japonicum)* has 7- to 11-lobed leaves, 2 to 5 inches in diameter, with sharply toothed margins and drooping clusters of purple flowers. Winged seeds spread in wide "V", 1.8 to 2 inches long. To 25 feet tall.

ENGLISH FIELD MAPLE *(Acer campestre)* is a small tree, to 30 feet tall, with a rounded crown. Its small leaves, 1 to 4 inches in diameter, have 3 to 5 blunt lobes with smooth margins or rounded marginal teeth. The greenish-white flowers are in clusters, and the winged seeds, 1 to 1.3 inches long, are spread wide, sometimes forming almost a straight line.

JAPANESE MAPLE *(Acer palmatum)* has deeply cleft leaves, 2 to 4 inches in diameter, with 5 to 9 narrow, pointed, toothed lobes. It bears erect clusters of purple flowers, producing widely spread winged seeds about 0.8 of an inch long. A shrub or small tree, to 25 feet tall.

AMUR MAPLE *(Acer ginnala)* has narrow, 3-lobed, toothed leaves. They are 1.5 to 3.5 inches long and 1.3 to 2.5 inches wide. Clusters of yellow flowers produce V-shaped, winged seeds about 1 inch long. A shrub or small tree, to 20 feet tall.

50-75 ft.

BOXELDER

ROCKY MOUNTAIN MAPLE

NORWAY MAPLE

PLANETREE MAPLE

ENGLISH FIELD MAPLE

JAPANESE MAPLE

FULLMOON MAPLE

AMUR MAPLE

217

HORSECHESTNUT (BUCKEYE) FAMILY
(Hippocastanaceae)

This family has but two genera, most important being the horse-chestnuts, or buckeyes, including about 20 species of trees and shrubs of North America, southeastern Europe, and Asia. Approximately one-third are native to the United States. All have opposite, palmately compound, deciduous leaves, the margins of the leaflets coarsely toothed. Large, showy, erect panicles of tubular or bell-shaped flowers develop after the leaves in the spring. Large, leathery capsules, 1 to 3 inches in diameter, are formed by fall. They split open when ripe and release the round, inedible seeds, 1 to 2 inches in diameter. Except for a large, lighter spot (hilum), they are a polished, dark chestnut brown.

The other genus in this family *(Billia)* includes two species of evergreen trees native to the area from Colombia north into Mexico.

YELLOW BUCKEYE *(Aesculus octandra)* leaves have 5 to 7 short-stemmed, obovate, pointed leaflets, each 4 to 6 inches long and 1.5 to 2.5 inches wide. The yellow flowers, hairy below and with stamens shorter than the petals, are borne in erect panicles, 5 to 7 inches long. The capsules, about 2 inches in diameter, are smooth on the surface and usually enclose two seeds, each about 1 to 1.5 inches in diameter. Brown bark is fissured and scaly. Grows 50 to 90 feet tall and 2 to 3 feet in diameter; crown oblong, rounded.

OHIO BUCKEYE *(Aesculus glabra)* resembles Yellow Buckeye but has narrower leaflets, stamens are longer than the petals, and surface of capsules is spiny. Also, leaves and twigs have an unpleasant odor when bruised. Texas Buckeye *(A. arguta),* once considered a variety, is similar to Ohio Buckeye.

PAINTED BUCKEYE *(Aesculus sylvatica)* leaves have 5 short-stemmed, oblong-obovate, pointed leaflets, each 4.5 to 6 inches long and 1.5 to 2.5 inches wide, with an orange midrib. Flowers are yellow, occasionally tinged with red, and hairless. Smooth-surfaced capsules usually contain only one seed. Painted Buckeye grows to 30 feet tall, 10 inches in diameter. It has brown, scaly bark.

RED BUCKEYE *(Aesculus pavia)* leaves have 5 short-stemmed, oblong-obovate leaflets, 4 to 5 inches long and 1.5 to 2 inches wide. Dark-red flowers produce smooth-surfaced capsules containing 1 to 2 seeds. A shrub or small tree, Red Buckeye grows to 25 feet tall; bark smooth, pale brown.

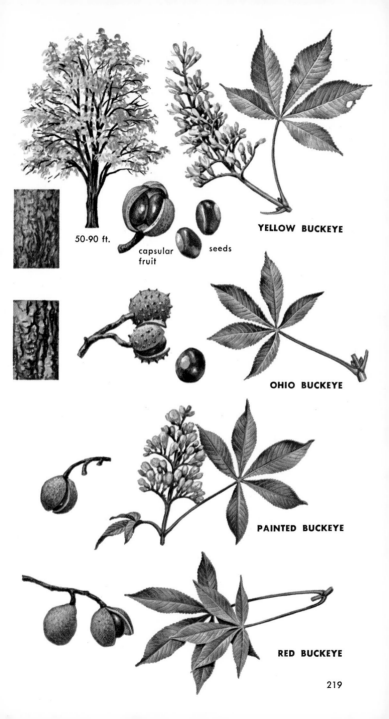

50-90 ft.

capsular
fruit

seeds

YELLOW BUCKEYE

OHIO BUCKEYE

PAINTED BUCKEYE

RED BUCKEYE

CALIFORNIA BUCKEYE *(Aesculus californica)* leaves have 4 to 7 (usually 5) distinctly stemmed, oblong-lanceolate leaflets. Each is 4 to 6 inches long and 1.5 to 2 inches wide. Trees growing in drier foothill regions usually lose their leaves early. White to pale-rose flowers are produced in panicles 5 to 10 inches long, and the pear-shaped, usually one-seeded capsules are 1.5 to 2 inches long and smooth-surfaced. California Buckeye may be a shrub or a small tree, to 40 feet tall and 8 inches in diameter. Its bark is smooth and light gray to brown.

AN INTRODUCED MEMBER OF BUCKEYE FAMILY

HORSECHESTNUT *(Aesculus hippocastanum)* leaves have 5 to 7 leaflets, each 4 to 10 inches long and 2 to 3.5 inches wide, distinctly widest near abruptly pointed apex. Creamy-white flowers are marked with red or yellow and are borne in erect panicles 8 to 12 inches long. Spiny capsules are 2.5 inches in diameter and contain 1 to 2 large seeds. Terminal bud large and sticky. Dark-brown bark is smooth or broken into irregular plates. A medium-sized to large tree, 25 to 60 feet tall, with rounded crown of wide-spreading branches. Horsechestnut is native to Asia and southeastern Europe; it is planted as a shade and street tree throughout central North America.

PAPAYA FAMILY (Caricaceae)

This is a small family of tropical and subtropical shrubs and trees. Best-known member is the Papaya, native from southern Florida southward into the tropics. Horticultural varieties are now widely planted in subtropical and tropical regions. The fruit is eaten raw or is processed to make juice. Papain, from the milky sap of stems and young fruit, is used as a meat tenderizer.

PAPAYA *(Carica papaya)* leaves are evergreen, 12 to 24 inches in diameter, palmately lobed, with pointed tips. The base is deeply heart-shaped, and the stout stems are 1 to 3 feet long, hollow, and enlarged at base. Staminate and pistillate flowers are borne in different clusters on separate trees or, less commonly, on the same tree. Staminate flowers are fragrant, with 5 spreading lobes at apex of narrow tube, clustered on long, many-flowered stalks; pistillate flowers tubular with separate petals, 1 to 3 on short stalks. Fruits melon-like, yellowish green to orange, about 4 inches long and 3 inches in diameter (much larger in horticultural forms), with a thick skin and sweet, whitish to orange flesh enclosing many dark seeds. Bruised twigs exude milky sap. Bark smooth, greenish gray. Papaya grows to 20 feet tall and 6 inches in diameter.

to 40 ft.

CALIFORNIA BUCKEYE

HORSECHESTNUT

pistillate flower

staminate flower

to 20 ft.

PAPAYA

221

BUCKTHORN FAMILY (Rhamnaceae)

Includes some 600 species of shrubs and small trees, largely tropical and subtropical. About 100 species in United States. In addition to the native species described here, Common Jujube (*Ziziphus jujube*), from Asia, Africa, and Australia, is grown as an ornamental in California and is naturalized in parts of the South.

CASCARA BUCKTHORN (*Rhamnus purshiana*) has usually alternate, broadly elliptical, deciduous leaves, 2 to 6 inches long and 1 to 2 inches wide; apex rounded or bluntly pointed, margins finely toothed and slightly curled under. Small clusters of tiny yellowish-green flowers occur in leaf axils. Black, globose, fleshy fruits, about 0.3 of an inch in diameter, contain several seeds. The bark is smooth and dark gray, often with cream-colored stripes; contains a drug used in laxatives. A small tree, to 40 feet tall. Birchleaf Buckthorn (*R. betulaefolia*) and the evergreen California Buckthorn (*R. californica* var. *ursina*), usually shrubs, grow in the Southwest.

CAROLINA BUCKTHORN (*Rhamnus caroliniana*) resembles Cascara Buckthorn but has tapered leaves and greenish-white flowers. The fruit has a drier flesh. The ash-gray bark is smooth to slightly furrowed, sometimes with dark markings. Carolina Buckthorn is a shrub or a small tree, growing to 30 feet tall.

LEADWOOD (*Krugiodendron ferreum*) has leathery, usually opposite, evergreen leaves, with smooth to wavy margins. They are broadly oval, notched at apex, and somewhat hairy above, 1 to 1.8 inches long and 0.5 to 1.5 inches wide. Clusters of 3 to 5 greenish-yellow flowers are in leaf axils. Fruit ovoid, black, about 0.3 of an inch long. Gray bark scaly, ridged. A shrub or small tree, to 30 feet tall, 10 inches in diameter. The wood of this species is the heaviest of any native tree.

DARLING-PLUM (*Reynosia septentrionalis*) leaves are evergreen, leathery, opposite, 1 to 1.5 inches long and 0.5 to 0.8 of an inch wide, usually oblong, with a notched or round, bristle-tipped apex. Greenish-yellow flowers, in small axillary clusters, produce dark-purple fruits, 0.5 of an inch long, with a pointed tip. Bark reddish brown and scaly; wood heavy. A shrub or small tree, to 25 feet tall and 9 inches in diameter.

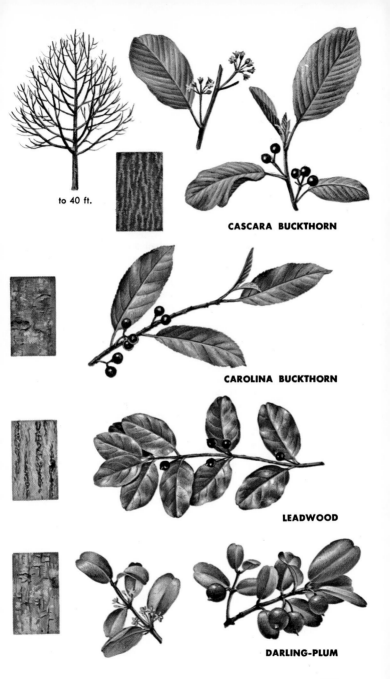

to 40 ft.

CASCARA BUCKTHORN

CAROLINA BUCKTHORN

LEADWOOD

DARLING-PLUM

223

SPINY CEANOTHUS *(Ceanothus spinosus)* has alternate, elliptical to oblong, evergreen leaves, about 1 inch long and 0.5 of an inch wide, with a stout midrib and pinnate venation. On young shoots, leaves are generally larger and .have three palmate veins. Blue, fragrant flowers, resembling lilacs, are borne in dense clusters 5 to 6 inches long. Bark greenish on branches and trunks of small trees; reddish brown on older trunks. A shrub or small tree, to 20 feet tall and about 6 inches in diameter, with a narrow, open crown of slender, angled branches, often with spiny tips.

BLUEBLOSSOM *(Ceanothus thyrsiflorus)* has alternate, oblong to oblong-ovate, evergreen leaves, 1 to 1.5 inches long, 0.5 to 1 inch wide, slightly hairy on underside; fine marginal teeth, 3 prominent palmate veins. Flowers, blue or occasionally white, in 2- to 3-inch axillary clusters. Fruits black, 3-lobed. A shrub or small tree, to 20 feet tall, 8 inches in diameter. Bark greenish on young trunks and branches; reddish brown on larger, older trunks.

FELTLEAF CEANOTHUS *(Ceanothus arboreus)* leaves are alternate, elliptical to broadly ovate, with rounded marginal teeth; dark green above, lighter and densely hairy below, prominently 3-veined; 2.3 to 4 inches long, 1 to 2.5 inches wide. Flowers pale blue, in dense axillary clusters 3 to 4 inches long, 1.5 to 2 inches wide. Black fruit, 0.3 of an inch in diameter. To 25 feet tall, 10 inches in diameter, with stout branches. Greenish bark becomes gray on older trunks.

SOLDIERWOOD *(Colubrina reclinata)* leaves are alternate, 2.5 to 3 inches long, 1.5 to 2 inches wide; elliptical to lanceolate; yellow-green with stout midrib; persist until second season. Yellow flowers in small axillary clusters. Capsules oval, dark orange-red, 3-valved, 0.3 of an inch in diameter. Thin, orange-brown bark peels off in large, papery scales, leaving light patches on trunk. To 60 feet tall, 4 inches in diameter. Coffee Colubrina *(C. arborescens),* found in same area, has leathery leaves hairy below.

SOME INTRODUCED BUCKTHORNS

GLOSSY BUCKTHORN *(Rhamnus frangula),* also from Europe, is generally a shrub. Twigs lack thorns but are somewhat hairy.

EUROPEAN BUCKTHORN *(Rhamnus cathartica)* is a shrub or small tree, resembling Cascara and Carolina buckthorns. Twigs often spiny.

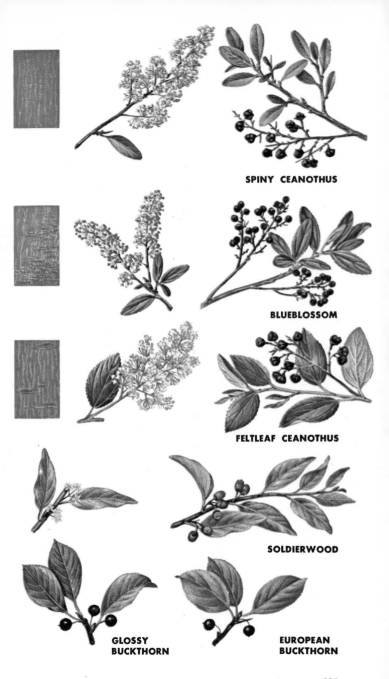

SPINY CEANOTHUS

BLUEBLOSSOM

FELTLEAF CEANOTHUS

SOLDIERWOOD

GLOSSY
BUCKTHORN

EUROPEAN
BUCKTHORN

CANELLA FAMILY (Canellaceae)

CANELLA *(Canella winterana)* leaves are evergreen, leathery, alternate, 3 to 5 inches long, 1 to 2 inches wide; apex rounded, margins smooth. White to purplish flowers, 0.1 of an inch in diameter, produce fleshy, bright-red berries, 0.5 of an inch in diameter, each with 2 to 4 seeds. Outer bark gray; yellow inner bark is source of commercial cinnamon. To 25 feet tall, 10 inches in diameter.

SOAPBERRY FAMILY (Sapindaceae)

This large family of trees and shrubs is primarily tropical. Chinese Lychee *(Litchi chinensis)*, from which lychee nuts are obtained, is a well-known foreign member of the family. Mexican-buckeye *(Ungnadia speciosa)* is a shrub or small tree ranging into Mexico.

WINGLEAF SOAPBERRY *(Sapindus saponaria)* leaves are evergreen, alternate, pinnately compound, 6 to 7 inches long. The 5 to 9 leathery leaflets (terminal leaflet sometimes lacking) are smooth-margined. Leaf stem winged between leaflets. Small, white flowers in panicles, to 12 inches long, appear in fall. Globular, orange-brown berries, 0.8 of an inch in diameter, have thin, juicy several-seeded flesh; when crushed, serves as a soap substitute. Bark gray, roughened, scaly. To 30 feet tall, 12 inches in diameter.

FLORIDA SOAPBERRY *(Sapindus marginatus)* resembles Wingleaf Soapberry but lacks winged leaf stems and has 7 to 13 leaflets, curved at pointed tips. Fruit keeled, yellow; bark ash gray. To 25 feet tall.

WESTERN SOAPBERRY *(Sapindus drummondii)* leaves are deciduous, even-pinnately compund; 8 to 18 leaflets 2 to 3 inches long, 0.3 to 0.8 of an inch wide, hairy below. Flower panicles 6 to 9 inches long. Yellow berries, 0.5 of an inch in diameter, turn black; may hang through winter. To 50 feet tall, 2 feet in diameter; bark scaly, reddish brown.

BUTTERBOUGH *(Exothea paniculata)* leaves are evergreen, alternate, pinnately compound, the 2 to 6 wavy-margined leaflets 4 to 6 inches long, 1.5 to 2 inches wide. Flowers white. Fleshy berry purple (occasionally orange), 0.5 of an inch long. Bark reddish brown, scaly. To 50 feet tall, 1 foot in diameter.

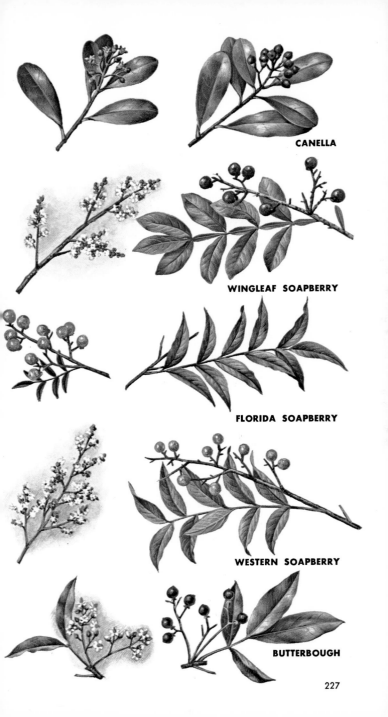

CANELLA

WINGLEAF SOAPBERRY

FLORIDA SOAPBERRY

WESTERN SOAPBERRY

BUTTERBOUGH

LINDEN FAMILY (Tiliaceae)

This family, consisting of over 40 genera with several hundred species of herbs, shrubs, and trees, is best represented in the tropics and regions south of the equator. One genus of trees—linden, or basswood *(Tilia)*—is widely distributed over parts of the Northern Hemisphere and includes four species native to eastern North America. They are distinctive for their simple, alternate, broadly ovate, deciduous leaves with coarsely toothed margins and unequally heart-shaped bases. The small clusters of creamy-white flowers develop later into nutlike fruits that hang on slender stalks attached to a narrow, leafy bract. Cordage was made from the tough inner bark by American Indians. An herbaceous Asiatic genus *(Corchorus)* is a source of jute, a widely used fiber.

AMERICAN BASSWOOD *(Tilia americana)* has the largest leaves, 5 to 6 inches long and 3 to 4 inches wide, of the native American lindens, or basswoods. The few-flowered clusters, each flower, 0.5 of an inch long, and the nutlike fruits, 0.3 of an inch in diameter, are attached to a leafy bract 4 to 5 inches long and 0.5 to 0.8 of an inch wide. On large trees the dark-gray bark is ridged and furrowed. American Basswood grows 60 to 80 feet tall and 2 to 3 feet in diameter. Its wood is light and strong. The tree is valued most as a shade and ornamental tree and for the flavor of honey from its flowers.

CAROLINA BASSWOOD *(Tilia caroliniana)* leaves are 3 to 4 inches long and 2.5 to 5 inches wide, often hairy-brown on the underside. The flower clusters contain 8 to 15 blossoms. The nutlike fruits, also covered with rust-colored hairs, are 0.1 of an inch long, smaller than American Basswood's.

FLORIDA BASSWOOD *(Tilia floridana)* is smaller than American Basswood, growing 50 feet tall and 15 inches in diameter. The leaves of Florida Basswood are 3 to 5 inches long and 2.5 to 3.5 inches wide, and silvery on their underside, especially in spring. They are not hairy when mature.

WHITE BASSWOOD *(Tilia heterophylla)* grows to 80 feet tall and 2.5 feet in diameter. The finely toothed leaves are 3.5 to 5 inches long and 2 to 3 inches wide; they are densely covered with white to brownish hairs on lower surfaces. Numerous (10-24) flowers are borne in each cluster. White Basswood's nutlike fruits are somewhat hairy.

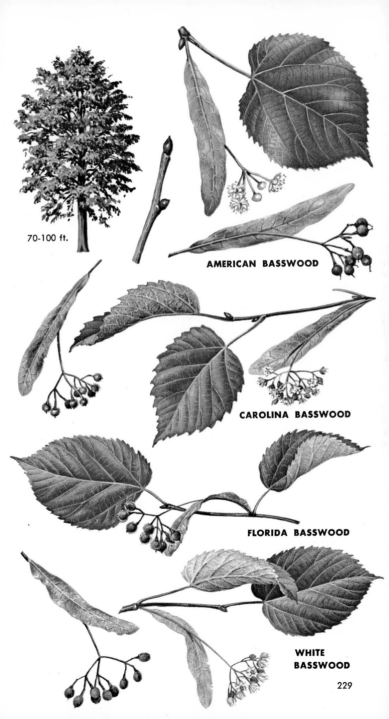

70-100 ft.

AMERICAN BASSWOOD

CAROLINA BASSWOOD

FLORIDA BASSWOOD

WHITE BASSWOOD

229

TEA FAMILY (Theaceae)

This family of several hundred species of largely evergreen trees includes the commercial tea plant (*Thea sinensis*) and also the camellias, prized ornamentals. The family is primarily Asiatic, but includes several small trees in southeastern United States, all with simple, alternate leaves. The rare Franklinia (*Franklinia alatamaha*) has not been recorded in nature since 1790, when it was found along the Georgia coast. It is believed to exist now only in cultivation.

LOBLOLLY-BAY (*Gordonia lasianthus*) has leathery, oblong to lanceolate, evergreen leaves, 4 to 6 inches long and 1.5 to 2 inches wide, with finely toothed margins; turn scarlet before falling. Long-stemmed, fragrant, white flowers, 2 to 2.5 inches in diameter, produce a hairy, ovoid, woody capsule, 0.8 of an inch long. Reddish-brown bark is broken into scaly ridges. Short-lived; to 70 feet tall, 20 inches in diameter.

MOUNTAIN STEWARTIA (*Stewartia ovata*) has elliptical to oblong, deciduous leaves, 2 to 5 inches long and 1 to 2.5 inches wide, with pointed tips and toothed, hairy margins. Flowers 4 inches in diameter; hairy capsule splits along 5 sutures. A shrub or small tree, to 25 feet tall. Virginia Stewartia (*S. malacodendron*) is less widely distributed, has smaller leaves.

CACTUS FAMILY (Cactaceae)

Cacti of more than 1,000 species grow largely in arid lands of the Western Hemisphere; a few range northward to British Columbia and southern New England. Most have leaves reduced to spines, photosynthesis occurring in the green, fleshy stems. Large, colorful flowers produced singly; fruit is a fleshy berry, edible in many species. Of native cacti in western North America, Saguaro and a few Mexican species are tree-sized with a single trunk. Organ-pipe Cactus, Senita, and others are tall but many-stemmed. Key West Cephalocereus (*Cephalocereus keyensis*) grows to tree size in the Florida Keys.

SAGUARO (*Cereus giganteus*) has clusters of gray spines, 0.5 to 2 inches long, on 12 to 30 prominent ridges around stout trunk. Funnel-shaped flowers, 4 to 4.5 inches long and 2 to 3 inches in diameter, occur at top of branches; open at night in May and June and have a melon-like odor. Red fruits, 2 to 3.5 inches long, are sweet, edible. Grows 25 to 50 feet tall, 1 to 3 feet in diameter.

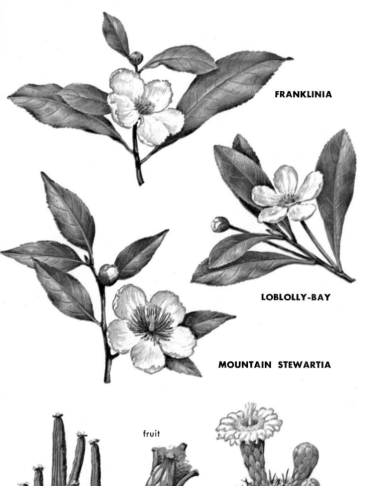

FRANKLINIA

LOBLOLLY-BAY

MOUNTAIN STEWARTIA

25-50 ft.

fruit

SAGUARO

MYRTLE FAMILY (Myrtaceae)

This family contains about 3,000 shrubs and trees native principally to the tropics and Australasia. Many are aromatic. A few species are native to Florida.

Eugenias spp.

EUGENIAS *(Eugenia spp.)* have simple, opposite, usually black-dotted, evergreen leaves; white flowers in axillary clusters and juicy, berry-like fruits. White-stopper Eugenia *(E. axillaris)* has leaves 1 to 3 inches long and 0.5 to 1 inch wide. The sweet, black fruits are 0.5 of an inch in diameter, and the tree's bark is light brown, ridged, and scaly. Grows to 30 feet tall and 1 foot in diameter, in sandy soil near tidewater. Red-berry Eugenia *(E. confusa)* is similar but larger, to 60 feet tall and 2 feet in diameter, with red fruits. Simpson Eugenia *(E. simpsonii)*, also with red fruit, may grow 50 feet tall and 1 foot in diameter. Twinberry Eugenia *(E. dicrana)* grows 25 feet tall and 8 inches in diameter and has reddish-brown, aromatic fruits. There are four other native species. Spiceberry Eugenia *(E. rhombea)*, common in the West Indies, and Bahama Eugenia *(E. bahamensis)* are rare, small trees. Small Eugenia *(E. anthera)* and Boxleaf Eugenia *(E. myrtoides)* are usually shrubs.

Lidflowers spp.

LIDFLOWERS *(Calyptranthes spp.)* have simple, opposite, evergreen leaves and clusters of small flowers lacking petals. Sepals capped in bud by a lidlike cover which is shed later. Fruits dry, berry-like, reddish-brown. Bark pale white, smooth to scaly. Pale Lidflower or Spicewood *(C. pallens)* is a shrub or small tree, to 25 feet tall, with leaves 2 to 3 inches long and 0.8 of an inch wide; fruits oblong. Myrtle-of-the-river *(C. zuzygium)* has smaller, elliptical leaves, nipple-like apex on floral lid, and globular fruits.

SOME INTRODUCED MEMBERS OF MYRTLE FAMILY

EUCALYPTUS *(Eucalyptus spp.)* is the most important genus in the myrtle family, with more than 500 species native to Australia. Many are grown in other parts of the world either for wood or as ornamentals. About 75 species have been introduced to California, including Red Ironbark *(E. sideroxylong)*, Manna Gum *(E. viminalis)*, and Bluegum *(E. globulus)*.

CAJEPUT-TREE *(Melaleuca quinquenervia)*, an Australian species, is grown in California and Florida where it has become naturalized. Bark thick, spongy.

COMMON GUAVA *(Psidium guajava)*, native to Central America, is widely planted in warm regions for its fruit but also grows as an escape. Bark is smooth.

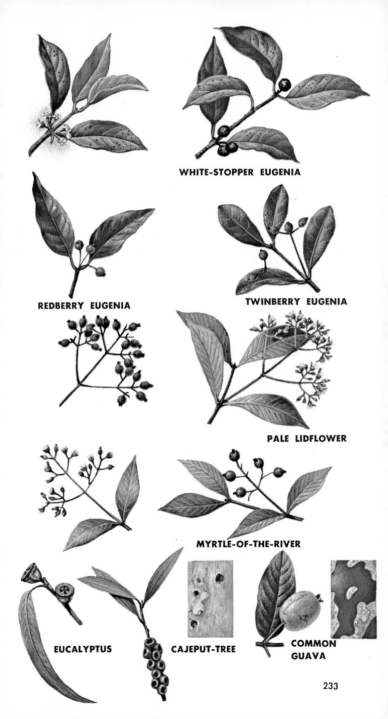

WHITE-STOPPER EUGENIA

REDBERRY EUGENIA

TWINBERRY EUGENIA

PALE LIDFLOWER

MYRTLE-OF-THE-RIVER

EUCALYPTUS

CAJEPUT-TREE

COMMON
GUAVA

233

MANGROVE FAMILY (Rhizophoraceae)

This tropical family includes about 60 species of evergreen trees and shrubs that form dense thickets in tidal creeks and estuaries. Soil and debris carried by the tides is washed into the network of stiltlike roots and becomes caught there. Over many years this process slowly extends the shoreline. Mangrove seeds germinate while still attached to the tree. Upon dropping, they float until contacting mud, then begin growth immediately. Bark yields tannin; the wood, charcoal. Commonly associated with Black-Mangrove (p. 262.)

RED MANGROVE *(Rhizophora mangle)* leaves are leathery, simple, opposite, ovate to elliptical, 3 to 5 inches long and 1 to 2 inches wide. Flowers are pale yellow, 1 inch in diameter and clustered. Fruit is a roughened, conical, rusty-brown berry about 1 inch long, with a short apical tube through which the dartlike radicle of the developing embryo protrudes, becoming 6 to 12 inches long. Bark gray to gray-brown, thick, scaly, and furrowed. Rarely over 20 feet tall in Florida; to 80 feet tall and 2 feet in diameter in tropics.

COMBRETUM (WHITE-MANGROVE) FAMILY (Combretaceae)

Species in this primarily tropical family have leathery, evergreen leaves. Many grow in tidewater flats. Oxhorn Bucida *(Bucida buceras)* has limited distribution in the Florida Keys. Indian-Almond *(Terminalia catappa)* is naturalized in southern Florida.

BUTTON-MANGROVE *(Conocarpus erectus)* leaves are simple, alternate, 2 to 4 inches long and 0.5 to 1.5 inches wide, with smooth margins and a pointed apex. Flowers in dense, globular heads, about 0.3 of an inch in diameter, on panicles 3 to 10 inches long. Tiny, leathery, reddish fruits in conelike heads about 1 inch in diameter. Bark brown to black, in scaly ridges. A shrub or tree, Button-mangrove grows to 60 feet tall and 2 feet in diameter.

WHITE-MANGROVE *(Laguncularia racemosa)* has simple, opposite leaves, 1 to 3 inches long and 1 to 1.5 inches wide, with a rounded or notched apex, red petioles, and glandular swellings along margin. Greenish-white flowers borne in 1.5- to 2-inch spikes. Fruit about 0.5 inch long, 10-ribbed, obovoid, leathery, reddish brown. Bark reddish brown, ridged, and scaly. A sprawling shrub in Florida, but may grow 60 feet tall in parts of the tropics.

to 20 ft.

RED MANGROVE

mature fruit

BUTTON-MANGROVE

WHITE-MANGROVE

235

DOGWOOD FAMILY (Cornaceae)

About 100 species, found primarily in the temperate regions, constitute the dogwood family. Two genera represented in the United States and Canada. Dogwoods (*Cornus*), the most familiar, include the diminutive Bunchberry (*C. canadensis*), a small herbaceous plant of spongy forest soils, and three species that are usually shrubs but sometimes reach tree size—two western species, Western Dogwood (*C. occidentalis*) and Blackfruit Dogwood (*C. sessilis*); and one eastern, Stiffcornel Dogwood (*C. stricta*). Wavyleaf Silktassel (*Garrya elliptica*) is a shrub or rarely a small tree on the Pacific coast.

FLOWERING DOGWOOD (*Cornus florida*) has simple, opposite, deciduous leaves, 3 to 6 inches long and 1.5 to 2 inches wide, usually oval with a pointed apex and with primary veins curving upward along smooth, wavy margins. Scarlet in fall. Small, greenish-white flowers are in compact heads, surrounded by four large, white (occasionally pink or rose), petal-like bracts, notched at apex. Clusters often erroneously considered to be single flowers. Bright-red, ovoid fruits, about 0.5 of an inch long and 0.3 of an inch in diameter, also clustered. Smooth, dark-brown to black bark of young trees breaks up into small, scaly blocks at maturity. Flowering Dogwood, often cultivated as an ornamental, grows 15 to 40 feet tall, 6 to 18 inches in diameter. It has a rounded, rather bushy crown and hard, heavy wood. Prefers moist, rich soils.

ALTERNATE-LEAF DOGWOOD (*Cornus alternifolia*) leaves resemble those of other dogwoods but are alternate. White flowers, in loose, flat-topped clusters (cymes), rather than heads. Fruits deep blue to black, 0.3 of an inch in diameter. Bark of young trees is dark reddish brown, smooth; on older trees, fissured. Alternate-leaf Dogwood is a shrub or small tree, growing to 30 feet tall and 8 inches in diameter. It has a broad, flattened crown.

ROUGHLEAF DOGWOOD (*Cornus drummondii*) has opposite leaves, rough above and woolly below. Flowers and fruit white, in open clusters. A shrub or small tree.

RED-OSIER DOGWOOD (*Cornus stolonifera*) resembles Roughleaf Dogwood but has reddish twigs. Usually a shrub, rarely growing to small-tree size. It commonly occurs along watercourses and in similar moist locations.

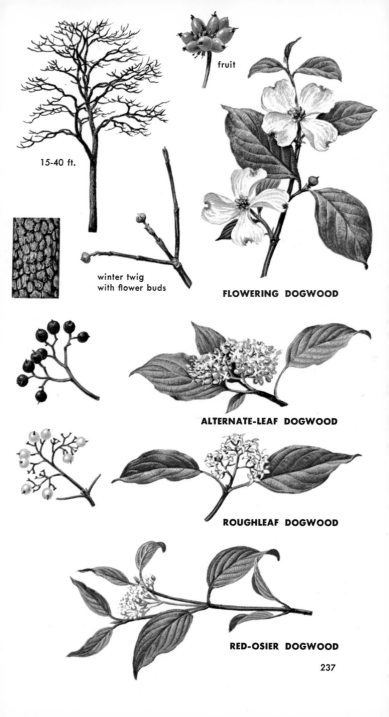

fruit

15-40 ft.

winter twig
with flower buds

FLOWERING DOGWOOD

ALTERNATE-LEAF DOGWOOD

ROUGHLEAF DOGWOOD

RED-OSIER DOGWOOD

237

PACIFIC DOGWOOD (*Cornus nuttallii*) leaves resemble Flowering Dogwood's but are larger and more ovate, 4 to 6 inches long and 1.5 to 3 inches wide. Greenish-white flowers, in larger heads, are surrounded by 4 to 6 bracts, not notched at apex; bright-red, ellipsoidal fruits in larger clusters. Dark-brown to black bark normally smooth, but breaks into scaly plates at base of large trees. Medium-sized to 60 feet tall and 2 feet in diameter, with a narrow, pyramidal crown. Pacific Dogwood grows at low elevations in shaded, coniferous forests. It is a popular ornamental.

TUPELO FAMILY (Nyssaceae)

Ten species in three genera make up this small family, closely related to dogwood family. Represented in North America only by tupelos, or black gums (*Nyssa*). The two other genera in the tupelo family occur in eastern Asia.

BLACK TUPELO (*Nyssa sylvatica*) has simple, alternate, usually obovate, deciduous leaves, 2 to 5 inches long and 1 to 3 inches wide, with smooth margins. Leaves are often clustered near ends of lateral branches; turn scarlet in fall. Small, greenish flowers are on separate stalks—the staminate in dense clusters and the pistillate few-flowered. Dark-blue, ovoid fruit, about 0.5 of an inch long, has thin flesh surrounding indistinctly ribbed seed. Bark is gray-brown and commonly in small, rectangular blocks. Young twigs greenish yellow, becoming gray to reddish brown. Grows 60 to 90 feet tall, 2 to 3 feet in diameter, mainly in moist soils.

WATER TUPELO (*Nyssa aquatica*) is similar to Black Tupelo but has larger leaves, 5 to 7 inches long and 2 to 4 inches wide, margins occasionally toothed. Fruit 1 inch long, the seed more prominently ribbed. Grows best in swampy situations, usually standing in water several feet deep during wet season. Base of trunk is usually swollen or buttressed, similar to Bald-cypress (p. 52).

OGEECHEE TUPELO (*Nyssa ogeche*) resembles Water Tupelo but differs in having less sharply pointed leaves and short-stalked, red fruits, 1 to 1.5 inches long. Seed has winglike ribs. Usually a shrub, occasionally a small tree. Bear Tupelo (*Nyssa ursina*), also most commonly a shrub, grows in northwestern Florida.

winter twig
with flower bud

fruit

PACIFIC DOGWOOD

60-90 ft.

BLACK TUPELO

WATER TUPELO

OGEECHEE TUPELO

239

HEATH FAMILY (Ericaceae)

Members of the heath family, more than 1,500 species, grow in acid soils in temperate regions throughout the world. All have simple and, in most, alternate leaves. Most are shrubs. Blueberries, cranberries, rhododendrons, and heathers are among the great variety of familiar plants in this family.

PACIFIC MADRONE (*Arbutus menziesii*) leaves are evergreen, leathery, oval to oblong, 3 to 6 inches long and 2 to 3 inches wide. The white, urn-shaped flowers, 0.3 of an inch long, are in drooping panicles 5 to 6 inches long. Fruits are orange or red, mealy, and berry-like, about 0.5 of an inch in diameter. Reddish-brown bark peels into thin, irregular sections exposing greenish-brown inner bark; scaly at base of large trees. To 100 feet tall and 4 feet in diameter, with varied form.

TEXAS MADRONE (*Arbutus texana*) leaves are evergreen, oval to lanceolate, 1 to 3 inches long and 0.8 to 1.5 inches wide. The flower clusters are 2.5 inches long, and the dark-red fruits are 0.3 of an inch in diameter. The bark is reddish brown. A rare tree with a crooked trunk, Texas Madrone grows about 20 feet tall and 10 inches in diameter, in dry soils.

ARIZONA MADRONE (*Arbutus arizonica*) resembles Texas Madrone in form, size, habitat, and size of flower and orange-red fruit clusters. But the evergreen leaves are lanceolate, 1.5 to 3 inches long and 0.5 to 1 inch wide. On trunks of older trees the bark is ash gray and scaly.

SOURWOOD (*Oxydendrum arboreum*) leaves are simple, alternate, elliptical, 5 to 7 inches long and 1 to 3 inches wide, margins finely toothed; turn scarlet. White, urn-shaped flowers, about 0.3 of an inch long, are in 1-sided, clustered racemes. Fruits are 5-angled, gray capsules. Bark gray, tinged with red; scaly and furrowed at base. Sourwood occasionally grows to 60 feet tall but is usually smaller.

TREE LYONIA (*Lyonia ferruginea*) has leathery, evergreen leaves, 1 to 3 inches long and about 1 inch wide, usually tipped with a stiff point. White, globular flowers, 0.1 of an inch in diameter, are in small, axillary clusters. The fruit is a light-brown capsule about 0.5 of an inch long. Bark on twisted trunk reddish brown, scaly, and ridged. A shrub or small tree, to 30 feet tall and 10 inches in diameter.

to 100 ft.

PACIFIC MADRONE

TEXAS MADRONE

ARIZONA MADRONE

SOURWOOD

TREE LYONIA

241

PACIFIC RHODODENDRON (*Rhododendron macrophyllum*) has oblong, leathery, evergreen leaves, 3 to 10 inches long, 1.5 to 2.5 inches wide, with smooth margins that are characteristically turned under. The flowers, 1.5 inches long, are white to pink, trumpet-shaped, and in compact clusters about 5 inches in diameter at ends of branches. The fruits are reddish-brown capsules about 0.5 of an inch long. Bark reddish brown. Usually a shrub, rarely to 25 feet.

ROSEBAY RHODODENDRON (*Rhododendron maximum*) resembles Pacific Rhododendron but has oval to obovate leaves, 4 to 12 inches long, 1.5 to 2.5 inches wide, often whitish below. Fruits slim, sticky. Usually a sprawling, twisted shrub, forming dense thickets. Rarely to 40 feet tall, 1 foot in diameter. Catawba Rhododendron (*R. catawbiense*), more southern and not as tall, has broader leaves and light-purple flowers.

ELLIOTTIA (*Elliottia racemosa*) leaves are deciduous, ovate to oblong, 3 to 4 inches long, 1 to 2 inches wide, with smooth margins, hairy below. White flowers, with 4 narrow petals, are in erect, terminal panicles. Fruit is a dry, 4-celled (rarely 3 or 5), globular capsule, about 0.3 of an inch in diameter. Bark smooth, gray-brown. A rare shrub or small tree, to 20 feet tall, 6 inches in diameter.

MOUNTAIN-LAUREL (*Kalmia latifolia*) has leathery elliptical to lanceolate, evergreen leaves, 3 to 4 inches long and 1 to 1.5 inches wide, alternate or in whorls. Deep pink to white, starlike flowers nearly 1 inch in diameter occur in compact clusters at ends of branches. Each produces a 5-celled capsule about 0.5 of an inch in diameter and ending in a slender style. Grows in moist soils, commonly forming thickets. Usually a shrub, rarely reaches a height of 30 feet and a diameter of 1 foot. Bark reddish brown and scaly.

TREE SPARKLEBERRY (*Vaccinium arboreum*) leaves are deciduous in North but persistent in South, oval to oblong, 1 to 3 inches long, 1 inch wide. Bell-shaped white flowers in axillary racemes produce tart, shiny, black, globular berries about 0.3 of an inch in diameter. Bark dark brown, ridged, and shreddy. Tree Sparkleberry is a sprawling shrub or small, crooked tree, growing to 30 feet tall and 10 inches in diameter.

25 ft.
(rare)

PACIFIC RHODODENDRON

ROSEBAY
RHODODENDRON

ELLIOTTIA

MOUNTAIN-LAUREL

TREE SPARKLEBERRY

GINSENG FAMILY (Araliaceae)

DEVILS-WALKINGSTICK *(Aralia spinosa)* has alternate, odd-bipinnately compound, deciduous leaves, 2 to 4 feet long and 2 to 3 feet wide, with spiny stalks. Each leaflet has a terminal and several pairs of opposite, ovate subleaflets, with a tapered apex and toothed margins, 2 to 4 inches long and 1.5 inches wide; midvein often spiny below. Small, white flowers in compound, terminal clusters, to 4 feet long, with yellowish stems. Fruit black, berry-like, and juicy, 0.3 of an inch in diameter. Coarse twigs bear stout spines. Bark brown, ridged, furrowed; inner bark yellow. Grows rapidly, to 30 feet tall and 10 inches in diameter, usually in moist soils.

MELASTOME (MEADOW BEAUTY) FAMILY (Melastomataceae)

FLORIDA TETRAZYGIA *(Tetrazygia bicolor)* has simple, opposite, lanceolate, evergreen leaves, 3 to 5 inches long, 1 to 2 inches wide. Dark green above, paler below, with 3 main veins and smooth, thickened, rolled-under margin. White flowers, 0.8 of an inch in diameter, in loose, terminal panicles. Ovoid, purplish fruits, 0.3 of an inch long, constricted at apex. Usually a shrub, Florida Tetrazygia occasionally grows to 30 feet tall and 4 inches in diameter.

MYRSINE FAMILY (Myrsinaceae)

MARBLEBERRY *(Ardisia escallonioides)* is a shrub or small tree, to 25 feet tall, with gray to pinkish bark. Leathery, evergreen leaves are simple, alternate, ovate to obovate, 3 to 6 inches long, 1 to 2 inches wide, with many dark dots on undersurface. Fragrant, starlike flowers have 5 petals dotted with red on inner surface; in rusty-haired panicles, to 5 inches long. Shiny-black fruit is round, 0.3 of an inch in diameter, with a sharp point and dotted with resin. Flesh thin and dry.

GUIANA RAPANEA *(Rapanea guianensis)* has leathery, simple, alternate, oblong to obovate, evergreen leaves, 2 to 4 inches long and 1 to 2 inches wide, notched at apex. Usually crowded near ends of branches. Small axillary clusters of white flowers, about 0.1 of an inch in diameter, are marked with purple; produce globular, dark-blue or black fruit, about 0.2 of an inch in diameter, with pointed apex. A shrub or small tree, to 25 feet tall, with smooth, gray bark.

DEVILS-WALKINGSTICK

FLORIDA TETRAZYGIA

MARBLEBERRY

**GUIANA
RAPANEA**

SAPOTE (SAPODILLA) FAMILY (Sapotaceae)

This family of about 500 species of tropical trees and shrubs includes the Central American Sapota, or Sapodilla (*Achras zapota*), from which chicle for chewing gum is obtained. The fruit is also delicious. Sapodillas grow wild in extreme southern Florida and on the Keys. Gutta percha, a gum, is derived from sap of species from southeastern Asia; other members of the family provide cabinet woods, oils, and other useful products. Only a few species, none of commercial importance, occur in temperate North America.

BUMELIAS (*Bumelia* spp.) of four tree-sized species are native to southeastern United States.

Gum Bumelia (*B. lanuginosa*) is a small, narrow-crowned tree, to 40 feet tall and 2 feet in diameter. Simple, ovate to oblong, evergreen leaves are alternate, appearing whorled; 1 to 3 inches long, 1 inch wide, with silvery or rust-brown hairs below. Most have blunt or rounded tips, some pointed. Small white flowers, clustered in leaf axils, produce black fruits about 0.5 of an inch long. Bark dark gray to black, scaly, and fissured.

Tough Bumelia (*B. tenax*), similar but smaller, has shiny, reddish-yellow hairs under leaves and on twigs, which often bear inch-long spines.

Saffron-plum (*B. celastrina*) leaves are 1 to 1.5 inches long and 0.3 to 1 inch wide. The black fruits are nearly an inch long.

Buckthorn Bumelia (*B. lycioides*) has deciduous leaves, 3 to 6 inches long and 0.5 to 2 inches wide. Black fruit about 0.8 of an inch long; twigs have curved spines.

FALSE-MASTIC (*Sideroxylon foetidissimum*), a medium-sized tree with an irregular crown, has simple, alternate, oval, evergreen leaves, 3 to 5 inches long and 1 to 2 inches wide. Tiny, yellow flowers in small, axillary clusters; inch-long, yellow, berry-like fruit has a thick, juicy flesh. Bark reddish brown and scaly.

WILLOW BUSTIC (*Dipholis salicifolia*) has simple, alternate, oblong to lanceolate, evergreen leaves, 3 to 5 inches long, 1 to 2 inches wide. Tiny, white flowers borne in small clusters, usually in leaf axils, have sepals covered with rusty-brown, silky hairs. Globular, leathery, black fruits are 0.3 of an inch in diameter. Bark reddish brown, scaly. Grows 50 feet tall and 18 inches in diameter, with a narrow, graceful crown.

GUM BUMELIA

SAFFRON-PLUM

TOUGH BUMELIA

BUCKTHORN BUMELIA

FALSE-MASTIC

WILLOW BUSTIC

SATINLEAF *(Chrysophyllum oliviforme)* has simple, alternate, oval, leathery, evergreen leaves, 2 to 3 inches long and 1 to 2 inches wide; shiny, coppery hairs make undersurface like suede. The small, white flowers in axillary clusters produce dark-purple, juicy berries 0.8 of an inch long. Reddish-brown bark is scaly. A shrub or small tree, Satinleaf grows to 30 feet tall, 1 foot in diameter.

WILD-DILLY *(Achras emarginata)* has simple, alternate, oblong to obovate, leathery, evergreen leaves, clustered at ends of twigs. They are 3 to 4 inches long and 1 to 2 inches wide, waxy above and covered with brown hairs below. Light-yellow flowers, clustered in leaf axils on slender, reddish, hairy stems. Fleshy fruit (berries), 1.5 inches in diameter, have a thick, brown, scaly skin. Each contains one seed surrounded by soft flesh with milky juice. Bark gray to reddish brown, scaly, fissured. To 40 feet tall, 18 inches in diameter, with a short, gnarled trunk.

THEOPHRASTA (JOEWOOD) FAMILY
(Theophrastaceae)

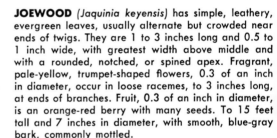

JOEWOOD *(Jaquinia keyensis)* has simple, leathery, evergreen leaves, usually alternate but crowded near ends of twigs. They are 1 to 3 inches long and 0.5 to 1 inch wide, with greatest width above middle and with a rounded, notched, or spined apex. Fragrant, pale-yellow, trumpet-shaped flowers, 0.3 of an inch in diameter, occur in loose racemes, to 3 inches long, at ends of branches. Fruit, 0.3 of an inch in diameter, is an orange-red berry with many seeds. To 15 feet tall and 7 inches in diameter, with smooth, blue-gray bark, commonly mottled.

SWEETLEAF FAMILY (Symplocaceae)

The one genus in this family contains about 300 species of shrubs and small trees, one of them native to southeastern United States. Others occur in the West Indies, Asia, and Australia.

COMMON SWEETLEAF *(Symplocos tinctoria)* has simple, alternate, oblong, leathery leaves, 5 to 6 inches long and 1 to 2 inches wide, with wavy margins. Leaves remain on tree most of year. White, fragrant flowers, 0.3 to 0.5 of an inch long, occur in clusters on silky stalks. Dry, brown, ovoid fruit is 0.5 of an inch long. Bark ash gray, with corky tubercles. A shrub or small tree, to 35 feet tall, 6 inches in diameter.

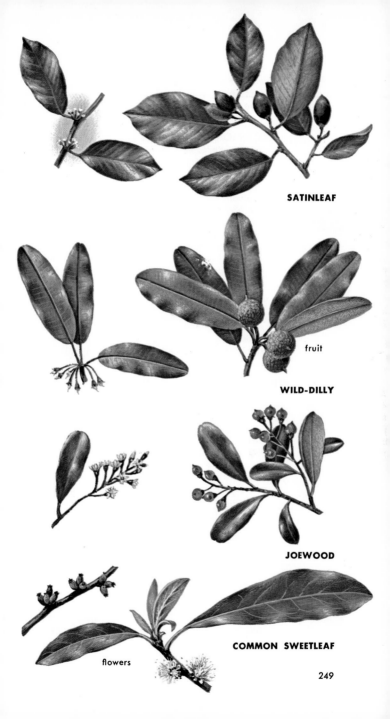

SATINLEAF

WILD-DILLY

fruit

JOEWOOD

COMMON SWEETLEAF

flowers

EBONY FAMILY (Ebenaceae)

Most of the more than 300 species in this family grow in the tropics and subtropics. The most famous is Ebony (Diospyros ebenum), a native of southeastern Asia; it provides the hard black wood used for piano keys and fine furniture.

COMMON PERSIMMON (Diospyros virginiana) has simple, alternate, ovate-oblong, deciduous leaves, 4 to 6 inches long and 2 to 3 inches wide and with smooth margins. Small staminate and pistillate flowers are on twigs of the current year on separate trees; the staminate in few-flowered clusters, the pistillate solitary. The fruit is orange to reddish purple and several-seeded, about 1.5 inches in diameter; astringent when green but sweet and edible when ripe. Bark is almost black, broken into small, rectangular blocks. The Common Persimmon grows to 60 feet tall and 2 feet in diameter, with a divided trunk and broad, rounded crown. It attains its best growth in moist, rich soils.

TEXAS PERSIMMON (Diospyros texana) resembles the Common Persimmon in form but has smaller, obovate leaves, with a rounded apex, hairy below. The flowers are on twigs of the previous season, the smaller fruit is black, and the bark is gray and scaly.

SNOWBELL (STORAX) FAMILY (Styracaceae)

Includes over 100 species of trees and shrubs native to North and South America, eastern Asia, the Malay Archipelago, and the Mediterranean region. Many have attractive flowers.

BIGLEAF SNOWBELL (Styrax grandifolia) has simple, alternate, obovate, deciduous leaves, 2.5 to 5 inches long, 1 to 3 inches wide; margins finely toothed or smooth; veins hairy below. White, 5-lobed, bell-shaped flowers, to 1 inch long, in axillary racemes to 6 inches long. The fruit is dry, oval, and 0.3 of an inch long. Bigleaf Snowbell grows to 40 feet tall and 8 inches in diameter.

Silverbells spp.

SILVERBELLS (Halesia spp.) are three species of deciduous shrubs or small trees. Leaves alternate, oblong to elliptical, hairy below, with toothed margins. Flowers showy, white, bell-shaped, to 2 inches long. Carolina Silverbell (H. carolina) has 4-winged, nut-like fruit; Two-wing Silverbell (H. diptera), 2-winged. Little Silverbell (H. parviflora), usually a shrub, has small flowers. The 4-winged fruit is club-shaped.

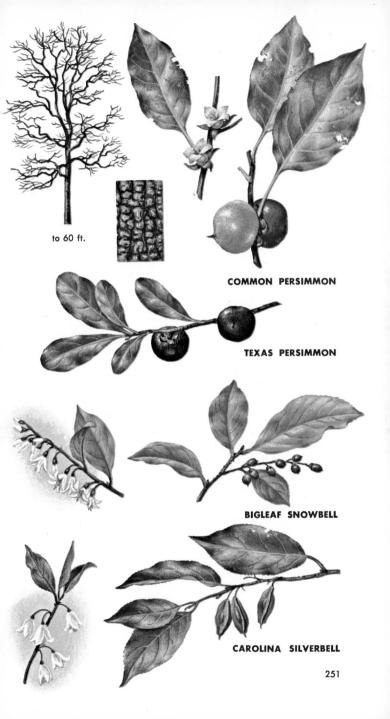

to 60 ft.

COMMON PERSIMMON

TEXAS PERSIMMON

BIGLEAF SNOWBELL

CAROLINA SILVERBELL

251

OLIVE FAMILY (Oleaceae)

This family, mainly of the Northern Hemisphere includes about 500 species of shrubs and trees. Olives and olive oil are provided by *Olea europa,* native to the Mediterranean Basin but now cultivated widely. Ashes *(Fraxinus)* and others are the source of timber. Lilac *(Syringa),* forsythia *(Forsythia),* jasmine *(Jasminum),* and privet *(Ligustrum),* well-known shrubs of the olive family, are widely used as ornamentals.

FRINGETREE *(Chionanthus virginicus)* leaves are deciduous, simple, opposite, ovate-oblong, 4 to 8 inches long and 0.5 to 4 inches wide; margins smooth to wavy, veins hairy beneath. Fragrant flowers, with 4 to 6 narrow, white petals, about 1 inch long, borne in clusters, 4 to 6 inches long; flowers dioecious or, rarely, perfect. Dark-purple, oval fruits, about 1 inch long, have thin, dry flesh enclosing one seed (occasionally 2 or 3). The fruit is sometimes covered with a white, powdery wax. Bark brown, scaly. A shrub or small tree, Fringetree grows to 30 feet tall and 1 foot in diameter, with a narrow, oblong crown. Planted as an ornamental.

DEVILWOOD *(Osmanthus americanus)* has simple, opposite, oblong-lanceolate, leathery, evergreen leaves, 4 to 5 inches long and 1 to 1.5 inches wide, with smooth, somewhat curled margins. Small, creamy-white flowers (perfect and unisexual on different plants) in axillary clusters. Fruit oval, dark blue, about 1 inch long, with a thin, fleshy covering over single seed. Bark gray-brown, scaly. A shrub or small, narrow-crowned tree, to 70 feet tall, 1 foot in diameter. Bigfruit Osmanthus *(O. megacarpus),* also a southern species, has plumper, greenish-yellow fruit, larger leaves, and hairy flower stems.

SWAMP-PRIVET *(Forestiera acuminata)* leaves are deciduous, simple, opposite, elliptical, 2 to 4 inches long and 1 to 1.5 inches wide, with small, widely spaced teeth above middle. Dioecious; small clusters of pistillate and yellowish-green staminate flowers, lacking petals, appear before leaves. Fruit is dark purple, narrowly oblong, 1 to 1.3 inches long, with thin, dry flesh enclosing one seed. Bark dark brown, ridged. Swamp-privet is a shrub or small tree, to 25 feet tall, usually in moist soils. Texas Forestiera *(F. texana),* Florida-privet *(F. segregata),* and Desert-olive Forestiera *(F. phillyreoides),* also shrubs, occur in southern United States.

FRINGETREE

DEVILWOOD

SWAMP-PRIVET

ASHES *(Fraxinus)*

Approximately 65 species of trees and shrubs belong to the genus *Fraxinus* in the olive family. Largely confined to temperate regions of Northern Hemisphere, but a few occur in the tropics. In addition to trees described here, four small trees, usually shrubby, grow in southwestern U.S. southward into Mexico—Berlandier Ash *(F. berlandieriana)*, Two-petal Ash *(F. dipetala)*, Goodding Ash *(F. gooddingii)*, and Chihuahua Ash *(F. papillosa)*.

Ashes are easily recognized as a group, but species are difficult to distinguish. Leaves are deciduous, opposite, and, with few exceptions, odd-pinnately compound. Some species are dioecious; others have polygamous or perfect flowers in clusters (panicles), appearing before or with the leaves. Flowers of most North American species lack petals; one has flowers with showy white petals. Fruit is a samara, with single terminal wing. In winter, naked twigs have blunt buds (terminal larger than lateral) with 1 to 3 pairs of exposed scales. In most species, the leaf scars are notched and half-round, with an elliptical line of tiny, vascular bundle scars.

WHITE ASH *(Fraxinus americana)* leaves are 8 to 12 inches long, usually with 7 (sometimes 5 to 13) oval to oblong-lanceolate leaflets, 3 to 5 inches long and 1.5 to 3 inches wide; margins smooth or finely toothed, essentially glabrous below. Stems of leaflets are very long and slender. Dioecious, flowers appearing before leaves. Samaras 1 to 2 inches long, with wing extending only part way along seed. Twigs round, usually not hairy, with half-round, notched leaf scars. White Ash has gray bark, with diamond-shaped ridges appearing on the trunks of older trees. To 80 feet tall, 3 feet in diameter.

GREEN ASH *(Fraxinus pennsylvanica)* resembles White Ash but has slightly smaller leaves, 6 to 9 inches long, with leaflets 3 to 4 inches long and 1 to 1.5 inches wide. Margins of the leaflets are toothed above the middle. The underside of the leaflets may be smooth to hairy. In addition, the dioecious flowers of Green Ash appear after the leaves have begun to unfold.

PUMPKIN ASH *(Fraxinus profunda)* has leaves 9 to 18 inches long. The lanceolate to elliptical, usually smooth-margined leaflets are 5 to 8 inches long and 1.5 to 4 inches wide; they are hairy below, especially on midribs and veins. Leaf stems and twigs also hairy. Pumpkin Ash samaras are 2 to 3 inches long and 0.5 of an inch wide, with the wing extending below the middle of the seed.

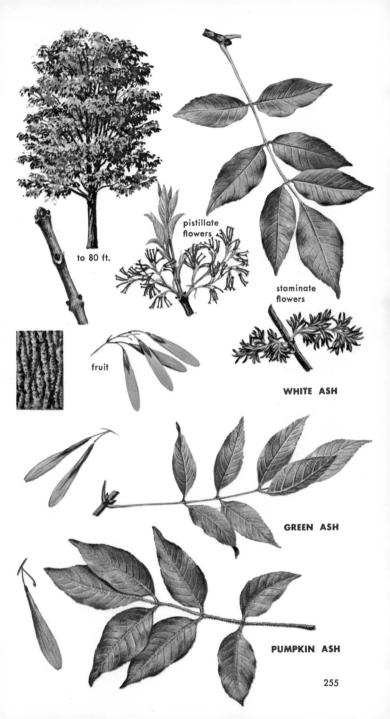

to 80 ft.

pistillate flowers

staminate flowers

fruit

WHITE ASH

GREEN ASH

PUMPKIN ASH

BLACK ASH *(Fraxinus nigra)* leaves are 12 to 16 inches long. They have 9 (sometimes 7 to 13) stemless, oblong to oblong-lanceolate leaflets, 4 to 5 inches long and 1.5 inches wide, with finely toothed margins; essentially glabrous below. Polygamous flowers appear before the leaves. Samaras are oblong to elliptical, 1 to 1.8 inches long, with a thin wing extending below the center of the indistinct seed cavity. Grows to 90 feet tall, 2 feet in diameter.

BLUE ASH *(Fraxinus quadrangulata)* twigs are distinctly 4-angled. The leaves, 8 to 12 inches long, have 5 to 11 stalked lanceolate to oblong-lanceolate leaflets, 3 to 5 inches long and 1 to 2 inches wide; margins toothed. Flowers are perfect. Samaras are oblong-ovate, 1 to 2 inches long with a thin wing extending to the base of the seed. Blue Ash grows to 60 feet tall and 2 feet in diameter. During pioneer days, a blue dye was obtained from the inner bark.

SINGLELEAF ASH *(Fraxinus anomala)* has simple (occasionally with 2 to 3 leaflets), long-stalked, broadly oval leaves, 1.5 to 2 inches long and 1 to 2 inches wide, with margins entire or toothed above middle. Polygamous flowers appear when leaves are nearly grown. Samaras, to 0.8 of an inch long, have a broad wing extending around seed. The twigs are 4-angled. Singleleaf Ash is a shrub or small tree, growing to 20 feet tall and 6 inches in diameter. Often occurs in dry or rocky soils.

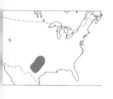

TEXAS ASH *(Fraxinus texensis)* leaves are 5 to 8 inches long. The 5 (occasionally 7) long-stalked, oval to obovate leaflets are 1 to 3 inches long and 1 to 2 inches wide, with toothed margins and tufts of white hair in axils of veins below. Dioecious flowers appear as leaves unfold. Spatulate samara, to 1 inch long, has a seed nearly round in cross section. To 50 feet tall and 3 feet in diameter.

CAROLINA ASH *(Fraxinus caroliniana)* leaves are 7 to 12 inches long. The 5 to 7 long-stalked, oblong-ovate leaflets are 3 to 6 inches long and 2 to 3 inches wide, with coarsely toothed margins. Glabrous below. Dioecious flowers appear before leaves. Samaras are to 3 inches long, the thin, broad wing surrounding seed sometimes 3-winged. Bark scaly, light gray. To 40 feet tall, 1 foot in diameter.

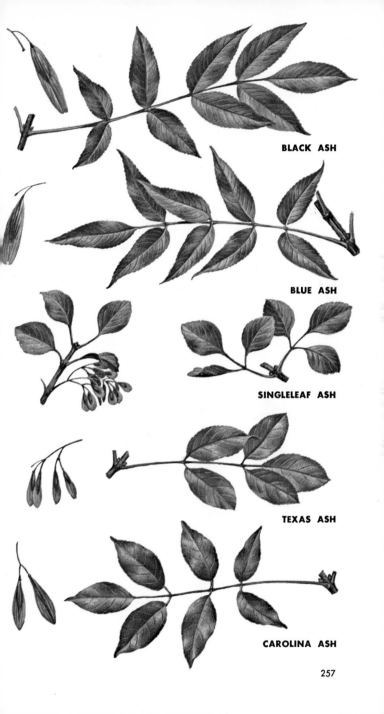

BLACK ASH

BLUE ASH

SINGLELEAF ASH

TEXAS ASH

CAROLINA ASH

257

GREGG ASH *(Fraxinus greggii)* leaves are 1.5 to 3 inches long, with winged main stem; they remain on the tree through the winter, until flowering time. The 3 to 7 leathery, obovate leaflets are 0.5 to 1 inch long and 0.3 of an inch wide; margins are smooth or inconspicuously toothed and the pale-green underside is marked with black dots. Polygamous flowers appear before the leaves. Samara is spatulate, to 0.8 of an inch long, with a broad wing extending to about the middle of the seed. A shrub or small tree, to 20 feet tall and 8 inches in diameter.

VELVET ASH *(Fraxinus velutina)* leaves are 3 to 6 inches long, with 5 (sometimes 3 to 9) elliptical to lanceolate leaflets, 1 to 2 inches long and to 1 inch wide; margins entire or finely toothed above the middle and often hairy below. Dioecious, the flowers appearing in spring before or with the leaves. The samara is obovate to elliptical, to 1 inch long, with wing extending only part way along the seed. Velvet Ash attains a height of 30 feet and a diameter of 1 foot. Its gray bark is ridged and furrowed.

OREGON ASH *(Fraxinus latifolia)* leaves are 5 to 14 inches long, with 5 to 7 (occasionally 9) ovate to obovate leaflets, 3 to 6 inches long and 1 to 1.5 inches wide, with smooth or finely toothed margins; usually slightly hairy below and lateral leaflets often stemless. Dioecious flowers appear with leaves. Samara elliptical to oblanceolate, to 1.5 inches long, with wing extending to middle of seed. Oregon Ash grows to 75 feet tall and 3 feet in diameter. In moist, fertile soils, it has a long, clear trunk, but on poorer soils, its form is often crooked and ragged.

FRAGRANT ASH *(Fraxinus cuspidata)* leaves are 3 to 7 inches long, with 3 to 7 long-stalked, lanceolate to ovate leaflets, 1.5 to 2.5 inches long and to 0.8 of an inch wide; margins entire or with widely spaced teeth above the middle. Perfect flowers appear with leaves; they differ from most ashes in being fragrant and having showy white petals. Samaras are elliptical to oblong-ovate, to 1 inch long, with wing extending nearly to the base of the seed. Scattered lenticels mark the reddish-brown twigs; bark of larger trunks is gray. A shrub or small tree, to 20 feet tall and 8 inches in diameter. A variety *(F. cuspidata* var. *macropetala)* has broader leaflets with entire margins, and occasionally its leaves are simple.

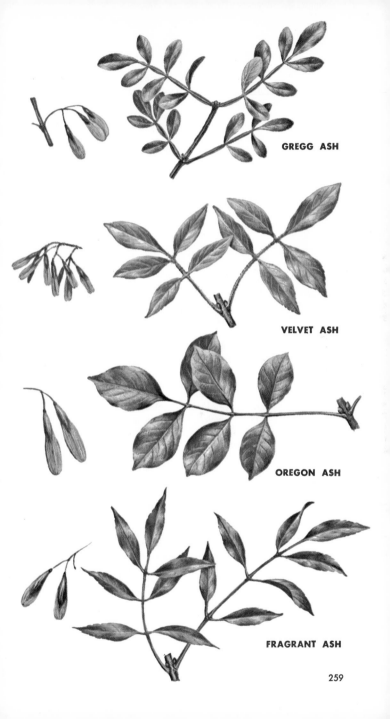

GREGG ASH

VELVET ASH

OREGON ASH

FRAGRANT ASH

BORAGE FAMILY (Boraginaceae)

The 90 genera and some 1,500 species of trees, shrubs, and herbs in this family are found primarily in warm regions. The family is represented most abundantly in the Mediterranean area and in Central Asia. Several species attaining the size of small trees are native to southeastern United States, southern Texas, and southward into Mexico and Central America. Heliotropes and forget-me-nots are familiar flowers of the borage family.

BAHAMA STRONGBARK (*Bourreria ovata*) has alternate, ovate to obovate, smooth, evergreen leaves, 2 to 3 inches long and 1 to 2 inches wide; margins smooth and apex rounded, notched, or pointed. Leaves hairy when young. White, bell-shaped flowers, 0.8 of an inch in diameter, in terminal clusters. Calyx of flower remains attached to orange-red fruit, 0.5 of an inch in diameter. Bark brownish gray, with thin scales. Bahama Strongbark grows in moist soils, to 50 feet tall and 1 foot in diameter, with a fluted trunk and an irregular, rounded crown. Rough Strongbark (*B. revoluta*), usually a shrub, is similar to Bahama Strongbark, but its leaves are rough.

GEIGER-TREE (*Cordia sebestena*) has simple, alternate, ovate, evergreen leaves, 5 to 6 inches long and 3 to 4 inches wide, with margins smooth or coarsely toothed above middle. Apex usually pointed; stout stem and underside of principal veins hairy. Trumpet-shaped, bright-orange flowers, 0.7 of an inch long and 1 to 1.5 inches across, in terminal clusters; hairy exterior. Fruit ivory, 1.3 inches long and 0.8 of an inch in diameter, with tail-like appendage at apex. Bark dark brown to black, ridged, scaly. Geiger-tree is a shrub or small tree, to 30 feet tall and 6 inches in diameter. Anacahuita (*C. boissieri*), a rare tree of southern Texas and Mexico, has white flowers, and calyx enclosing fruit is ribbed.

ANAQUA (*Ehretia anacua*) almost evergreen, has tardily deciduous, simple, alternate, oval to oblong leaves, 3 to 4 inches long and 2 to 3 inches wide. The apex is pointed, and the margins are toothed above the middle. Small, white flowers occur in loose terminal clusters about 2 inches long; blooms in late winter and spring. Fruit, 0.3 of an inch in diameter, is light yellow to red, fleshy, and edible. Brownish-gray bark is scaly. Anaqua grows to 50 feet tall and 3 feet in diameter, with stout branches forming round-topped crown.

BAHAMA STRONGBARK

GEIGER-TREE

ANAQUA

261

VERBENA FAMILY (Verbenaceae)

Shrubs and trees are included in the 80 genera and 1,200 species of largely herbaceous plants. Teak *(Tectona grandis)* is one of several valuable timber trees in this family.

BLACK-MANGROVE *(Avicennia nitida)* has opposite, oblong to elliptical, evergreen leaves, 2 to 3 inches long and 0.8 to 1.5 inches wide, with smooth, slightly curled margins; they are hairy below. White, 4-lobed flowers, 0.3 to 0.5 of an inch across, are in terminal clusters to 1.5 inches long. Fruit is a compressed, 2-valved and 1-seeded capsule, to 1.5 inches long and 1 inch wide. Bark of larger trees is dark reddish brown and scaly, with orange-red inner bark sometimes exposed between the scales. Forms dense thickets just inshore of Red Mangrove (p. 234). In Florida and adjacent Gulf Coast areas, a shrub or small tree, to 30 feet tall and 6 inches in diameter. To 70 feet tall in parts of wide range.

FLORIDA FIDDLEWOOD *(Citharexylum fruticosum)* leaves are evergreen, simple, opposite, oblong to obovate, 3 to 4 inches long and 1 to 1.3 inches wide, with curled margin. Small, white, fragrant flowers are tubular, with small, rounded petals; in axillary racemes 2 to 4 inches long. Blooms throughout year. Lustrous reddish-brown to black fruit, 0.3 of an inch in diameter, has thin, sweet, juicy flesh. Bark reddish brown, scaly. A shrub or small tree, to 30 feet tall, 6 inches in diameter.

NIGHTSHADE FAMILY (Solanaceae)

This is a family of some 85 genera and more than 1,800 species of herbs, vines, shrubs, and trees of temperate and tropical regions. Includes such valuable plants as potato, tomato, eggplant, tobacco, and petunia. Tree Tobacco *(Nicotiana glauca)* is a South American shrub or small tree naturalized in extreme southern United States.

MULLEIN NIGHTSHADE *(Solanum verbascifolium)* leaves are evergreen, simple, alternate, ovate to elliptical, hairy, and with wavy margins. Lower leaves are 5 to 7 inches long, 1 to 3 inches wide; smaller near growing tip. White, starlike flowers in axillary clusters 2 to 4 inches long; fruit yellow, round, 0.5 to 0.8 of an inch in diameter. Greenish to yellowish-gray, warty bark. A shrub or small tree, to 20 feet tall, usually in rich, moist soils. May be a naturalized species.

30-70 ft.

BLACK-MANGROVE

FLORIDA FIDDLEWOOD

MULLEIN NIGHTSHADE

263

BIGNONIA (TRUMPET CREEPER) FAMILY
(Bignoniaceae)

Some 700 species of trees and shrubs belong to this family. Most common in the tropics; a few species occur in temperate regions.

NORTHERN CATALPA *(Catalpa speciosa)* leaves are deciduous, long-stemmed, heart-shaped; 10 to 12 inches long and 7 to 8 inches wide, whorled or opposite. Tubular, white flowers, marked with purple and yellow, bloom after leaves develop; they are 2 inches long and 2.5 inches wide, in showy, 5- to 6-inch panicles. Each produces a brown capsule, 9 to 20 inches long and 0.5 to 0.8 of an inch in diameter, containing many fringed seeds about 1 inch long. Brown bark often scaly. To 100 feet tall and 4 feet in diameter, usually with a short trunk, stout branches, and a broad, rounded crown.

SOUTHERN CATALPA *(Catalpa bignonioides)* is smaller (60 feet tall; 3 feet in diameter). Flowers in denser clusters and with more yellow and purple. Capsules have thinner walls.

BLACK-CALABASH *(Enallagma latifolia)* leaves are evergreen, leathery, and alternate, widest above middle, 6 to 8 inches long and 1 to 4 inches wide. Creamy-white to dull-purple flowers, 2 inches long, in spring and fall; usually have a disagreeable odor. Oval fruit, 3 to 4 inches long and 1.5 to 2 inches in diameter, has a shiny-green, hard, 4-ridged, and somewhat roughened husk. Contains many seeds about 0.5 of an inch long. Bark reddish brown, scaly. Grows to 20 feet tall.

DESERTWILLOW *(Chilopsis linearis)* leaves are 6 to 12 inches long and 0.3 of an inch wide; deciduous. Tubular, white flowers, tinged with purple and yellow, are 0.8 to 1.5 inches long and in clusters 3 to 4 inches long. Narrow fruit capsule is 7 to 12 inches long. Bark dark brown, ridged, and scaly. To 30 feet tall, 1 foot in diameter, with narrow crown.

AN INTRODUCED SPECIES

ROYAL PAULOWNIA *(Paulownia tomentosa)* resembles a catalpa, but fragrant, deep-purple flowers appear before leaves. Twigs at first hairy, later smooth. Ovoid, woody capsules, 1 to 1.5 inches long. To 40 feet tall and 1.5 feet in diameter. Native to China; widely planted in the U.S., mainly in southeastern states.

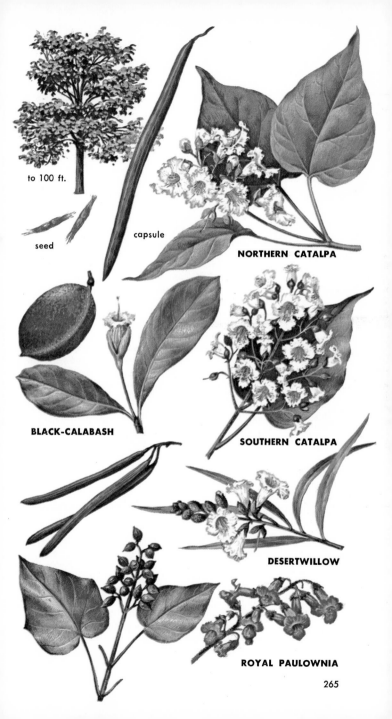

to 100 ft.

seed

capsule

NORTHERN CATALPA

BLACK-CALABASH

SOUTHERN CATALPA

DESERTWILLOW

ROYAL PAULOWNIA

265

HONEYSUCKLE FAMILY (Caprifoliaceae)

Most of the 275 species in about 10 genera are shrubs; a few attain small-tree size. Some of the shrubs are grown as ornamentals for their fragrant, showy flowers or for their colorful fruit. Represented most abundantly in temperate regions of the world.

ELDERS (*Sambucus* spp.) of more than 12 species grow in North America. All have opposite, odd-pinnately compound, deciduous leaves, with 5- to 7-toothed leaflets. Pith of twigs is large, spongy. Small, usually white flowers are in elongated or flat-topped clusters, and fruits are about 0.5 of an inch in diameter. Common native species that occasionally attain tree size include Pacific Red Elder (*S. callicarpa*), with red fruit; Blueberry Elder (*S. glauca*) and American Elder (*S. canadensis*), with blue fruit; Blackbead Elder (*S. melanocarpa*), Mexican Elder (*S. mexicana*), and Florida Elder (*S. simpsonii*), which have black fruit. Velvet Elder (*S. velutina*) has black fruit, hairy leaflets, and yellow flowers.

VIBURNUMS (*Viburnum* spp.) of some 20 species occur in North America. Their leaves are simple, opposite, and usually with toothed margins; in some species turn red in fall. Creamy-white flowers are in flat-topped clusters, 3 to 5 inches across. Fruits, about 0.3 of an inch in diameter, are black or blue. Native species that may attain tree size are Walter Viburnum (*V. obovatum*), which has scented, stemless leaves; Nannyberry (*V. lentago*), with sharply toothed leaf margins; Blackhaw (*V. prunifolium*), which has finely toothed leaf margins; and Possumhaw Viburnum (*V. nudum*), which usually has smooth leaf margins and long-stalked flower clusters.

COMPOSITE (SUNFLOWER) FAMILY (Compositae)

BIG SAGEBRUSH (*Artemisia tridentata*) leaves, with a pungent "sage" odor, are 1.5 inches long, alternate, wedge-shaped, and 3-toothed at apex. Small, drab-brownish flowers occur in long, narrow clusters. Usually a gnarled shrub, 4 to 5 feet tall, but grows to small-tree size in fertile bottomlands. Eastern Baccharis (*Baccharis halimifolia*), found along the Atlantic and Gulf coasts, is the only other native member of the composite family that may be tree-sized. Usually, however, it is a shrub.

to 25 ft.

PACIFIC RED ELDER

AMERICAN ELDER

FLORIDA ELDER

VELVET ELDER

NANNYBERRY

BLACKHAW

WALTER VIBURNUM

POSSUMHAW VIBURNUM

15-20 ft. (rare)

BIG SAGEBRUSH

MADDER FAMILY (Rubiaceae)

These are mainly tropical trees, shrubs, and herbs forming 350 genera and nearly 6,000 species. Coffee, the South American cinchonas (the bark of which yields quinine), and such ornamentals as Cape Jasmine and gardenias belong to this family. Seven-year Apple *(Genipa clusiaefolia)*, Scarletbush *(Hamelia patens)*, Bahama Balsamo, or Wild Coffee *(Psychotria ligustrifolia)*, and Seminole Balsamo *(P. undata)* are small trees or shrubs of southern Florida and the Keys.

COMMON BUTTONBUSH *(Cephalanthus occidentalis)* leaves are deciduous, opposite or whorled, 4 to 7 inches long, 2 to 3.5 inches wide, hairy along midvein below. Fragrant flowers in globular heads, 1 to 1.5 inches in diameter, on slender stems 1 to 2 inches long. Seeds in greenish to reddish-brown balls. Bark gray-brown (black on older trees), ridged, scaly. Shrub or small tree, to 30 feet tall, 8 inches in diameter; swampy ground.

CARIBBEAN PRINCEWOOD *(Exostema caribaeum)* has opposite, orange-stemmed, leathery, evergreen leaves, 1.5 to 3 inches long, 0.5 to 0.8 inches wide. Fragrant, solitary, axillary flowers 3 inches long with 5 narrow petals at apex of a thin tube. Capsule 2-celled, many-seeded, 0.7 of an inch long; black when mature. Bark thin, gray. A shrub or small tree, to 25 feet tall.

ROUGHLEAF VELVETSEED *(Guettarda scabra)* leaves are leathery, evergreen and opposite, 2 to 5 inches long and 1.5 to 3 inches wide, rusty-hairy below. Flowers white, tubular, about 1 inch long, on slender, few-flowered, axillary stalks. Fruit fuzzy, red at first but purple when ripe; 0.3 of an inch in diameter. To 30 feet tall and 15 inches in diameter; in sandy soil near salt water.

EVERGLADES VELVETSEED *(Guettarda elliptica)* resembles above species but has silky-haired leaves, 1.0 to 2.5 inches long and 0.5 to 1 inch wide. Creamy-white flowers. To 20 feet tall, 6 inches in diameter.

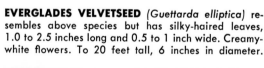

PINCKNEYA *(Pinckneya pubens)* leaves are deciduous, simple, opposite, 5 to 8 inches long, 3 to 4 inches wide. Tubular flowers, 2.5 inches long, in few-flowered clusters. Globular capsule 2-celled, about 1 inch long. Bark brown, scaly. Pinckneya grows to 30 feet tall and 10 inches in diameter.

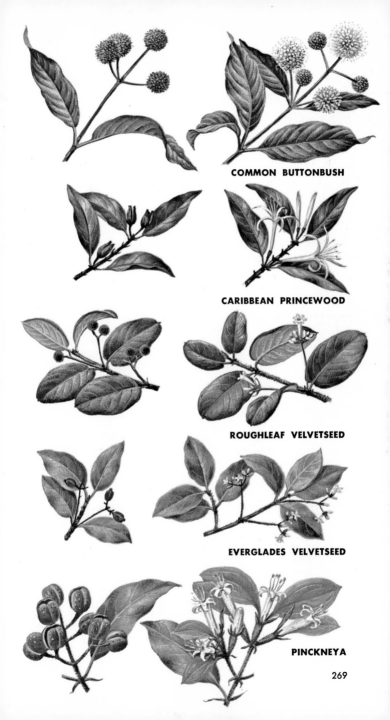

COMMON BUTTONBUSH

CARIBBEAN PRINCEWOOD

ROUGHLEAF VELVETSEED

EVERGLADES VELVETSEED

PINCKNEYA

269

ADDITIONAL EXOTIC SPECIES IN MISCELLANEOUS FAMILIES

HORSETAIL CASUARINA (*Casuarina equisetifolia*), one of 25 species of the family Casuarinaceae, is native to Australia and nearby lands. Evergreen leaves are tiny, toothlike scales, whorled at joints on the wiry, pale-green, drooping branches. Fruit conelike. Also called Australian-pine, Ironwood, and Beefwood. Naturalized in Florida and California. Grows 100 to 150 feet tall. Similar C. *glauca* used as a windbreak.

CHINESE PARASOLTREE (*Firmiana platanifolia*), of the chocolate family, Sterculiaceae, has 3- to 5-lobed, heart-shaped, deciduous leaves, 6 to 12 inches across. Crown rounded. Bark smooth, greenish. Grown in warm parts of North America and now naturalized in Southeast. Native to China and Japan. To 40 feet tall.

SILK-OAK (*Grevillea robusta*), in the family Proteaceae, is a native of Australia grown as an ornamental in California, Texas, and northern Florida. May grow 30 to 70 feet tall. Leaves evergreen, fernlike, bipinnately compound, 4 to 12 inches long, silvery below. Flowers yellow to reddish, in clusters 3 to 5 inches long. Wood lustrous, silky.

SHRUB-ALTHEA (*Hibiscus syriacus*), from Asia, and the naturalized Sea Hibiscus (*H. tiliaceus*) are both members of the mallow family, Malvaceae. Large flowers are bell-shaped. Shrub-althea's flowers are often bluish; those of Sea Hibiscus are yellow when they open in the morning, changing to maroon. Usually shrubs.

HORSERADISH-TREE (*Moringa oleifera*), in the family Moringaceae, is an East Indian species grown as an ornamental in southern Florida. Leaves deciduous, alternate, bipinnately (sometimes tripinnately) compound, to 2 feet long. Fragrant, white flowers about 0.8 of an inch across, in clusters 4 to 8 inches long. Capsules 7 to 14 inches long; cooked and eaten when young. Roots have horseradish odor and taste. To 30 feet tall.

SMALLFLOWER TAMARISK (*Tamarix parviflora*) and the smaller Five-stamen Tamarisk (*T. pentandra*), in the family Tamaricaceae, are native to the Mediterranean region. Branches graceful, slender; foliage small, scalelike; pink flowers in clusters 1 to 1.5 inches long. Shrubs or small trees, to 15 feet tall.

BIBLIOGRAPHY

Bailey, L. H. *The Cultivated Conifers.* N.Y., Macmillan, 1933

Benson, Lyman, and Robert A. Darrow. *The Trees and Shrubs of the Southwestern Deserts.* Tucson, Univ. of Arizona Press, 1954

Blakeslee, A. F., and Charles D. Jarvis. *Trees in Winter.* N.Y., Macmillan, 1931

Bonhard, Miriam L. *Palm Trees in the United States.* U.S.D.A., Forest Service, Agric. Inf. Bull. No. 22, Wash., D.C., Gov. Printing Office, 1950

Brown, H. P. *Trees of Northeastern United States, Native and Naturalized,* N.Y., Christopher, 1964

Canada, Department of Forestry. *Native Trees of Canada.* Ottawa, Queen's Printer, 1966

Collingwood, G. H., and Warren D. Brush (revised and edited by Devereux Butcher). *Knowing Your Trees.* Wash., D.C., Amer. Forestry Assoc., 1964

Dallimore, W., and Bruce Jackson (4th ed., revised by S. G. Harrison). *A Handbook of Coniferae, including Ginkgoaceae.* London, Edward Arnold, 1966

Harlow, W. M. *Trees of the Eastern and Central United States and Canada.* N.Y., Dover, 1957

Harlow, W. H., and E. S. Harrar. *Textbook of Dendrology.* N.Y., McGraw-Hill, 1968

Harrar, E. S., and J. G. Harrar. *Guide to Southern Trees.* N.Y., McGraw-Hill, 1946

Hough, R. B. *Handbook of the Trees of the Northeastern States and Canada (east of the Rocky Mountains).* N.Y., Macmillan, 1947

Lawrence, G. H. *Taxonomy of Vascular Plants.* N.Y., Macmillan, 1951

Ledin, R. Bruce (ed.). *Cultivated Palms.* Amer. Hort. Mag. (special issue), Vol. 40, No. 1, January 1961

Little, Elbert L., Jr. *Check List of Native and Naturalized Trees of the United States (inc. Alaska).* Forest Service Tree and Range Plant Committee, Agric. Handbook No. 41, Wash., D.C., Gov. Printing Office, 1953

Little, Elbert L., Jr., and Frank H. Wadsworth. *Common Trees of Puerto Rico and the Virgin Islands.* Agric. Handbook No. 249, U.S.D.A., Forest Service, Wash., D.C., Gov. Printing Office, 1964

Little, Elbert L., Jr. *Southwestern Trees, A Guide to the Native Species of New Mexico and Arizona.* Agric. Handbook No. 9, Wash., D.C., Gov. Printing Office, 1950

McMinn, H. E., and E. Maino. *Illustrated Manual of Pacific Coast Trees.* Berkeley, Calif., Univ. of Calif. Press, 1947

Muirhead, Desmond. *Palms.* Globe, Ariz., D. S. King, 1961

Peattie, Donald Culross. *Natural History of Trees of Eastern and Central North America.* Boston, Houghton Mifflin, 1950

Peattie, Donald Culross. *A Natural History of Western Trees.* Boston, Houghton Mifflin, 1953

Preston, R. J. *North American Trees (exclusive of Mexico and Tropical United States).* Cambridge, Mass., M.I.T. Press, 1961

Sargent, C. S. *Manual of the Trees of North America (exclusive of Mexico).* Boston, Houghton Mifflin, 1923

Sudworth, George B. *Forest Trees of the Pacific Slope.* Wash., D.C., U.S. Gov. Printing Office, 1908

Trelease, William. *Winter Botany,* N.Y., Dover (paperback), 1967

U.S.D.A. *Trees—The Yearbook of Agriculture.* Wash., D.C., Gov. Printing Office, 1949

U.S.D.A., Forest Service (compiled and revised by H. A. Fowells). *Silvics of Forest Trees of the United States.* Agric. Handbook No. 271, Wash., D.C., Gov. Printing Office, 1965

Vines, R. H. *Trees, Shrubs and Woody Vines of the Southwest.* Austin, Univ. of Texas Press, 1960

West, Erdman, and Lillian E. Arnold. *The Native Trees of Florida.* Gainesville, Univ. of Fla. Press, 1956

In addition to the above, many regional books and pamphlets are available locally in forestry offices, educational institutions, and libraries.

INDEX

Common names are indicated by two text page numbers for species that are illustrated —the even page number for the text, the odd for the illustration. Single text page numbers (even) are for scientific names and also for species not illustrated. Inclusive page numbers are given for families and for some genera or groups in which a number of species are listed. For explanation of names used in this book, see p. 4.

273